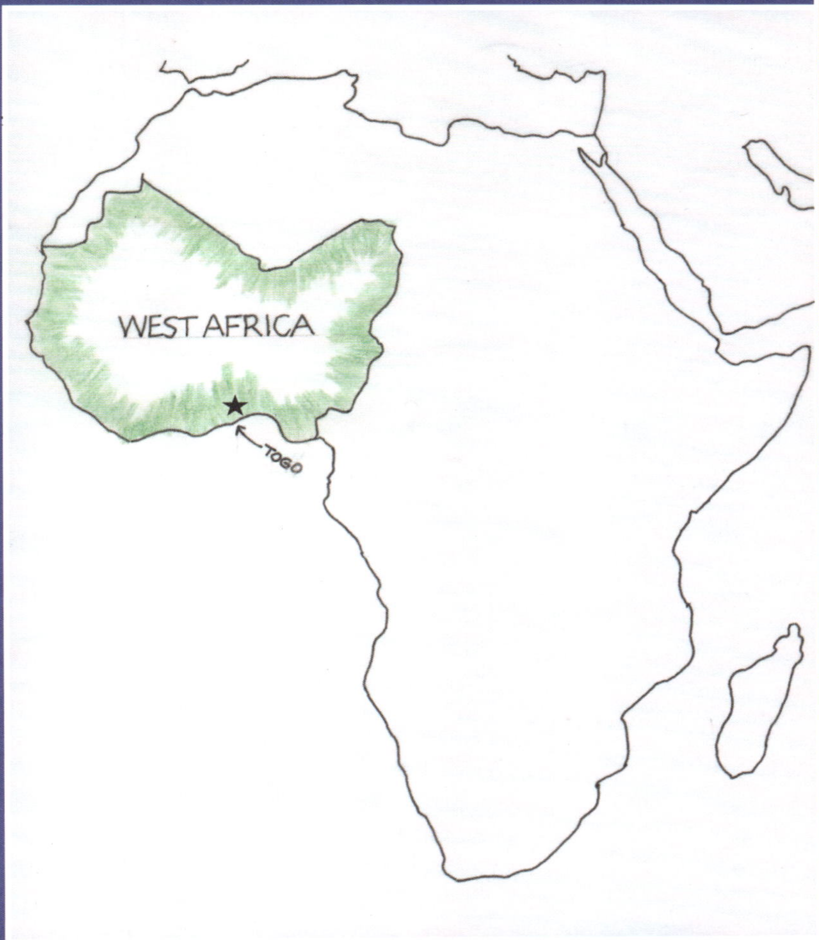
WEST AFRICA
TOGO

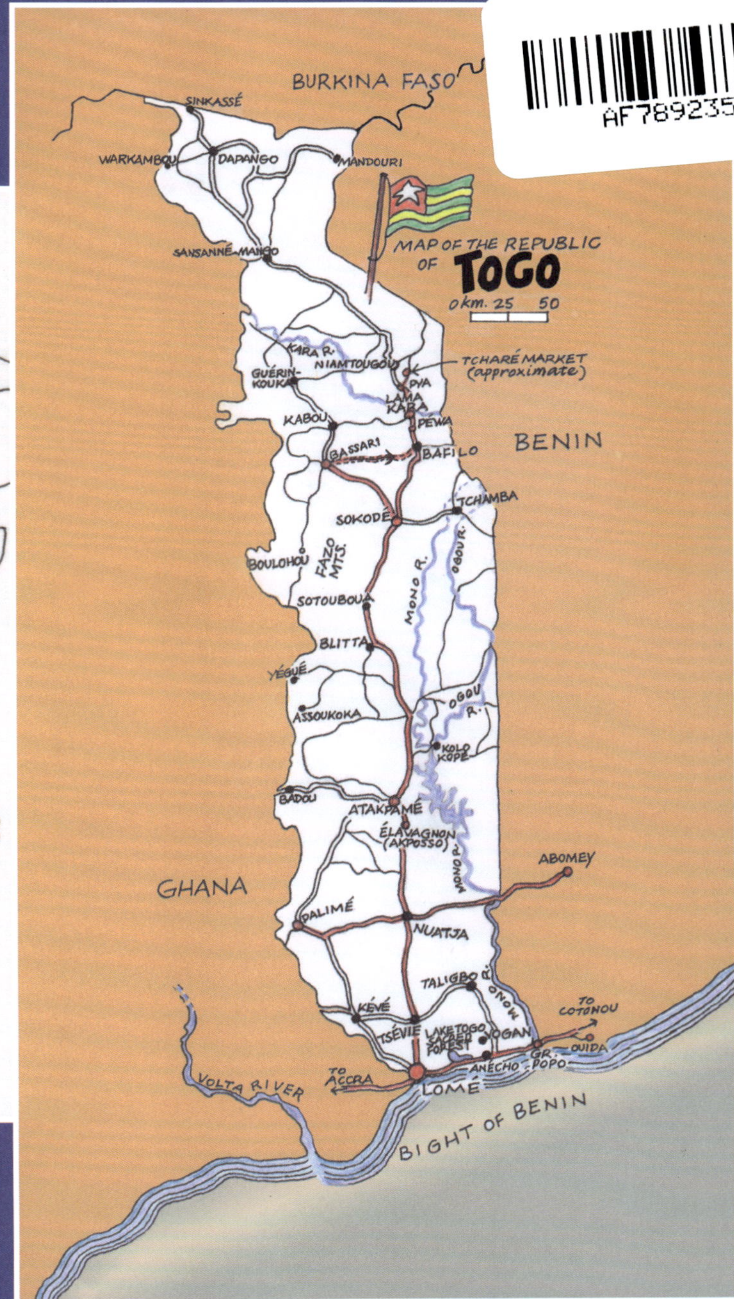
BURKINA FASO
SINKASSÉ
WARKAMBOU
DAPANGO
MANDOURI
SANSANNÉ-MANGO
MAP OF THE REPUBLIC OF TOGO
0 km. 25 50
KARA R.
NIAMTOUGOU
TCHARÉ MARKET (approximate)
GUÉRIN-KOUKA
PYA
LAMA KARA
KABOU
PEWA
BASSARI
BAFILO
BENIN
TCHAMBA
SOKODÉ
FAZO MTS.
BOULOHOU
OGOU R.
MONO R.
SOTOUBOUA
BLITTA
YÉGUÉ
ASSOUKOKA
OGOU R.
KOLO KOPÉ
BADOU
ATAKPAMÉ
ÉLAVAGNON (AKPOSSO)
MONO R.
ABOMEY
GHANA
PALIMÉ
NUATJA
TALIGBO
MONO R.
KÉVÉ
TSÉVIE
LAKE TOGO
SACRED FOREST
VOGAN
TO COTONOU
OUIDA
GR. POPO
ANÉCHO
TO ACCRA
LOMÉ
VOLTA RIVER
BIGHT OF BENIN

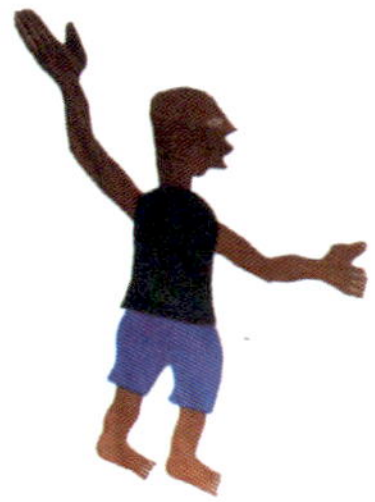

TOGO

Being Human

TOGO

Being Human

1969 ***West Africa*** *1971*

by PHILIP HECKSCHER

Seapoint Books
2021

TOGO

Being Human

1969 West Africa 1971

Seapoint Books + Media LLC

PO Box 21, Brooklin, ME 04616 USA

www.seapointbooks.com

Design and composition by Claire MacMaster

barefoot art graphic design

Printed by Printworks Global Ltd., London & Hong Kong

First Edition

ISBN: 978-1-7325470-3-2

June12,1943 **Eric Johannes Kiers** October 15, 1994

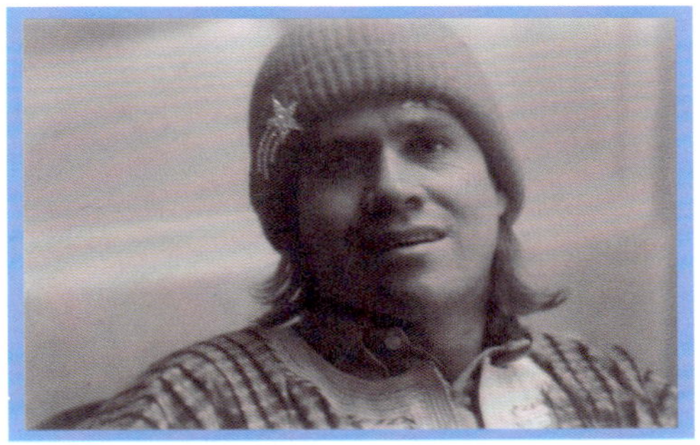

for you
Eric,
because you
were so happy there

THANKS

Thanks to my spouse, Michael Reid, whose love and devotion kept me going, and whose technical expertise made this book happen.

Lucas Kiers, with great liberality, allowed me to use many of his extraordinary photographs.

Thanks to Clare Monfredo, Maxim Lowe and Aaron Morris for typing from a hand-written draft. In addition, Clare's musical transcription of Stephen's song in the Endnotes brought it to life after fifty years.

Yawo Frédéric Yévu of the Togolese Mission to the United Nations offered invaluable insights and corrections. Ayodeji Otuyelu, photographed by Geoff Sokol, expressively modeled the West African clothing in this book.

Thanks to Roger Pasquier for reading the draft and making helpful changes; and to many friends for their interest and encouragement.

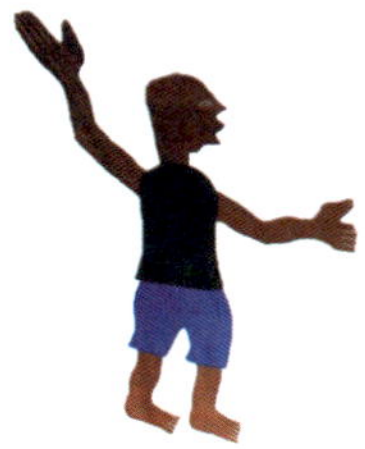

CONTENTS

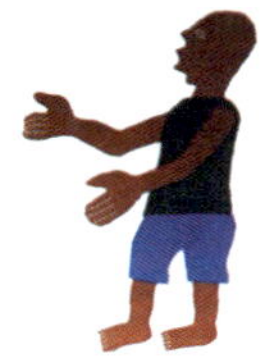

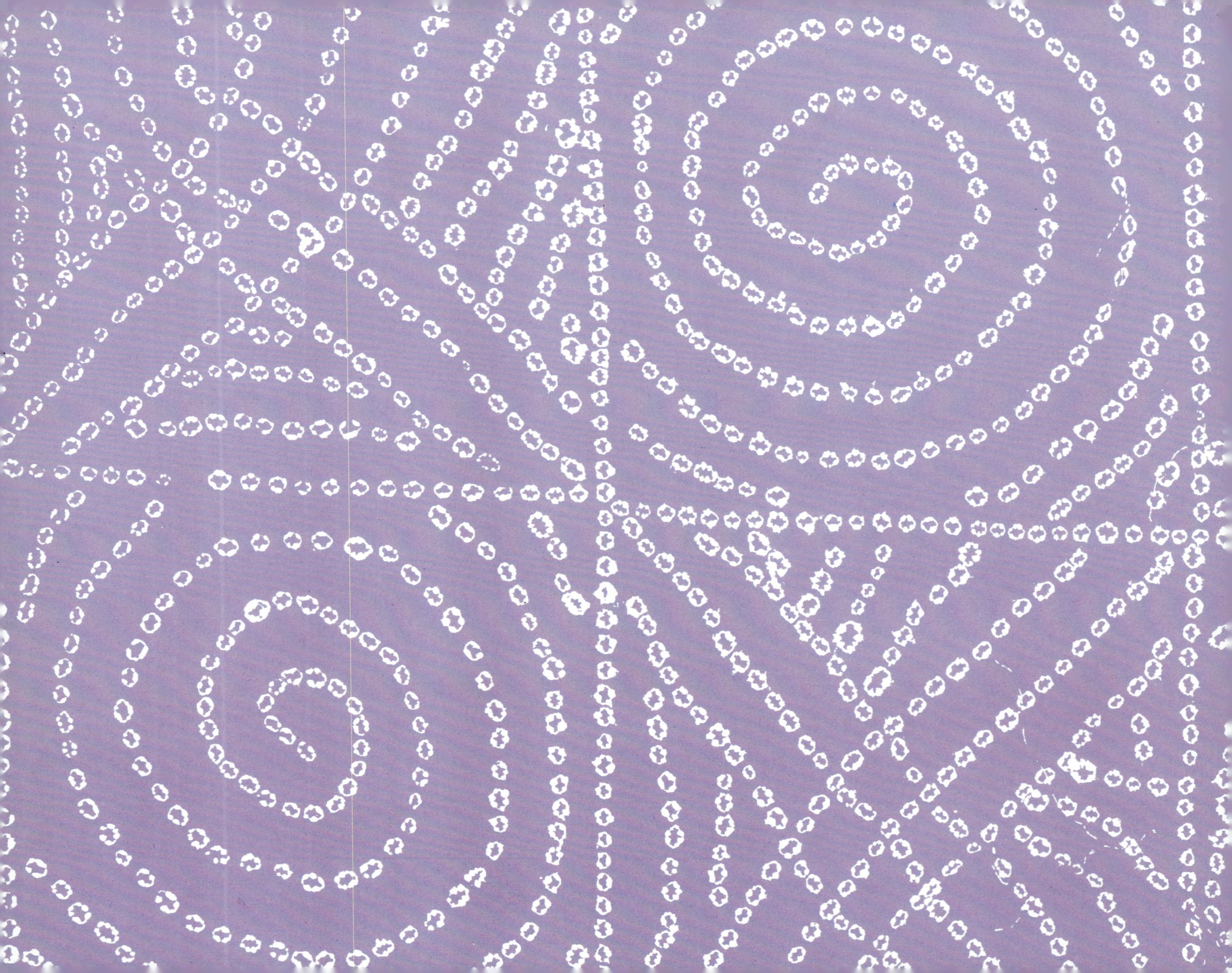

INTRODUCTION

In 1969 and again in 1971, I visited my friend Eric Kiers in Togo, West Africa. Eric had been living in the Togolese capital, Lomé, where he helped organize and administer the International Dialogues, a program of conferences, on behalf of the Society of Friends (Quakers). Because his work took him all over the French and English-speaking countries of the region, where he recruited participants and made friends among students, academics, journalists and politicians, he was the perfect guide and companion to the still deeply traditional, post-colonial, aspiring cultures of the many places we traveled through together.

Eric and I had been graduate students in the same class at the Woodrow Wilson School at Princeton University, where we both felt out of place. Eric was an activist, impatient with the powers in place, indignant at the social injustices he perceived and eager to use his graduate degree in Public Affairs to engage with the world.

I was a dreamer. The Woodrow Wilson School program, I thought, would prepare me for work in a non-governmental organization. I would learn several languages in addition to the English and French of my bilingual childhood, and mediate between differing cultures, winning hearts and minds for international understanding. The school, however, I soon found, was not a place for idealists or even polyglots. Foreign languages and comparative cultures were not on the program; instead, we studied economics and the functioning of federal bureaucracies.

Eric was miserable there. For my part, economics so puzzled me that I failed to graduate, despite the benevolence of my classmates who gave their time to tutor me. After graduation, Eric went to West Africa to work for the Quakers and I taught elementary school in Harlem, New York City, to avoid the unfathomable violence of the war in Vietnam. We kept in touch and discovered that we both thrived as cultural outsiders, and that his experience in the African homeland and mine in the African diaspora had many similarities. "Come to Togo," Eric wrote, and after two turbulent years at Public School 46, Manhattan, I joined him in Lomé. This book is an account of our travels along the West African coast in Togo and Ghana, Benin and Nigeria and northwards into the Sahel, the threshold of the Sahara Desert, through northern Nigeria, Niger, Mali and Burkina Faso.

When I came home from Togo in 1971 to my loft on West 28th Street in Manhattan, Eric joined me as soon as his work with the Quakers was done. After the graceful, leisurely comportment of West Africans, New Yorkers seemed possessed, striding hard-eyed and compulsively towards events and obligations governed by clocks; or vacant-eyed, oblivious of their surroundings, drifting towards nothing at all. We tried to keep the spirit of Togo alive in our lives. Eric took a job at International House at Columbia University, where he was responsible for many West African students. He seemed to come fully alive, however, only after midnight, when he threw himself into the nascent disco club culture around Times Square.

Meanwhile, I worked in Riverside Park as a Recreation Director for the Parks Department; and I joined the choir of a storefront church in Harlem, the First Tabernacle of Deliverance Spiritual Church. We loved Jesus, for sure; but perhaps not as much as the Holy Ghost. We dressed all in white and sang great thunderous Gospel music choruses that made passers-by stop to peer through the big plate glass window and drew the Spirit itself down among us. Someone in the choir or congregation would start speaking in tongues, uttering intense unintelligible things, spreading their arms wide, bending double convulsively. Then someone else would spring up and start dancing in rapid, precise steps, head back, eyes closed. The whole church would put its hands together, a tambourine would take up the rhythm, the organ begin to growl, then to roll, and all of a sudden everyone was in the aisle dancing and the folding chairs were scattered to the walls. From my seat in the tenor section, I too, rejoiced and welcomed what I recognized as an African spirit, joyous, tuneful and intense.

Eric was living in Malibu, California in the early 1990s when he was diagnosed with AIDS. He called to say he wanted me to come to his funeral—his funeral *party*, that is. He was determined to see his friends one last time, so we were invited to gather at his house on the beach for a three-day period. He suggested I ask for a "bereavement discount" from the airlines. The ticket agent expressed sympathy and asked for the name of the funeral home. I had to explain that my friend hadn't actually died yet, not until he had seen all his friends one last time. There was a moment of hesitation, then "Why that's the nicest thing I've ever heard," she said, and gave me the discount.

Dozens of us came to Malibu from other parts of California, from the East Coast and even from overseas, including a group of French women who had sung madrigals with Eric long ago and came all the way from Paris. We traded stories about our experiences with him as we walked on the beach or sat down to eat the elaborate catered meals he had ordered. He was too weak to leave his bed upstairs, so he had installed video cameras in the living room and watched everything on screen. From time to time, he would ask us to come up, singly or in groups, to sit on the edge of the bed while he recalled details of our friendship and suggested, with the acumen and frankness of a man who knows the end is near, how we should live the rest of our lives. He and I talked about our time in West Africa and how our experiences there had sharpened our sense of what it is to be human. Eric died on October 15, 1994 at 51 years old.

When we traveled together, we had called each other Flotsam and Jetsam to express our willingness to put our own culture on hold and float without resistance on the currents that carried us around West Africa. Through the International Dialogues, Eric's youthful activism made a difference after all; and he gave me the chance to be the wandering diplomat I'd dreamed of, switching languages, bridging cultures, learning to love humanity more widely.

Philip Hofer Heckscher
Mount Desert Island, Maine 2019

PREFACE

THE PATH

From the road where my bus is passing, a footpath of beaten red earth crosses a bright green field to a dense line of trees. I look closely at the trees to see if there's a village behind them. I've been in West Africa long enough not to underestimate the significance of a footpath: even the faintest ones lead somewhere, to a village or a market, a charcoal-burner's clearing or a grove of palm wine trees....

A little girl is walking along the path, hopping over puddles of water that lie across it. The path twists and turns around rough ground or an anthill or sunken places left by puddles from previous rainy seasons. That's definitely a village it leads to, now I can see smoke behind the trees and smell wood fires and something else, something like aromatic leather: the scent of people living closely together.

The bus lumbers on, but the red path in the green field is still in my mind's eye. It's been made by the people's feet, by the repeated passage of their broad, calloused feet falling rhythmically on the earth, the red dust flying up between their spreading toes or clinging as mud. The earth is stronger than they are: where it rises, they must climb; where rock protrudes, they must go around it. But they persist and the path is redirected. It shifts and twists and evolves, hardening or dissolving in dry season or wet, avoiding obstacles that may come and go, always shaped by the people's feet or sandals or even laced shoes sometimes, their steps weighted by a pail of water balanced on their head or a book bag, a single melon or a sack of charcoal. Their feet fall with a real immediate contact on the ground, creating a momentary bond of gravity with the earth then springing up, falling again, simultaneously making and following the path.

Someday, I suppose, the path may become a road, and the land graded and surfaced so that the people walk straight and dry on it, or ride unheeding on wheels. But, meanwhile and immemorially, people make the way, yielding and persisting in their patient, wily partnership with the earth. And I know that if I could see behind those trees and beyond the village, there would be more paths leading in all directions to other villages and I would see and understand the whole West African countryside, connected and organized by the people treading out the intricate organic accommodating network of footpaths.

BLACK STAR SQUARE

On my way out of Kotoka airport in Accra, Ghana in March, 1971, I was startled to see a rack of newspapers with huge banner headlines: *"GHANA GOES GAY!"* My old friend and classmate, Eric Kiers, was there to meet me and explain what was going on. "It's the Soul to Soul Festival, a huge first-ever rock concert of Afro-American and Ghanaian musicians to help celebrate Ghana's Independence Day. We'll be there tomorrow, in Black Star Square. No, it's not gay, stupid—that's just Ghana English."

Eric had come all the way from Lomé, the Togolese capital, four hours south of Accra over bad roads, to meet my plane. Ever since my first visit in 1969, he'd been writing me, describing his adventures and reminding me of the charms of living there: perpetual sunshine, warm Togolese relationships, a slow pace of life, and an interesting job with the Society of Friends, the Quakers, who furnished him with a fine house and garden. "Life is lovely in Lomé," he wrote. "Come back to Togo, Philip." So I quit my teaching job, rented my loft on West 28th Street in Manhattan, held a farewell party for my fellow bohemians who lived all around me in similar skylight-lit lofts above the Flower District, promised my parents I'd write, and booked a flight to Accra.

That first night in Accra, Eric and I ate at the Black Pot, a determinedly Ghana-themed restaurant serving traditional food. The dining room was lined in *adinkra* cloth, an Ashanti fabric of black symbols stamped on white cotton. Door curtains made of tiny shells rippled with a tinkling sound as we entered, and we ate chicken-groundnut stew out of rough black pottery bowls with spoons shaped from calabash gourds.

The restaurant was busy with people who were here for the Soul to Soul Festival. Our party had grown to include several of Eric's friends from Lomé, including Julie Toland, who worked at the American embassy. Julie was charming, confident and well-connected, and immediately hailed a friend at a neighboring table. He was Les McCann, an American jazz performer, with his drummer, Eddie Harris, and a Ghanaian gourd player from the north whom he had invited, soul-to-soul, to join his band for their performance in Black Star Square. In a moment, they had waved us over to their table, and we spent the rest of the evening in their jovial and unstinting company.

The next morning, Eric and I went to the botanical garden at Aburi, in the highlands above the city. At that cooler elevation, shaded by well-grown trees of every kind, we bought some plants for Eric's garden and bantered with an excursion of Ghanaian schoolgirls in vivid pink uniforms. I climbed into a massive, hollow baobab tree. We dozed on benches, surrounded by many Ghanaians doing the same, singly, in couples and family groups, seated or asprawl, all blessed with the temperament to fall asleep instantly, anywhere. Later, as we were speaking to a friendly student, he put his face up to mine and surprised me by blowing very hard into my eye. This is the West African way to clear the eye of an irritant, and I soon learned to appreciate the concern it implies, the sudden egalitarian way it's administered and the disconcerting lack of physical distance that goes with it. Personal space, it seems, is a peculiarly European requirement. Is it because Westerners equate physical closeness with erotic intimacy, and eroticism with something fraught, fearful, and forbidden? I think my student friend would have laughed at these complications, and I soon learned to give up my inhibitions and loll in unreproved closeness with my Togolese friends, doze on the shoulders of strangers, and relax into the lovely West African fellowship of touch.

That night, emboldened by my new cultural consciousness, I plunged happily into the vast crowd in Black Star Square. I learned only later the formidable dimensions of the event: 100,000 people in the square, 14 hours of performances. The American musicians included big stars like Wilson Pickett, Ike & Tina Turner, Santana, Roberta Flack, the Staple Singers, the Voices of East Harlem and of course, Les McCann and Eddie Harris. Their acts alternated with sets by Ghanaian performers playing western-influenced rock music or traditional village music involving large choruses of women, prancing *griots*,* and barrages of drums. The stage was enormous, bristling with towers of lights and speakers and exploding with sound, but it seemed almost remote in the huge sweep of the square. Eric and I spurned the roped-off seats near the stage and bought 50¢ tickets that allowed us to roam through the whole ecstatic, gyrating, delirious crowd. Everybody was dancing with everybody, and it was easy for us to join in. A young man named Auric danced up to tell us what a great country Ghana was and how little credit it received from Europeans. He was disrespected, he said, at his job with the National Cash Register Company. We shared his indignation, we deplored the heartless multinationals and assured him that this moment in Black Star Square was the best in our lives. Our enthusiasm was real, and before dancing off, Auric declared he had to leave me with something "from my person," and put a string of shell beads over my head.

* A West African troubadour who sings and recites oral history.

We were showered with names and addresses scrawled on scraps of paper, deluged with invitations to visit homes in every part of Ghana. Willie, a journalism student who had studied in Philadelphia, assured us that if we drove north with him, we'd meet his family and he'd take us through that whole remote countryside. Willie wasn't wearing much, just a pair of cut-off shorts, with "SOCK IT TO ME" painted across his chest.

We left Black Star Square nine hours later, around three in the morning. The music and dancing were still going strong and we felt we had friends now all over Ghana. Our ears buzzed, our feet ached, we were profoundly happy. After a few hours of sleep, somehow we woke up in time to get on a bus for Lomé.

While our passports were examined and stamped at Aflao, the border crossing, I watched as two men in the crowd greeted each other. They must be close friends, I thought, and hadn't met in a long time; but even so, what pleasure their greeting expressed, with such warmth! Broad, brilliant smiles, lengthy handshakes ending in a brief Moslem tap of the breast, inquiries into the well-being of their villages, families, households, livestock; renewed cries of surprise and delight, more handshakes, eyes often averted in respect as is the African custom, but shining with pleasure. There's an element of ritual in such greetings, inquiries are made and answered in a customary call and response, but there was no feigning the delight that these men showed in each other, in their encounter, in their very familiarity.

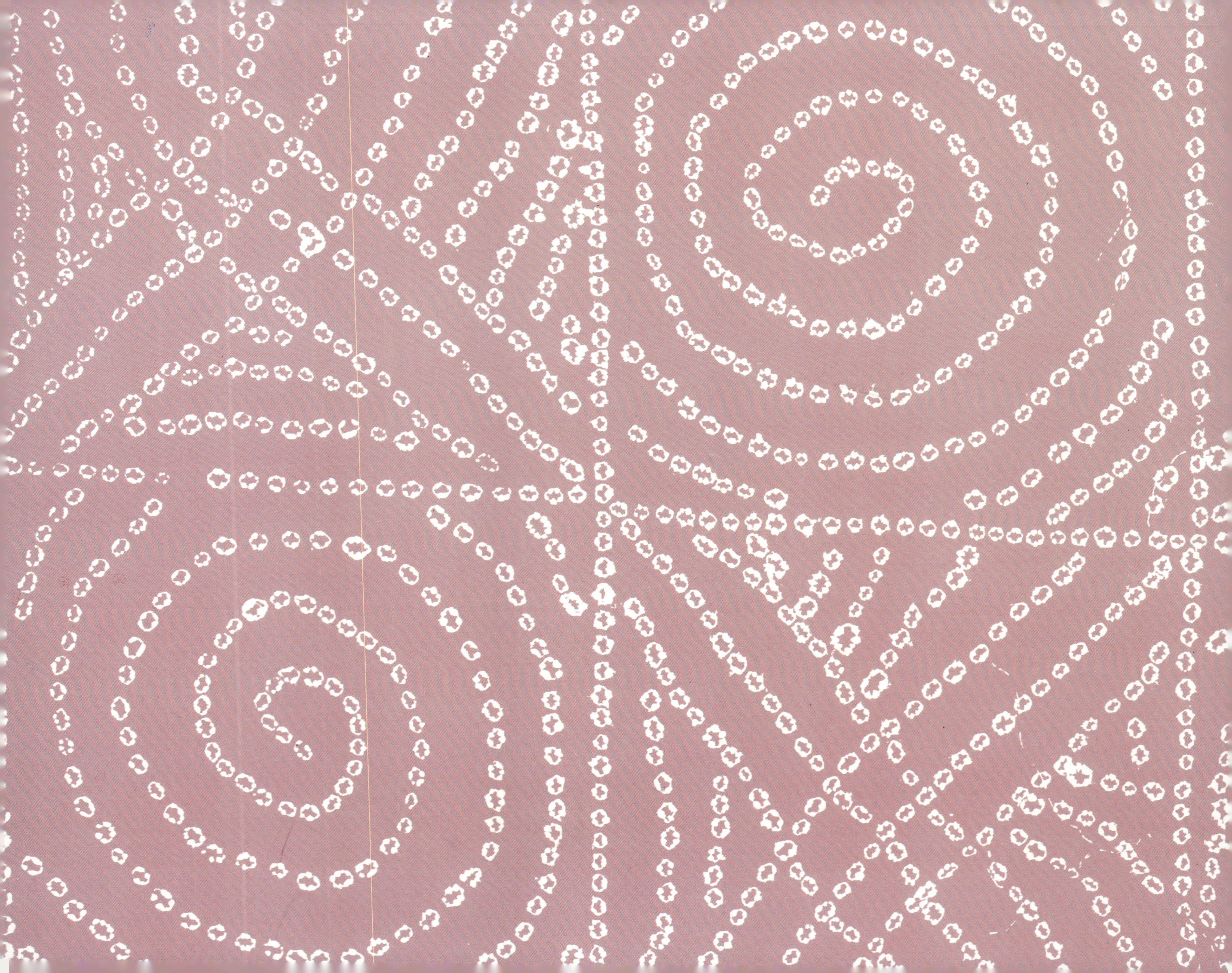

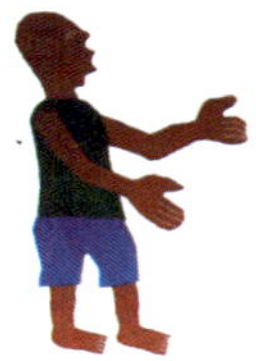

LOMÉ AND THE COAST

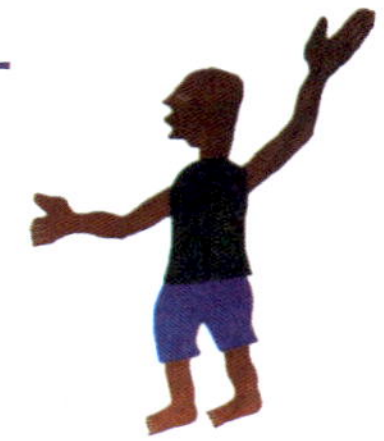

LOMÉ

The night wind soughs through the philodendron trees outside Eric's house in Lomé. I'm lying in bed, listening to the rising and falling sound, like bolts of silk being drawn through the branches. Pools of light tremble on the sandy surface of the street as the sea wind shakes the streetlamps. At intervals, I can hear the watchman's little radio playing pop songs: "*Nouké me wo...?* What did I do?" Jean, the watchman, comes and goes around the house all night. A lot of houses in Lomé have watchmen, although break-ins are not that common. Perhaps it's a prestige thing left over from French colonial times. Anyway, it provides employment to many up-country men like Jean who come to the capital. He patrols Quaker House with a spear, a machete, and a club, but I think he places more confidence in the little protective amulets he drops at strategic locations. Maybe he gets these amulets ready-made at the Grand Marché downtown, which has an extensive stock of practical magic objects. Or maybe they're made just for him, because I know that recently, he's had a lot of contact with.....what English word can I use that doesn't sound pejorative? "Witch doctors" won't do; popular stories and Hollywood have demonized them. In French, the official language of Togo, they are "*fétisheurs*" (or "*fétisheuses*," as many are women), although their work goes well beyond sticking pins in wooden figures. Eric had sent Jean to a neighborhood fetish-man for psychological counseling after he began waking the Quaker household in the middle of the night with stories of spirits bent on killing us all. The fetish-man interviewed him, then sent him to the Marché for a certain kind of ground-up animal bone and some expensive Scotch. This cocktail not only banished Jean's fears, but so relaxed him that Eric found him asleep on the living room couch, his weapons at hand, the radio crooning, "*Nouké me wo...?*"

Lomé is an architecturally unpretentious capital. Of course, there's the gleaming white presidential palace and a concrete Gothic cathedral on the Rue du Commerce, where you can also find the Michelin garage and salesroom, Walter's Bookshop, the Gulf Hotel (evocative of Graham Greene), the French patisserie of course, the Air France office, a Monoprix department store and the African Grand Marché. Everything one needs can be found on the Rue du Commerce—in limited quantities. I remember the relief I felt at the ease of buying plates at Monoprix. There was a choice of three styles, and I made a quick selection without agonizing as I would have in New York over which one was "me" or which went with what we had, or any of the refined considerations required by the consumer society.

The rest of Lomé is made up of compounds: that is, narrow, one-story residential structures arranged around a rectangular courtyard. They accommodate the owner and his or her extended family, renters, sometimes a small manufactory or a shop on the street side. The courtyard and the sidewalk are immaculately swept at first light by women or children with short-handled brooms. The women hitch up the babies tied to their backs, gather their bright enveloping wraps with one hand, and bend over gracefully to sweep with the other. Palm trees raise their spiky silhouettes behind the rooflines, sometimes the denser foliage of an orange or mango tree appears over the walls, but generally the African sky full of burning sunlight or towering clouds, uninterrupted by residential towers or office buildings, lords it over the low-lying town.

The compounds, full of life and built up closely against each other, make up extensive neighborhoods with names like Le Frigo (the Fridge), Lom Nava ("call and I'll come to you"), Tokoin ("little hill"), Amoutivé ("a god hides in the forest"), and Ablogamé ("the joy of liberty"). Quaker House was in Nyakponapwé, which means "look behind you", and was made up of the same low compounds with blank walls lining narrow, sandy streets. Quaker House, however, was an exception. The fine, high, brightly whitewashed two-story house with blue shutters dominated a luxuriant garden and the outbuildings that framed it. Eric lived on the ground floor and his colleagues, John and Sonja Willey, lived above. Together, they ran the International Dialogues and invited participants from both French-speaking and English-speaking countries to discuss general topics like education and women's

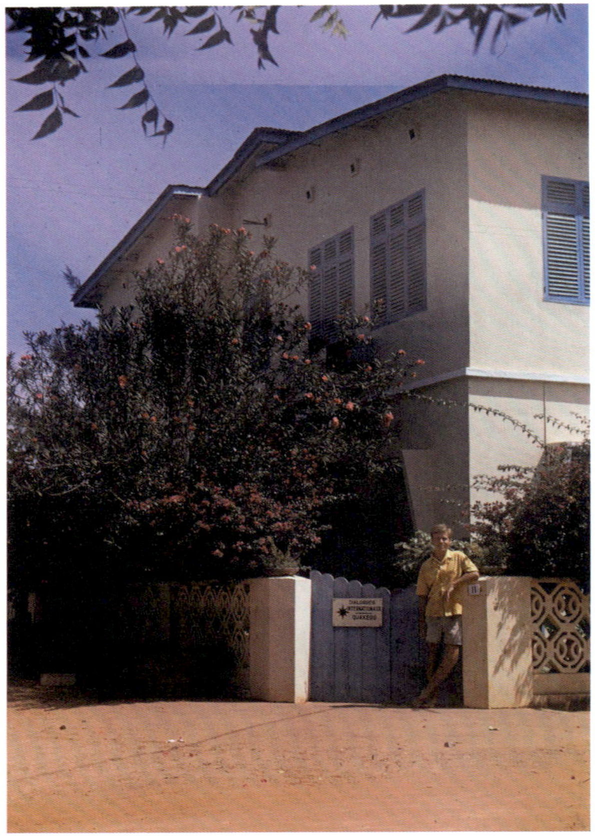

Quaker House, Eric Kiers at the gate

rights, at hotels and conference centers all over West Africa. The real purpose of the Dialogues, Eric confided to me, was less to air the problems of the region than to heal the rifts of colonization. Even a decade after independence, communication still ran

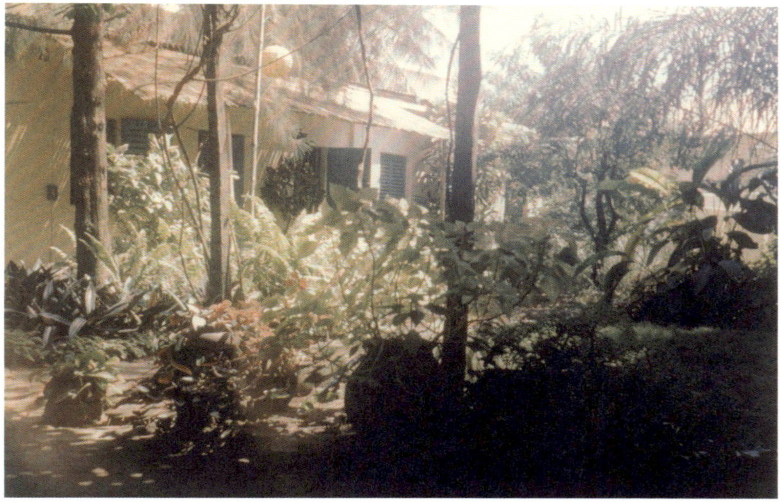

Eric's garden, Quaker House

through the former colonizers. A telegram from Lomé to Accra, for example, had to go first to Paris and then London before finally being sent to Ghana. The Quaker conferences were several days long, simultaneous translation was provided at the formal sessions and there was plenty of informal contact, too. The hope was that these exchanges would help substitute an African identity for the post-colonial French or English orientation, and that the journalists and media personalities, students and cabinet ministers who debated, ate together and shared their leisure, would go home subtly redirected away from Europe. "Or," as Eric said with shining eyes, "*married*!" The conferences had spurred several romances among participants and he regarded these as real proof of their efficacy.

In the early morning, Eric would work in his office in the garden, where he might pause to encourage the orchids growing in a row of pots outside his door. The garden's papaya tree would have produced another fruit that Justin Allagbé, the cook, would prepare for breakfast. Certainly the hibiscus bush would have replaced overnight the gorgeous red blossoms fallen during the previous evening. The new ones were perfect and fresh at this early hour, but fated to fall by twilight in a colorful litter on the bit of lawn before Théo, the gardener, swept them up. Cocks crowing all over Nyakponapwé would wake me a little later than Eric, and I might lie in bed, listening to the neighborhood come back to life. The Baptist church over the wall rang its bells at 5:30. Bells on bicycles took over as people went to work; then the breadman's little horn announced the availability of baguettes and croissants in the basket on the back of his bicycle. Choir practice in the church followed, full mellow voices singing in soaring unfamiliar harmonies. Finally the sun itself appeared, demanding that I join the day, with a chorus of its own if it had rained during the night: the loud fluttering of hundreds of resplendent sunbirds in the philodendron trees, drying their feathers.

Justin calls us to breakfast. He has sharpened the papaya with lime juice. The eggs were still in the henhouse a quarter hour ago. There's plenty of honey and butter for the breadman's baguette, and Eric (Dutchman that he is) pours lots of strong tea. He will have less to do today, as his colleague is gradually taking over the Dialogues program, so I know that he won't say no to a trip after breakfast to the Grand Marché, and soon we set off downtown on foot. We make a detour to cross the wide esplanade of the Post Office just to see the animation that prevails there. All of

West Africa seems to be here in the sunny plaza under its shading trees, on the broad flight of steps that leads up to the porch or in the cavernous cool interior thronged with people waiting in line or gathered to talk. Tall thin men in white robes and Moslem caps talk to sturdy bare headed Togolese businessmen in safari suits. Full-fleshed women dressed in bold patterns from head to foot and coiffed in intricately wound turbans bargain, laugh and scold. Country folk in homespun ponchos and wide straw hats look around bemusedly. I love this scene for its variety and social warmth.

In the surrounding street are the shops or work tables of a small army of tailors, who will assemble any cloth you bring them into shorts or trousers or shirts, embroidered robes or simple tunics. I brought them my blue jeans and asked that they embroider the left leg with the gorgeous gold or red arabesque embroidery usually applied to formal robes. They looked puzzled, they wanted to do both legs, but soon I was walking around the city in asymmetrically splendid jeans.

Eric and I are climbing up into the Grand Marché, an unassuming concrete construction that reminds me of a parking garage: four or five open-sided floors crammed with stalls selling everything from food to hardware to monkey skulls. It's dark on the inside of the floors but the open outer sides admit daylight and big fresh breezes from the sea that vie with the musty smells of the monkey skulls and animals skins among the fetish supplies, the fishy odors from the morning's catch and pungent fragrances arising from piles of hot peppers and dried spices. Each display is presided over by an immense seated woman swathed in yards of cloth that cover her enormous bust and are artfully wound around her head. Many of these market women, especially the sellers of cloth, recognize Eric, who has amassed from them a collection of cloth printed, tied and dyed in indigo or kola nut, figured with wax, rice paste or mud-based resists, painted, appliquéd, woven in strips on hand looms, artfully slashed, embroidered, beaded.... West Africans love cloth, and the whole region nourishes an astounding variety of techniques, many of which identify the wearers as Yoruba, Tuareg, Fulani, Bambara, Kabré, Evé, etc. Cries of "Ça va?" greet us from every side. *"Viens, viens, tu dois regarder ça."* ("Come, come, you should look at this.") We are urged to look, feel, buy. The women know that Eric is a hard bargainer and they start high, shaking with laughter and calling others to witness as he obliges them to come down and down. They shake their heads, they slap the back of one hand into the other palm, they implore him not to ruin them, their voices climb in feigned disbelief; and then the final price, acceptable to both, suddenly emerges. I myself purchase a length of cloth from Grand Popo on the nearby border with Benin. It has a name, *avobabla*, and is dark with a dark, subtle pattern of something like ferns. The good-humored women show me how to wear it: rolled down around the waist like a sarong in the day, crossed over the chest and tied behind the neck for more coverage in the cool of evening, and draped over the shoulder, toga-like, for formal occasions.

The peanut ladies, too, call out in welcome as we make our way through their displays, for we are devoted to the taste of their freshly roasted groundnuts and never leave the market without buying some. Eric was my guide at first, since I'd never seen peanuts ground and shaped into balls, hefty softball-sized golden balls neatly organized in rows according to their degree of heat—for

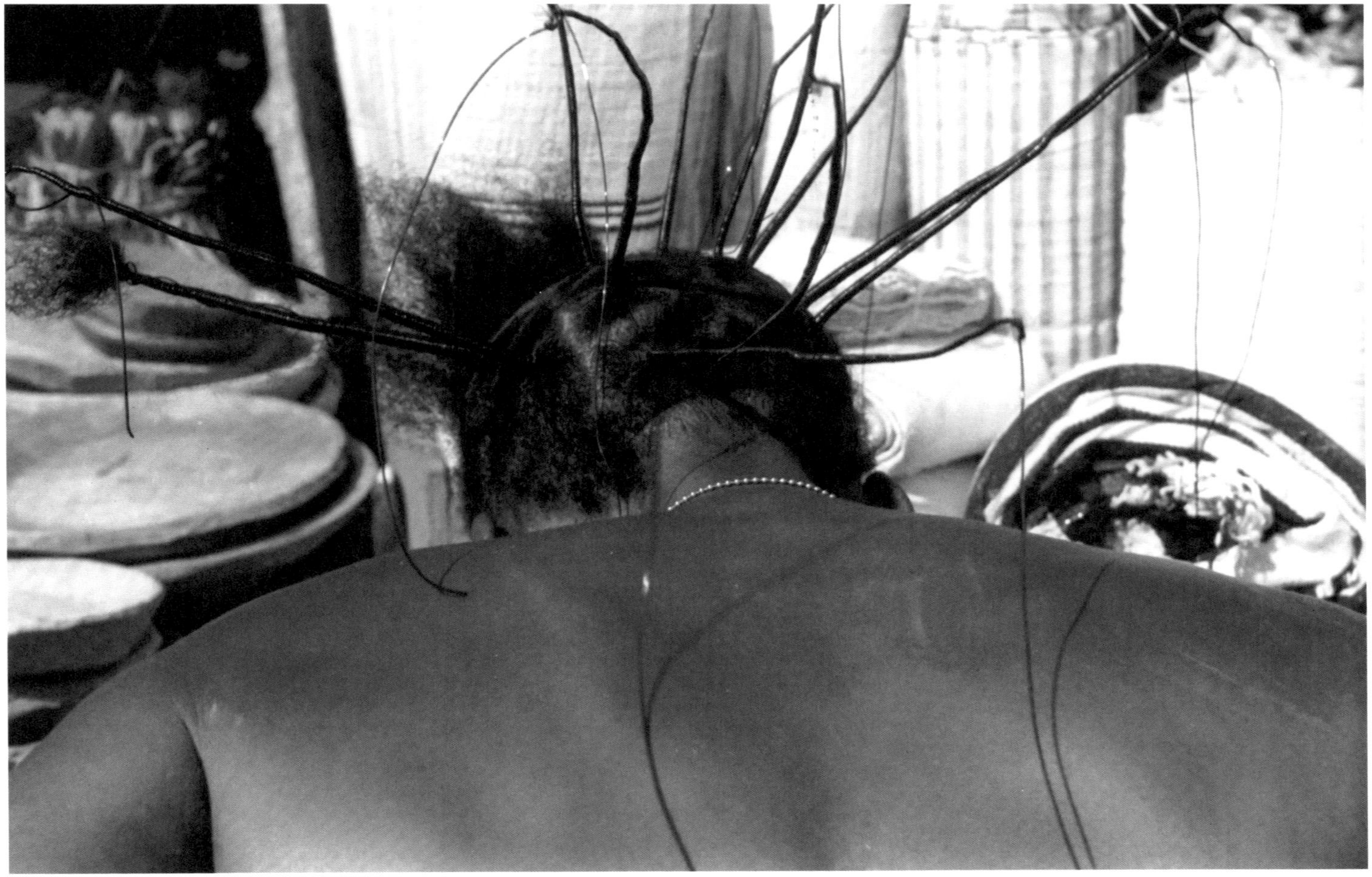

Lomé market lady having her hair done. Photo by Lucas Kiers

they are mostly incorporated into the peppery soups and sauces that, along with a starch such as rice or yam, make up the bulk of the West African diet. Eric steered me away from the hotter ones, which make a dish so fiery as to be inedible to the average *yovo* (white person). The market ladies are amused by our wariness and insist that a dish is only good when it's as hot coming out as it was going down! But in any case, we're really looking for the Johnnie Walker bottles. The best grade of peanut, carefully sorted and roasted and left whole, is sold in the appropriately prestigious bottle of that expensive Scotch, whereas less coddled grades may end up in an old wine bottle. The difference in taste is marked, and the addictive, delicately oily, unsalted, freshly roasted taste of the Grand Marché peanuts spoiled me forever for anything out of a can or bag. We would take home a Johnnie Walker bottle or two, make ourselves comfortable in the garden or on the beach, brew tea or roll a joint, and "drink" them down right out of the bottle as if they were, indeed, the most delicious of spirits.

The fetish, or *gris-gris** market is very popular with *yovos*. We're taught to look askance at magic, and so it exercises the fascination of a discredited and more instinctual power. To many West Africans, Moslem or Christian, *gris-gris* is much more deeply part of their lives than any other system of belief. When our Togolese friends wanted to pass a school exam or triumph in a soccer game, they saw a *fétisheur* as a matter of course; and needless to say, the opposing teams did the same. If something were lost or stolen, specialized *fétisheurs* promised to find it. Others foretold the future or assured the success of a love affair. The *gris-gris*

* *Gris-gris* (gree-gree) refers to particular magical charms as well as to the whole system of West African magic.

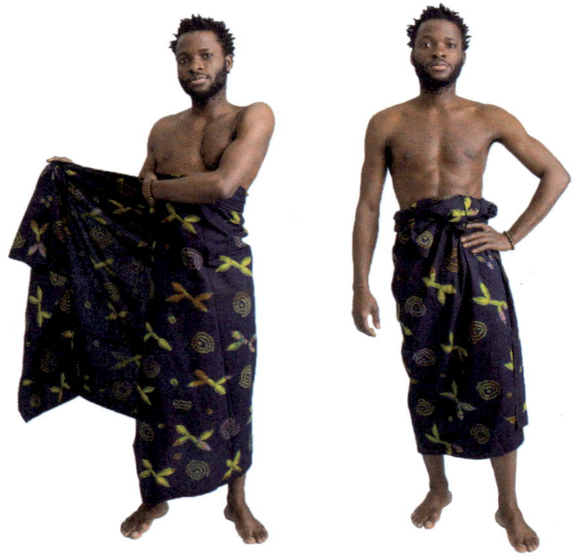

Rolled down around the waist during the day...

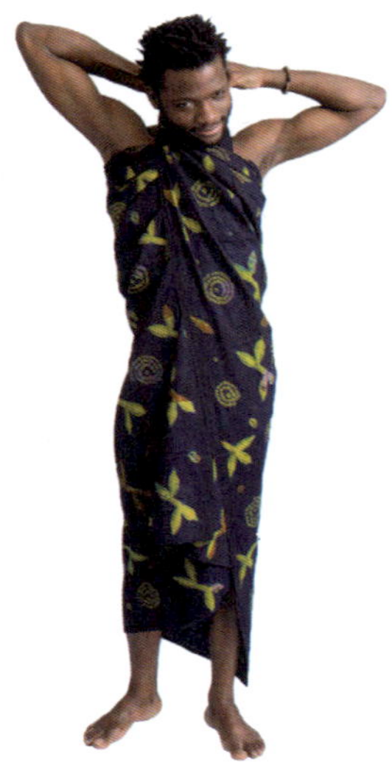

Crossed over and tied...

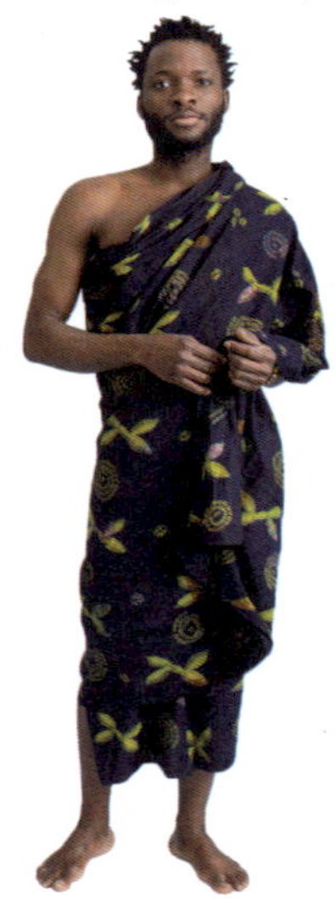

Draped over the shoulder.

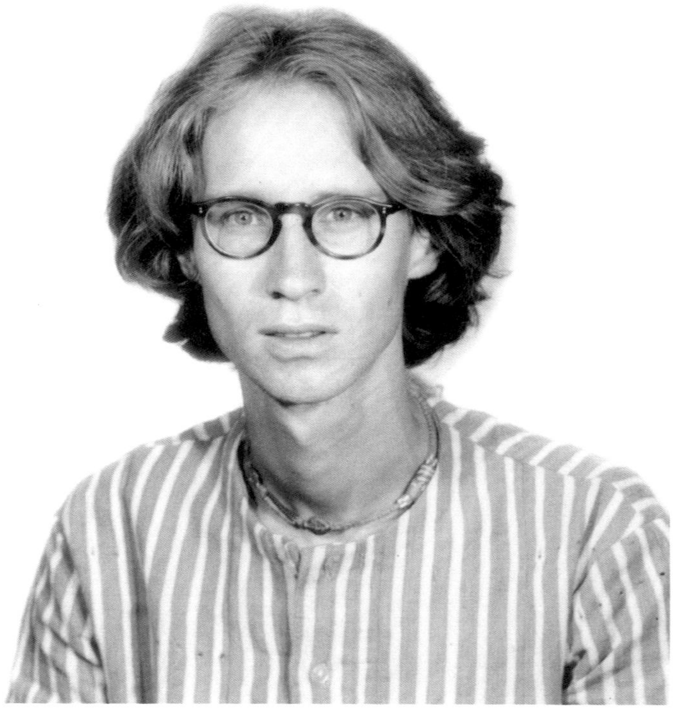

The author with beads

market in Lomé abounded in magical paraphernalia: oils and powders in little bottles, figured clay ritual vessels, leaves and roots, animal skins and bones in bins, and a profusion of beads of every color and material including bone, ceramic, glass, wood and tooth, sometimes strung but most often loose, waiting to be combined as the *fétisheur* prescribed. The visitor, having seen too many movies, perhaps, dwells on the malevolence of these charms; but they are more often intended for defensive purposes, for protection. Justin, I noticed, wore a string of beads around his waist. *"Ça se porte dans ma famille,"* ("People in my family wear these") he explained with a shy smile, and offered further that he didn't wear them around his neck in Lomé because the Togolese might deride them or even feel provoked to test the efficacy of a charm from across the border in Benin, where Justin is from.

I was entranced by the market beads when I first saw them, and bought some to work into macramé ornaments. Sitting by the roadside waiting for a bus, I would pass the time stringing them, feeling quite African in my artisanship. I noticed, however, that the reaction from passersby was not always frankly approving. And if I actually wore them, people would look from me to the beads and back at me with a changed expression. Maybe they wondered whether my beads really had power, or whether I even knew what they were for. I didn't, and quickly understood that it would never have occurred to most people to wear these kinds of beads as ornaments, and I put them away.

When we return from the Marché, Justin has a salad on a big green platter for lunch. Shrimp, hearts of palm, beets, cucumber, avocado, lettuce and julienned carrots are set out with a mound of *rémoulade* in the center and accompanied by a bowl of broth made of some of these same vegetables. Papaya again for dessert, or a sweet, brilliant-yellow pineapple, ripe to the core. Eric would set out a plate of sugar water for the gecko lizards from the garden that have come to stare at us. We stare at them. They are a beautiful green color. They lift their throats and roll their eyes as they stand on spread adhesive toes and breathe rapidly, their sides collapsing and filling like tiny bellows. Eric claims he has

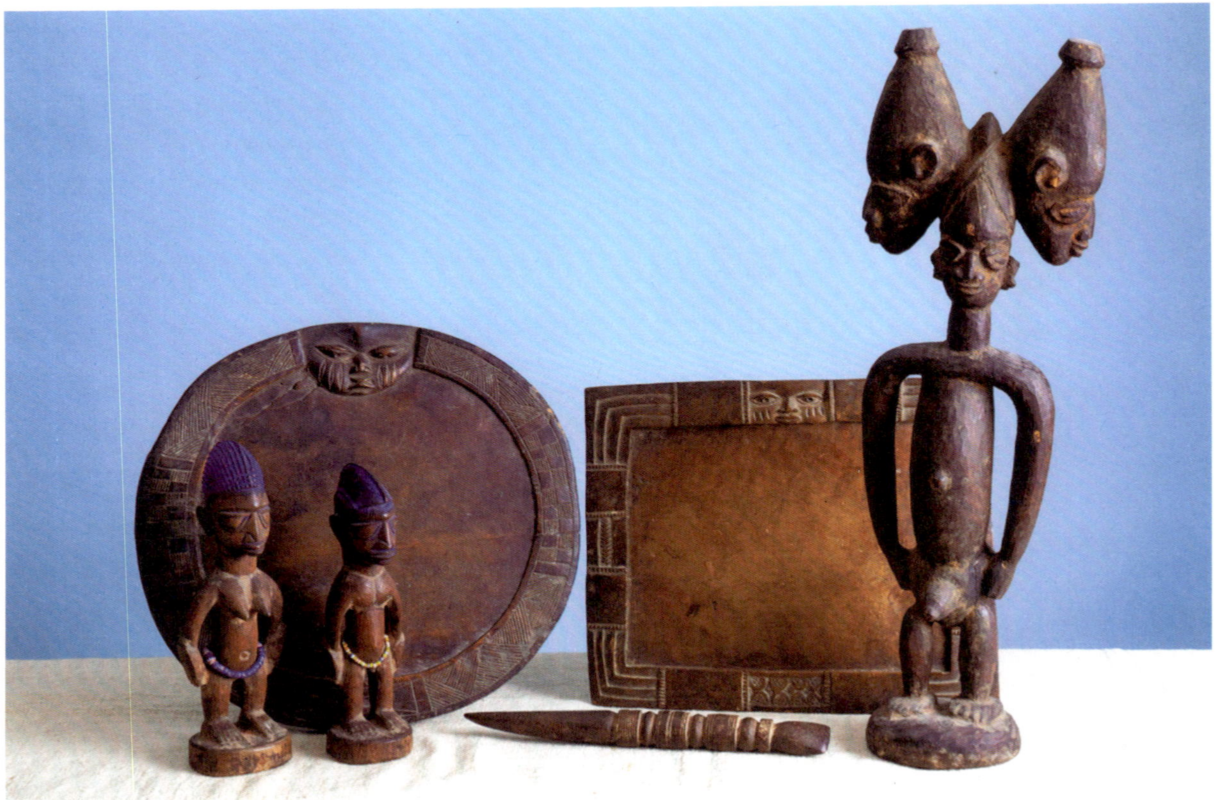

Fetish figures

domesticated them.

In the garden after lunch, tired from rising early, replete with Justin's meal and our experiences at the Grand Marché, we could easily nap in the afternoon shade. More often than not, however, we have visitors. Some of them are commercial, like the Nigerian art dealer who comes often enough so that by now we recognize the sound of his bicycle bell at the gate. He brings in a number of cloth bundles from the bike rack and opens them on the table: mostly "fetish figures," wooden representations of spiritual beings. One is a 20-inch tall figure with three heads and a protuberant penis; another has little horns, a cheerful expression and a curious symbol engraved on its chest. There are several pairs of *ibeji*, small figures representing twins who have died and that a Yoruba mother may carry at her waist in commemoration—two of these are dressed in little leather ponchos covered with cowrie shells. I'm drawn to the *oponifa,* divination boards used in Nigeria. They are carved with the face of the operative oracle spirit, which bears the three parallel cheek scars of the Yoruba. Shells or beans are scattered on the board, the soothsayer makes them jump around with a wooden tapper and reads the patterns they fall into.

Eric and I have promised each other not to buy anything that someone is actually wearing—too obviously rapacious, we think, and disrespectful of person. These carvings, however, have already been torn from their contexts and seem like fair prizes. Now they are "art." Once I drove through a village in Benin where a curious crowd gathered around the car. Those nearest suddenly broke into vehement exclamations, and everyone fell silent and took a step backwards. I had several fetish figures in the front seat, fetishes unfamiliar to this village and therefore untrustworthy, potentially troublesome. When someone asked me why I had them, I tried to explain that I had bought them because they were expressive, as art. Total incomprehension from the villagers, of course, to whom the carvings were spiritually, not aesthetically, expressive. They had power. They were real. I was asked how much I had paid for them, and everyone shook their heads in disbelief. No wonder, I thought, the *yovo* is often a figure of fun.

This afternoon, I buy an oracle board, Eric one of the *ibeji* pairs, and we urge our dealer friend to come back soon. Then we settle down in the garden again, confident that someone else will show up. Sure enough, Justin calls out that Ben is here, and we rise, smiling, to welcome the tall, gentle, and somewhat threadbare figure who appears at the door.

Ben and the bicycle he rides resemble each other: lean, black, worn. He speaks very low and smiles readily, and does typing for Quaker House to make ends meet. Perhaps there was no one else like him in Togo, a lone black American who had decided that it was better to try living in West Africa than to stay in the U.S.; a kind of refugee. Ben had found that the Togolese didn't really accept him as one of them because he was too different. It seemed to me a cruel irony, to flee color-racism to a place where color wasn't the problem, but cultural differences were.

As Ben was leaving, there was a sound of clapping and a strong, young, self-amused voice said, "*Ago, Ago!*"—the Evé way to announce yourself. But Lexy, our next visitor, is not Evé, nor even Togolese. His village is Agué, in Benin. He calls himself a "Lagos Boy," but that's his hip identity; he'd *like* to live in Lagos. Hence the amusement in his voice, as it pleases him to move up and down the coast from Accra to Lagos, adopting identities along the way.

Lexy is wearing a well-cut safari jacket and dark glasses. He's told me that he's been to "naked parties" in Lagos and taken LSD, but I don't know whether to believe him. Sometimes he seems as much part of his village as of the big cities, as when he sings us a derisive pop song about the African "*akada,*" (academic) who studies abroad and has lost touch with his village. In Agué, Lexy's name is Todejrapou, "the river cannot overcome the ocean," inherited from his powerful grandfather. This leads him to be habitually respectful of strangers, he says, any one of whom might be his ancestor come to see how his namesake is behaving.

This time, Lexy has brought all the ingredients for an okra

gumbo and proposes we cook together. We protest: we just ate. By the time this gumbo is ready, he says, you'll be hungry again. We do, indeed, spend all afternoon in the kitchen. Lexy cooks, Justin steps in when he hesitates, Eric tastes everything and I take notes. My notes, looking at them now, are somewhat chaotic; I think we were enjoying ourselves to distraction. Among the things Lexy puts in the gumbo are fresh, dried and powdered shrimp, fresh and smoked fish, tiny green peppers, dried red peppers, ground pork, palm oil, okra of course, and a mystery ingredient, a nugget of something to add viscosity that he calls *akamé*. Chop the okra fine, my notes read, boil it with the *akamé* until it falls thickly, glutinously from the spoon. Grind an onion, some ginger and anise seed together on a grinding stone (we used a rolling pin), add to the okra. We've boiled the pork and the shrimp, they are added with their broth; then red pepper (not too much!), and a Maggi cube of all things, then everything else. Finally, half a Coke bottle of palm oil, salt and five of the little green peppers, breaking each one as it's added and inspecting it for worms, and a handful of chopped lettuce. The gumbo is dark red and its consistency is fairly thick, thick enough to be eaten with our hands, with rice. We are giddy from our cooperative cooking and so hungry we can hardly wait for the gumbo to cool. Justin has provided a bowl of water, a bar of soap and some *eau de lavande* (lavender cologne). We wash our hands, take up the rice in balls, dip it in the sauce, and push it with our thumbs into our eager mouths. Of course it's delicious, glutinous in texture and complex in taste—and quite spicy. But, as Lexy says, "You need a peppery meal from time to time to make your blood alive." By now, the garden is deep in twilight.

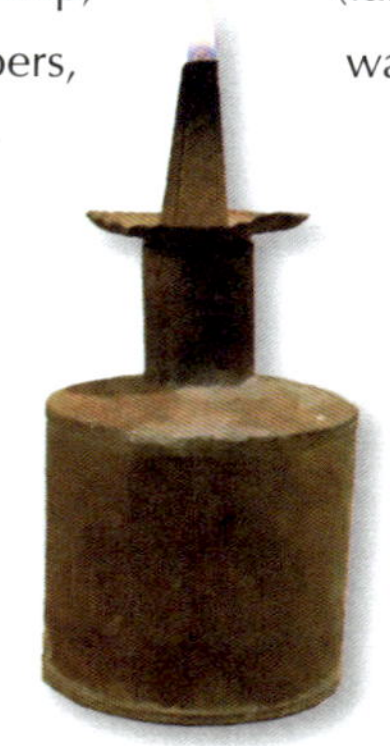

Oil or petrol lamp

Lomé by night is a surprisingly lively place. Justin is too good a cook for us to need to frequent any of the several excellent restaurants downtown. Usually we take showers at the end of the day, Eric brings his Walkman into the garden and plays some Mahler or Mozart, and we set out mosquito coils and a couple of oil lamps (lamps made of empty condensed milk cans that cast a small warm light), and enjoy Justin's dinner: fish in a tomato sauce with *abló* (Togolese polenta) and maybe a chocolate soufflé. Tonight, however, we've eaten too much gumbo to think about dinner. The evening sounds of Nyakponapwé are rising from behind compound walls all around: women calling to each other, children playing, a goat bleating… and drums! Several drums are beating nearby, adding a bass note to the neighborhood noises. I have seen enough Hollywood movies for the drumming to sound slightly sinister, announcing hostilities perhaps, or relaying information about strangers like me. Justin shrugs it off. "*La mort d'un vieux*" ("the death of an elder"), he says. Now a rhythmic clapper has joined the drums, and a chorus of voices; Eric and I decide to go have a look, and soon we are standing at the doorway of a nearby compound.

"*Bonsoir, Monsieur*. May we come in?"

"Sure, sure, come in," says a genial man in a traditional cloth, and we step into the compound. Eric has overruled my reluctance at crashing the party. He's learned that African hospitality is boundless and the *yovo* is usually treated as an honored guest. Sure enough, chairs are brought for us as a mark of welcome. No matter how hard we protest or insist on standing with the crowd, we are invariably seated. I dislike being singled out like this but it would be ungracious to refuse. No one pays any further attention to us, and we can take in the scene at leisure. A pressure lamp has been set in the middle of the compound and sheds its harsh light on a temporary palm frond pavilion at its center, on a crowd of people standing in a square formation before it and on a chorus leader, two drummers, and someone on clappers. Everyone is singing and dancing a kind of shuffling step to the volleying drums. I'm trying to understand the mood of the event. Outside the lighted area, all over the shadowy expanse of the compound, little groups are dancing, too—children, mostly, with older people showing them the steps. Not far from us, young men are clowning around. Two of them dance under the same cloth, slapping each other's behinds. I ask one of them what's going on, and he grins and says, *"C'est pour faire vivre les gens."* ("It's just to have fun.") The general merriment is palpable; I think I've never seen social joy so richly expressed. But there's more. A commanding figure in whiteface, dressed all in white, with a white cloth over his head anchored by a kind of tinsel crown, appears in the square of dancers. He raises his hand, the drums fall silent. White, I know, is the color of the fetish man; maybe this is a religious event. He begins to strut around the square, reciting loudly something the audience seems familiar with. They respond in unison. He moves jerkily, talking in a rapid guttural way that makes the young men around us titter hysterically. He stops suddenly, throws down his crown and cloth, and walks away in an exaggerated huff.

The drums and clapper take up their rhythms again. The young men urge us, too, to dance, but all their friendliness doesn't overcome my shyness and a feeling that I'm an outsider at this boisterous, joyful, puzzling event; but I vow, inwardly, that I *will* join the dance *next* time, and we say goodnight, *"Bonsoir, bonsoir,"* to all those incandescent smiles.

In the street outside the gate, the drums sound suddenly remote behind the high compound wall, and the glare of the pressure lamps is effectively eclipsed. The streets we follow are dark and silent, eerily lit from below by sand drifts reflecting the light of a brilliant full moon rising over Lomé.

"Eric," I ask, "was that a party or a religious event we just witnessed?" He shakes his head. He's long since resigned himself to not understanding many things in Togo. Sometimes, he says, people turn aside his questions because it's difficult to explain in French; sometimes it's not for outsiders to know, and they won't tell.

"Let's go get some ice cream," he says.

We walk into downtown Lomé. The night warmth is all-enveloping and the streets are lit at intervals by streetlamps throwing pools of light every 20 feet or so. Often, someone will be reading in the light, perhaps students who may not have good light at home. We've learned that conversation comes easily here, and have spent hours talking under the streetlights. Tonight, however, we don't stop but continue to another neighborhood called Lom Nava. The streets here are mostly unlit. Once in a while, the headlights of a passing car throw walls and facades into harsh brilliance for a moment, or a door opens and light spills out. Most of the time, however, we walk in the dark along streets full of unseen residents enjoying the warm night, gathering and talking in low tones or walking by noiselessly with only the whisper of their clothes or the snap of a flip-flop to let you know they're passing. I feel out of place, straining to see, afraid I'll bump into someone.

Eric says the Lom Nava ice cream bar is the only one in Lomé officially approved by the American embassy, because the drinking water is boiled. Certain other aspects of the place, however, might have struck an earnest Foreign Service officer as peculiar. The wide-open storefront has no sign, no soundtrack, no strings of colored lights. Within, the only illumination is from a single neon tube on the ceiling, positioned to throw its uncompromising blue-white glare directly onto an impressive rectangular white enameled freezer with three black rubber hatches along its top. The light and the freezer are in a kind of recess behind a counter where two immaculately white-uniformed young Togolese women mutely await our order. Their stillness, their downcast eyes, their symmetrical positions in front of the brilliant freezer, make me think of priestesses serving at an altar. I order coconut and kirsch, Eric banana and durian fruit. The little black hatches are briefly opened and scoops of ice cream placed in glass stem cups which come on a tray with a glass of the embassy-sanctioned water. There are no other customers. The usual Togolese *bonhomie* seems to have been banished from this place. The pitiless neon light casts harsh shadows as if we were in outer space and seems to reduce the furnishings— ceiling fan, metal tables and chairs—to skeletal forms. We order seconds because the flavors, decocted from local fruit, are sublimely fresh and intense. The silence and the unnerving light, however, are a little oppressive, and we speak in low voices. "Let's go to the Rex," Eric says in a whisper.

The Rex Cinema is blazing with light. There's a movie in progress, and it's partly visible from the street because the Rex is a mostly open-air cinema. Impossible, though, to distinguish the soundtrack, which is overwhelmed by the sounds of the audience talking, whistling, calling, and commenting on the storyline. This commotion rises from the unroofed front of the cinema, where the seats are cheaper and where the younger crowd sits on bare concrete blocks. Some of them are sleeping, some empathizing aloud with the film, many passing up and down visiting friends. The volume and animation increase suddenly whenever the film becomes violent; and since the Rex shows a lot of spaghetti westerns (cowboy movies made in Italy in the '60s) and war movies, it's not unusual for the whole audience to be convulsed. People stand on their seats mimicking the action onscreen and mock-machine-gunning the actors or each other, with all the appropriate sound effects. Our friend Bernard has told us that as a teenager, after his first time at the Rex, he was so wrought up by all this violence that he seized the family duck as he returned to his courtyard, twisted its neck and flung it away into the darkness!

Eric and I usually sit further back on chairs or benches in the 100 franc section among older Togolese professionals, wealthy market ladies and Peace Corps volunteers. We used to enjoy sitting up front with the students, but that audience had a particular inconvenience for Eric, who looked a lot like Klaus Kinski, star of Werner Herzog's *Aguirre, the Wrath of God* and father of the actress Natasha Kinski. Kinski had made a lot of spaghetti westerns early in his career, and during the screening of one of them at the Rex, Eric had to go to the men's room at the back of the theatre. His progress up the aisle created pandemonium as many in the audience rose, incredulous, to catch a glimpse of him, many shouting, "Kinski!," laughing and trying to shake his hand.

Thereafter, we sat in back of the theatre and I could enjoy the spectacle of the night sky through the open roof up front. When

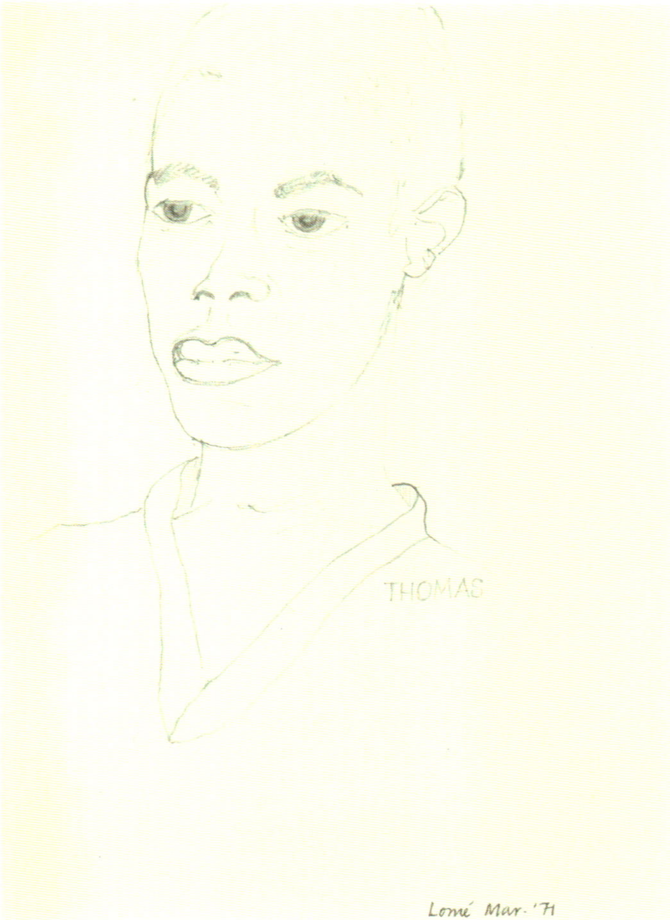

Sketch by the author

the movie was less than riveting, there might instead be a leisurely moon to watch as it traversed the velvety tropical sky, or an unfamiliar constellation to ponder and, occasionally, a shooting star. On the other hand, rain could be a problem. The roof extended only over the back of the hall, and as soon as the typically intense tropical downpour began, the younger crowd would storm up looking for shelter and you might find several damp strangers eager to share your seat with you. Resistance was futile; everything in West Africa is shared as a matter of course, and arguments like, "Hey, pal, I paid for this seat," fall on culturally deaf ears. As a matter of fact, there's a lot about the Rex experience that's explained by traditional African ideas about audience and performance. Western audiences focus forward to watch the stage or screen, and a certain formality is imposed: no talking, stay in your seat, try not to fall asleep. These rules isolate audience members from each other and from the performers, too. In a traditional event such as we had seen earlier in our neighbor's compound, however, the audience faces inward on itself and is as active as the artists. The people are the chorus, clapping and chanting and enhancing the instrumental music. When a celebrant calls out, everyone responds. When someone steps forward to dance, someone else follows to dab the sweat from the dancer's face. The drummers may be the only specialists. It's a participatory experience, as is a movie at the Rex. The Rex audience—like Bernard—seems to think it's actually part of the movie.

Tonight, Eric and I are looking for Thomas on the sidewalk outside the cinema. Among the bicycle racks and knots of idlers examining posters for the next movie, a number of vendors are selling snacks from small tables. Our friend Thomas is there, smiling in greeting across the brightly wrapped candy bars, loose kola nuts, tea bags, instant drinks, and AA batteries that he's selling. He makes hot chocolate for us on a little burner and we sit with him on chairs of blond varnished wood that match the table. All this he bought with the modest capital that Eric and I provided.

We had met Thomas during a morning walk on the beach, where he had spent the night after smuggling chickens over the border from Ghana to sell in Lomé. The border is a complex of lagoons that has to be negotiated carefully, and the border guards beat you if they can catch you. Thomas told us this with such appealing diffidence, in such a gentle voice, that we felt we had to make ourselves responsible for him. Eric tells him he can sleep at Quaker House whenever he needs to; I frankly fall in love with him. Together, we set him up in business outside the Rex. He comes by the house from time to time to wash his clothes and let us know how he's getting on. Either he is not so inclined, or wiser than his 17 or 18 years, but my passion for him remains unrequited. I figure I've fallen in love with the gentleness that pervades his speech and manner, and is new to me and my New York self-assertion. How disarming, this pervasive mildness of Thomas', the softness in his eyes and quiet voice! I found that it's not an unusual characteristic of the Togolese. Once on a rustic up-country bridge, an imposingly tall local man stopped me to ask me where I was from. When I said the United States, he laughed and mimed the fast draw of a frontier gunslinger. Oh, so he sees *us* as violent, I thought. We talked for a moment and I felt the same charm of an immense gentleness and of the benevolence with which he regarded me from his great height. In parting, he said, "*Alors, on s'est rencontrés sur un pont,*" ("So, we've met on a bridge") and there seemed to me a lovely significance in that.

On our way home from the Rex, we stop at the night market by the railroad tracks for a snack. There are no streetlights and the market appears as an extension of the night sky, a field of darkness lit by hundreds of little petrol lamps like stars. Open-faced lean-to stalls shelter large, steaming black pots full of different stews sitting on beds of charcoal that glow with the petrol lamps. From one of these, we get some rice and stew, a rich spicy sauce with bits of meat and leafy vegetables swimming in red palm oil, generously ladled into Chinese enameled tin plates by a woman who shakes with laughter at the idea that these two *yovos* are going to enjoy her cooking; or is she laughing at the comments that are coming out of the surrounding dark from her jocular sisters minding other black pots in adjacent stalls? We sit on benches to eat at a board table. The darkness is full of animation, men and women only glimpsed in the limited glow of the little lamps, coming and going, calling and laughing. The good humor is as thick as the night.

We each take away an ear of roasted corn to eat on the way back to Nyakponapwé. The students have gone home by now and the pools of lamplight are deserted. Most of our local friends would probably say it would be better to be home at this time of night. They might urge us to go down to the port in the darkness to see Olympio's ghost; but they would balk at coming with us. Sylvanus Olympio was Togo's first president, assassinated in a military coup in January 1963. The man who claims to have fired the fatal shot is Étienne Eyadéma, the current president. Olympio's ghost, our friends tell us, is to be seen every night at the port, making endless rounds in a white Mercedes. Eyadéma is a Kabré tribesman from the north of Togo. I wonder whether the persistence of Olympio's ghost might be an expression of the coastal Togolese's resentment of the northern usurper.

For more midnight thrills, our friends tell us to look for a giant tree under which an entire court—king, wives, ministers and subjects, all shadows of living persons—gathers at night. A witch has ensnared them, and if the tree is cut down, they will die with it. We're told with a grin that the witch is now being held in the fearsome military barracks outside the city; she ensnared the wrong people. Despite their grins, our friends give credence to these stories and stay home at night.

We walk home on the hard wet sand of the beach, watching the big waves come ashore. In the moment before they break and send sparkling foam up around our ankles, their arching crests cast a fleeting moon-shadow below onto their towering indrawn mass. The moonlight flashes and skips on the turbulence, subsides into a languid watery hula dance offshore, and is concentrated like crinkled silver leaf on the black featureless far horizon.

By the time we get home, the night watchman is asleep in his chair, confident that his amulets will protect us. Justin, however, is still up. He is the true guardian of Quaker House, keeping an eye on Eric's collections of cloth and sculpture and making a discreet triage of people who visit. Sometimes, after dark, he comes into my room when I'm already in bed and sits on the opposite end, giggling and looking shyly down as he asks whether I like a new dish, suggests that a new acquaintance is not to be trusted, or compliments me on the latest Liberian tie-dye I've hung on the wall. Tonight, he wants to hear where we've been and sits on the bedcover, speaking softly. Around the house, Justin rarely wears anything but shorts and sandals, and in New York I would have certain expectations of a shirtless, well-muscled man on my bed who smiles at me and speaks in low, intimate tones. But Justin's is an African intimacy, physically casual but not intentionally erotic, full of his own ease of being and his strong, slightly amused devotion to Eric and me. I love him back from my end of the bed, and to this day think of him as a best, true friend.

Eric is very much a creature of the beach. That could be because his parents are from Friesland is northern Holland, a moist, cool, cloudy region innocent of beaches. The Kiers left when Eric was very young, but sometimes he seems to be still drying out, and declares that he's only really happy sitting in the sun. So in the afternoon, after work, he invariably walks the quarter mile to the beach to get a tan, to breathe sea air, to chat with all who pass, to just sit in the sun.

Lomé beach is so long, it loses itself in haze at both ends, but it's really just a small part of the long, sandy coast of West Africa. In 1971, most townsfolk couldn't swim, and European tourists hadn't yet arrived in any numbers. There were no cabanas, no waterfront restaurants, no parasols or folding chairs, no pale bodies spread-eagled on towels. Lomé town and the beach met without fanfare along an oceanfront boulevard, itself often covered with sand blowing between the decaying concrete posts of an ornamental balustrade built by the Germans colonists, before the French arrived. The sand just kept on blowing, blowing across the boulevard, down the streets, into the walled compounds and around your feet until Lomé seemed one with the beach, uncertain of its urban nature and insouciant of the ocean waters which stretched away, unimpeded by bays or sandbars or islands, into the true deep. One day, out of that empty sea and sky, a tempest of wind struck us.

I was at a window, talking to Eric in his office across the lawn. Suddenly, the sun went out like a light bulb. The garden looked oddly colorless for a moment, then a tremendous blast of wind made the palm trees bend over double and the roaring air was full of flying leaves and branches. I stepped back as a big piece of corrugated tin from someone's roof went cartwheeling by. Eric's mouth was still open, saying something inaudible over the sound of the wind. A moment later, the wind stopped. Total silence. A moment more, and voices were raised, children were bawling, a goat bleating. Seeing that the blast was brief and not much damage done to the house, we walked out into the neighborhood. The roof of the school showed big holes, and someone over the wall was whimpering. I don't remember any sirens or ambulances. Things went back to normal pretty quickly. *"Le Cyclone,"* the Lomé papers called it; but the sky very soon turned blue again, and by the time we'd reached the beach, an untroubled sea beat on the sand as usual.

In addition to the concrete balustrade, the Germans built a steel pier on the beach opposite the center of Lomé. The pier goes straight out to sea for 300 feet or so, standing in the water, it seems, without any masonry elements to support it. The effect is almost lacy, a delicate Erector-set structure; but it used to handle large ships and still has a railroad track running its length. We follow the tracks to the end of the pier and look back at Lomé's modest panorama: a row of palms, horizontal rooflines, the cathedral spire and the Hôtel Benin.... it's as if we were in a skiff offshore, at sea but not on it. We get down on all fours to watch the waves passing beneath us through the fragile-looking steel. Way

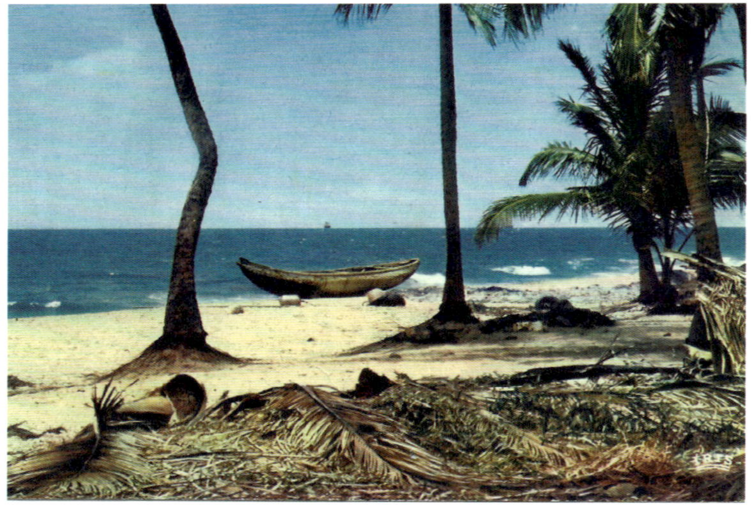

Beach at Lomé

out here, these are still the waves of the open ocean, silent, inexorably regular, powerfully compact as they race by below us. We hear them break with a roar as they meet the sand.

Walking back, we have to be careful not to trip over the fishing lines that crisscross the pier. There are always fishermen on the pier, silent, concentrated men lining its length. *"Alors, messieurs, c'est le retour?"* ("And so, gentlemen, you're back?"), one of them says with cheerful irony— as if there were any other way to go. We stop to talk, and he tells us he's an electrician ashore and a member of the national table tennis team. He fishes just for sport. His fellows, he says, indicating with a gesture the men who are leaning over the rail in rapt expectation of a catch, or speaking to each other in undertones so as not to alarm their prey, are much more experienced, and fish to eat. By the way, he adds with a smile, would we like to see some professional ping-pong later in the week?

We walk back onto the beach, charmed by the pier and its devotees. Abandoned by the colonizers who built it to exploit a conquered people, it's become an unplanned marine park, an informal nature observatory poised between waves and clouds, supporting a little community of the patient and the taciturn.

The beach has other regulars. Loiterers and the unemployed, or people on the margins of the economy like Thomas, may sleep there at night. Early in the morning, a few joggers appear. They are often Peace Corps volunteers, young women who run to lose a few pounds. The Togolese men are puzzled. Why do the girls want to be skinny, when a gentle plumpness is so erotic—like the rolls of flesh at the back of the neck when a woman tilts her head back, which drive a man crazy?

The beach is put to spiritual uses, too. The powerful, elemental blankness of the sea appeals to the soul, and fetish ceremonies on the beach are quite common. These ceremonies leave unmistakable traces: an area of sand scored and trampled by a crowd, and drifting feathers from sacrificed fowl whose bedraggled remains are tumbled around in the surf.

This evening, Eric and I have come across a sea-ceremony opposite the Hôtel de la Plage. It's a good-humored affair. An audience of beach boys and passersby are commenting aloud and grinning at the fetish women who sit chanting and swaying in place in a semi-circle with its open end to the sea. The women are dressed in white with white head cloths, and their faces and hands are white with talcum powder. They sing in unison over candles burning on a mound of sand before each of them. Several tall wooden staffs banded with ivory and topped with carved human figures are planted here and there in the sand. I can see, further down at the water's edge, large enameled basins piled high with fruit topped with decapitated pigeons.

The women's swaying is becoming more pronounced; some roll their eyes back in their heads. One woman springs up, still singing, to give a resounding high five to a tall man in a white robe who is part of the ceremony. Another and another follow, leaping up with a whoop, staggering around the semi-circle and slapping the tall man's palm with a huge theatrical movement and a rich, percussive smack. He in his long robe with a golden emblem of some sort on his forehead seems to be a kind of director, striding around, guiding and exhorting the fetish women.

The setting sun is approaching the horizon. The chanting picks up and the trance becomes more agitated. The women start to convulse as they are possessed. Several of them jump up and sprint towards the surf. They're trying to throw themselves into the sea! But the beach boys are ready for this, and tackle them at the water's edge. A few get through and splash into the water, wallowing full length on their backs in the waves. The boys are laughing as they haul the women back up the beach, wet through, eyes rolling back, still dancing with exaggerated, cocky, exalted expressions. They move jerkily, making guttural sounds, shaken by little whoops; finally, they sit down to eat rice and sauce and a raw egg each, served in silence by more men in white. By now, the palm trees along the beach are deeply silhouetted against the sunset orange sky and a band of dark clouds has appeared out to sea.

From time to time, we go to the little beach house we've rented down the coast from Lomé, where we spend hours swimming nude in the clean warm sea water. There's a village of fishermen nearby, but the men are usually out in the boats and the women don't seem to mind our nudity. Jerry and Claudine Karzen, our co-renters, usually come with us. Jerry works as a vaccinator attached to the American embassy. He has a high forehead over a craggy face, twinkling eyes, and an earnest, empathetic voice. His wife, Claudine, is a French woman, darkly tanned and thin as pulled taffy, and her sharp-elbowed skepticism is a foil to Jerry's earnestness. She's up for anything; once I asked her how to make a shirt with some fabric from the market and we spent all afternoon cutting and sewing, finally producing something comically misshapen and dwarfish. Their house in Lomé had a long room on pillars over the garden, and we spent hours there getting high and dancing up and down the long unpartitioned room to "Oh Happy Day" by the Edwin Hawkin Singers. When we got hungry, we had recourse to a freezer full of food from the embassy commissary, especially those sweet Sara Lee cakes that haunt the dreams of every ex-pat.

At our shared beach house, we'd walk up the beach, feeling a little exposed in our nakedness under the wide-eyed sun, and float down with the current past Claudine, who kept watch on us from in front of the modest palm-frond house...and then we would start all over again, for hours at a time. This was our ritual whenever we left Lomé, and Eric has just announced that we're going to Benin to meet his parents at the airport in Cotonou. We'll be taking them to remarkable sites in Benin and then to a village in rural Togo where, although they don't know it yet, they have family. The Europeanized coast will seem far away, and we fortify ourselves against the rigors of up-country travel and the unfamiliar complexities of a deeper Africa by blissful immersion in this effervescent surf.

ABOMEY

We are eating in a stall at a street market in Cotonou with Eric's parents. They have just arrived after long flights from Santa Barbara, California, and I'm watching to see how they will take to West African food: *gari* (cassava meal), *abló* (steamed cornbread), fish sauces and rice, everything eaten with the hand. Trudi Kiers asks for a spoon but Luc takes some *abló* in his fingers, plunges it into a sauce, pops it into his mouth, and declares it delicious. They are both very good sports. I'm not sure my own parents could arrive from New York City and share so wholly and heartily their son's enthusiasm for an unfamiliar cuisine and culture. But the Kiers emigrated to the U.S. from the Netherlands with four children and moved across the whole continent from city to city before settling on the West Coast, and this odyssey may account for their admirable adaptability. Reassured by their willingness, we set off the next day for the interior of Benin and the old royal capital of Abomey.

The kings of Abomey founded their capital in 1625 and flourished there as warriors and slave-dealers until the French took the city in 1892. The last king, Béhanzin, fought fiercely to keep his kingdom and capital from colonization. His army, a third of which was made up of well-armed virginal women warriors ("Amazons" to the Europeans), battled the French in two successive wars. Béhanzin set fire to Abomey as he abandoned it, but fortunately for posterity, most of it survived. This may have been because of its sheer extent: there had been twelve kings in the dynasty, and each built his own sprawling palace of thatch-roofed adobe halls, courtyards, residences and storehouses. The defensive wall around them grew to be six kilometers long.

Before we tour the city, Eric wants his parents to meet his deaf-mute friend, Tokonou. We bump along an unpaved road into the city through fields of yam and peanuts and groves of palm and mango trees. The car edges past a family on a bicycle. The father pedals with his young son on the handlebars. The mother rides sidesaddle over the rear wheel with a baby on her back and a plastic bucket on her head. The Kiers express alarm at their perilous balance, and then astonishment as the whole family combusts into smiles and waves and shouts of welcome as we drive by.

It's hard to know how Luc and Trudi will react to Tokonou. He is a strongly built young man with a beautiful, broad face. His complete deafness and consequent lack of speech make him a startlingly original personality in a traditional culture that demands a high degree of socialization. It's evening by the time we catch up with him. He's just showered and runs to greet us, glistening, radiant in the car headlights. Recognition and delight wring strange, high-pitched cries from him. We try to explain that Luc and Trudi are Eric's parents, but I'm not sure he fully understands. No matter, communication is mostly physical. We shake hands repeatedly, laughing and smiling and patting each other on the back. He holds his head high and back, breathing through flared nostrils like a stallion, and indeed, I feel that horses do run up and down inside him and behind his eyes, untamed horses of the Id. A passerby in the dark taunts him and he's off, chasing him good-naturedly down the road, returning a moment later in a state of undiluted delight that courses through and over him. Everything about him seems passionate, pure, unpremeditated. Trudi and Luc shake hands with Tokonou again and again before they get back in the car. They are silent in the back seat, as if turning things over in their minds.

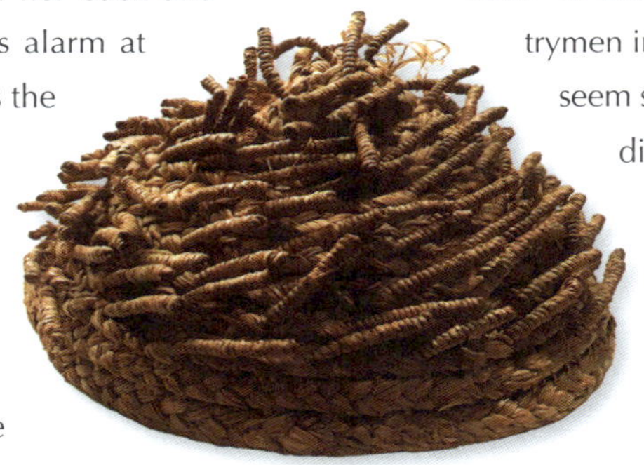

The river god's cap

We leave them at the Hôtel Campement in downtown Abomey and head out to the night market to eat. A loud cry of "Hey, white man!" in down-home accents startles us. Some of our countrymen in a car want to know where there's a hotel. They seem so loud, so self-consciously out of place, that we direct them to the *other* hotel.

At the side of the road in a little tin-roofed cabana, a noisy gasoline-powered mill is grinding corn into flour for a group of people who stand around waiting for their turn, each with a bag or basket of grain. The racket, the vibrations and the rhythmic agitation of the little machine contrast with the silence and stillness of the people waiting. They crouch or stand or lean around in the tiny space, staring down at the mill and lit only by a petrol lamp in a little girl's lap. Its glow catches a profile here, the line of an arm there, the liquid flash of an eye…. the rest is in shadow. Everyone's expectancy centers downwards. It's as beautiful as a Nativity, except for the striving incongruous clatter of the mill engine.

In the absence of streetlights, the dark sky is powdery with stars in which Orion blazes. The night market, too, seems like a

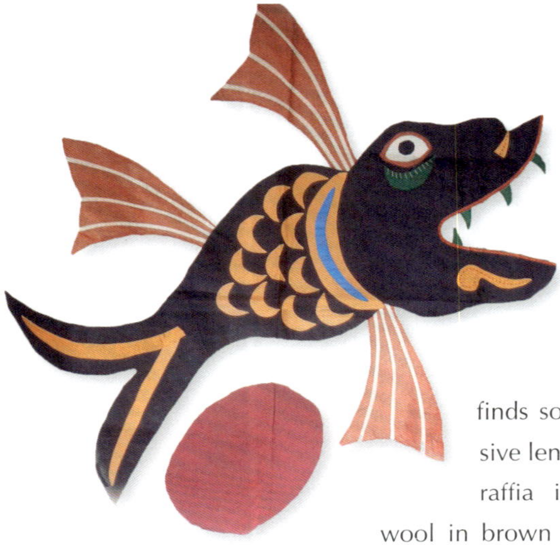

starry field of petrol lamps. I buy a conical cap covered with raffia curls that mimic the hair of Tohossou, a river god. Eric finds some curious, inexpensive lengths of roughly woven raffia inset with panels of wool in brown and green, and buys a half-dozen of them. We attract some surprised looks as we leave the market draped with them, and Eric inquires at the hotel what they might be for. Shrouds, it turns out, to wrap a corpse. Each mourner is expected to contribute one, hence their low price and throw-away manufacture. We creep back to the market early in the morning to leave them in a neat bundle in front of the stall where we'd bought them. Eric has developed an African respect for spirits stronger even than his collector's instinct.

Abomey appliqué: King Béhanzin

Beginning our tour of the palaces, our guide, Michel Glélé (himself descended from an Abomey ruler), tells us how Béhanzin confounded the French one last time. After his defeat, the king used his fetish powers to stop the engines of the steamship that was taking him to exile in Martinique, leaving it wallowing helplessly in the waters off the port of Ouidah. He was devoted to the long African pipe that he had been smoking, he claimed, since he was an infant. The French were obliged to send to Abomey for the pipe, Michel says, before the ship could proceed.

The palace halls and courtyards we pass through seem to still resonate with the power and personalities of the dynasty. The adobe walls are inset with colorful bas-reliefs, vivid heraldic emblems of each king. Appliqué tapestries on the wall repeat the narrative, and royal regalia and utensils take it up on a smaller scale. I feel we're surrounded by voices that speak of the kings loud and clear, in primary colors and declamatory symbols drawn directly from nature. The figure of a chameleon, for example, represents a king who wasn't crowned until he was 60; like the immobile lizard, he won the prize by patience. Another king is represented by a buffalo wearing a tunic; once it's on him, it's not easily taken off—a warning against rebellion. We see the image of a covered gourd vessel that holds traditional mysteries not to be questioned or revealed. The vessel appears within the rough outline of a Christian church, recalling the king's subjects to their ancestral beliefs. Two hands support a clay pot full of holes; only if all the people help plug them, will the kingdom be whole. The images are fresh, lively, and pervasive. I feel the history of Abomey as something alive, eerily present.

As we press deeper into these palace compounds among the bright speaking symbols, we arrive unexpectedly on a broad courtyard where a real royal audience is unfolding. Today

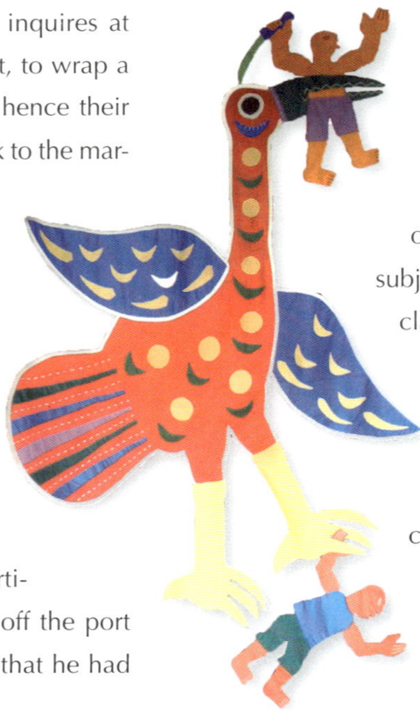

Abomey appliqué: King Gangnihessou

is a market day in Abomey, and the market women have come to make obeisance to an ancient man on an armchair throne who must be Béhanzin's descendant. Fifty or so women, jingling with tin jewelry and wrapped three and four times in bright cloth, some bearing great wooden broadswords (could they represent the famous Amazons?), kneel with their heads to the ground in front of the old king. His crown is an appliqued cap, his glasses have lenses like bottle bottoms, his shoulders are sunken and his bones seem to stick out through his skin ("Over 100 years," Michel whispers); but his movements are sprightly as he acknowledges the women, who kowtow, clap and chant in unison and then carry a pinch of earth to their foreheads or throw it with a graceful gesture over their shoulder. Suddenly they withdraw in a body, leaving the king surrounded by his wives and counselors in the vast courtyard. Almost immediately, their places are taken by a delegation of mostly elderly men performing the same obeisance. Then begins a long recitation of the Abomey dynasty from reign to reign. The *griot* is a young man with the *agogo*, the iron double bell of his profession, resting on his hip. Suddenly, repeatedly, he raises it high and strikes it, *Pong-PING!* to punctuate his narrative. When his account falters, an elder prompts him. And twice, without visible cue, someone fires an old musket into the air—a long, muzzle-loading musket with a violent head of smoke and flame and an enormous roar that bounces around the compound walls and nearly knocks us off the log we sit on. Between discharges, the musketeer trots off to the back of the courtyard to reload from a powder horn. At one point, a latecomer arrives, makes venerable haste across the broad court, falls to his knees among his colleagues and very beautifully presses a pinch of earth to his brow.

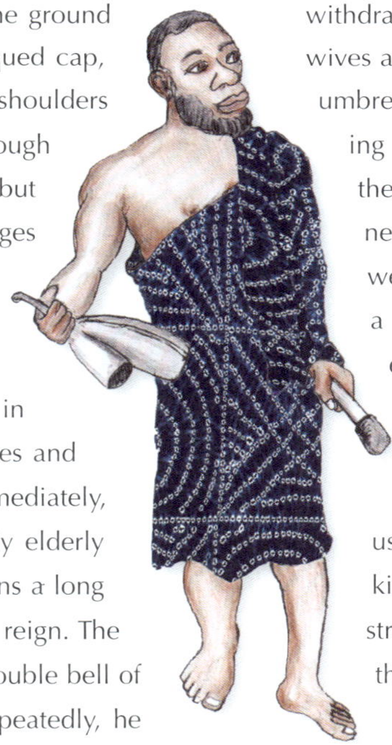

Sketch by the author

Suddenly, the recitation is finished. The king rises, the elders withdraw. A procession forms behind the king: counselors and wives at either elbow, another wife behind holding an appliqued umbrella over his head, more courtiers, and lastly, a wife carrying the throne upside down on her head. The old man leads them briskly out a gateway. In the ensuing silence and blankness of the wide, dun courtyard, we are a bit stunned by what we've seen. Michel Glélé tells us that this ceremony, part of a cyclical veneration of the last dynasty, occurs only once every eight years.

As part of these ceremonies, the tombs of the Abomey kings are refurbished. They lie deep within the neglected ruins of the palaces, and Michel takes us through the tumbled-down adobe courtyards of an early king, Ouégbadja, to his tomb, a substantial low round structure whose eaves of new thatch come right down to the ground. We're greeted by Ouégbadja's wives—that is, descendants of his wives, who care for the tomb and welcome supplicants like us. They maintain the same relationship to each other that their forebears had during the king's lifetime: one is his first wife, another his cousin-wife, etc.

Following Michel's example, we take off our shoes, which seems to make a good impression on the women. They prostrate themselves before a low opening in the thatch eaves and explain to the king that his "white children" have come to ask a blessing on their travels. I'm struck by their tone: no low incantations or prayerful whispers here, they are almost shouting through the little doorway, as if the king's spirit were slightly deaf. They pause occasionally to listen, as if in conversation. I sense a blurring of time, a strong simultaneity of past and present. The spirit of Ouégbadja is right here, right now. His wives live on in their descendants. Things that were, coexist with things that are. I feel suddenly less assured of my habitual linear perception of time as a continually advancing present that leaves the past irretrievably behind.

Mr. Kiers announces that he would like to see the inside of the tomb. Eric and I frown; is this inquisitiveness appropriate to a high sacred site? Aren't some things best left unexamined? But the wives hesitate only for Michel's translation. One of them accompanies him, both crawling on their hands and knees, posteriors side-by-side, through the low opening into the dark interior of the tomb. The only thing to be seen there, Luc emerges to say, is the king's bedstead.

PALIMÉ

We're arriving in Palimé in western Togo. From Abomey, we've driven through Ganvié on the Benin-Togo border, and from there back across the modest girth of Togo. Ganvié is unusual, a village of houses built on stilts over a lake. Ouidah is a nearby coastal town with a dark history of slave trafficking and a reputation for strong *gris-gris*; but we have pressed on to Palimé, for Eric is eager to introduce his parents to his elderly friend, Tobui Apetor. The red laterite road leads from cultivations surrounding the town down to urban streets lined with residences and shop stalls, towards a

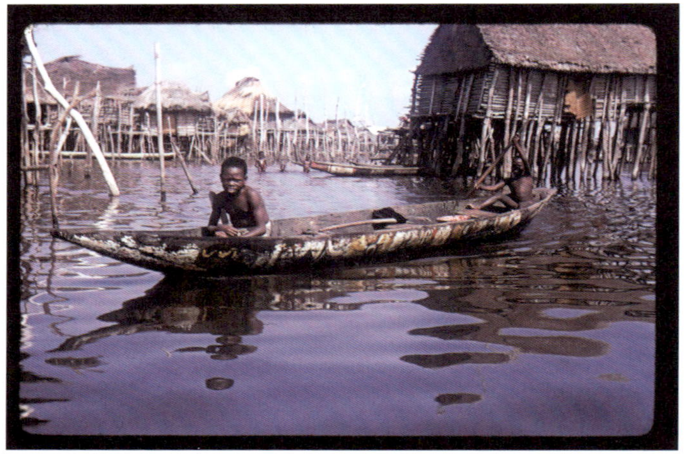

Village of Ganvié, in Benin

cathedral spire. We see very few cars, everyone is walking or bicycling, carrying all kinds of things on their heads: a crushing load of firewood, a high stack of multi-colored plastic basins, a sewing machine. Chin down, nape of the neck stretched, shoulders relaxed, straight back and conscious gait: the posture required to carry things on your head makes everyone move in a strong beautiful way, even when they're not carrying anything.* The streets of Palimé are full of men and woman walking in this graceful and leisurely way. No one hurries.

Alongside the cathedral at the center of town, there is an

* A heavy burden on your head requires help to get down. Someone takes it neatly from you as you bend the knees slightly and put one hand up to steady the load, inclining your head a little to help it slide off. It happens very quickly, but it's always graceful and wonderfully cooperative.

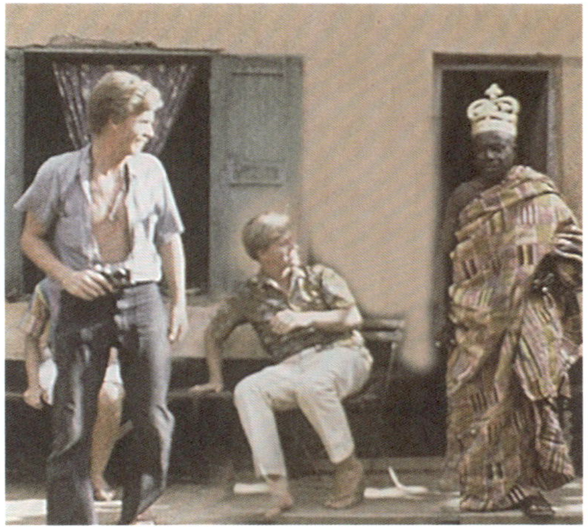

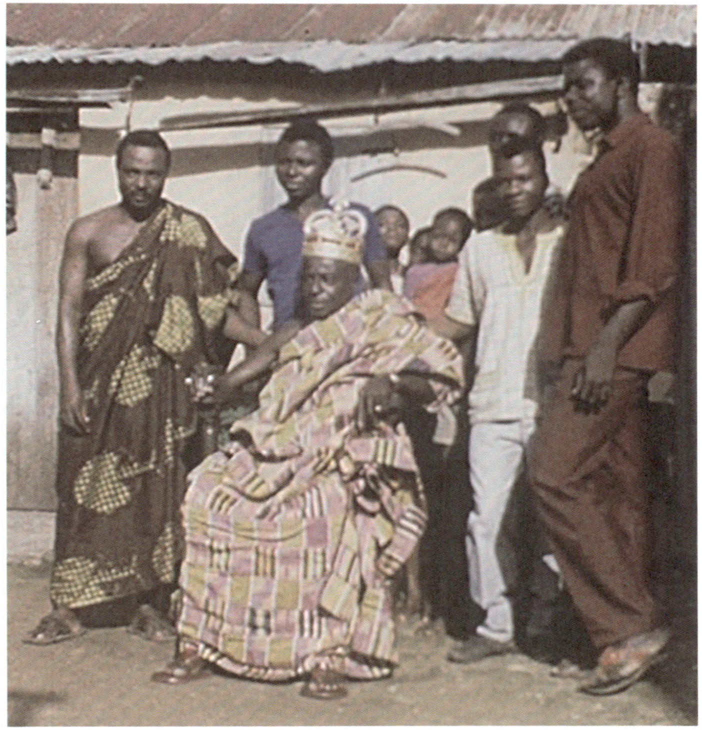

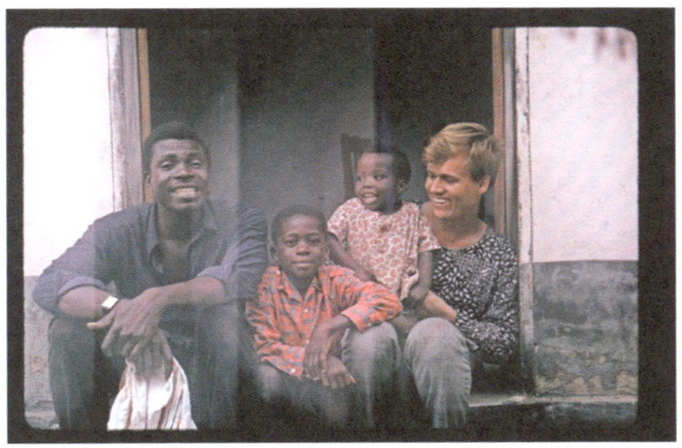

TOP LEFT: Lucas, Eric, Tobui Apetor; ABOVE: King and court; LEFT: Julien Koumako, Eric with children.

open-sided kind of courthouse or tribunal where local disputes are settled according to tribal law. Inside, I can see crowded benches, a panel of elders, a man facing them, talking and gesturing. Over the door is a sign with the name TOBUI APETOR II. This is the person, a chief of the Éwé people, whom we've come to see.

The chief is not at home. Behind the tribunal is his house, a haphazard complex of interlocking open spaces between adobe buildings with tin roofs. We're happy to follow our guide, Julien Koumako, the chief's nephew and a medical student in Dakar, through the maze. Julian introduces us to a bewildering number of aunts and cousins who are washing clothes or cooking or just sitting around talking. But the old man, they say, is in his fields, supervising the cultivation of the yam crop.

One of the red laterite roads leads us out of town to the fields from which the chief's extended family gets all its oranges and yams, corn, tomatoes, and coconuts. Corneille, his son, leads us through a dense grove of fruit-bearing trees: mango, coconut, cacao, orange, banana and grapefruit. It looks like a jungle in here, the air is full of birdsong and the underbrush runs wild. We start across a more open area of long grasses and massed vegetation. Corneille and Eric laugh hugely when I ask impatiently, "So where are the fields?" Everything you see here is cultivated, Corneille explains; but only the corn and the yams are actually planted in rows. "Fields" are not, then, the surveyed rectangles filled with neat rows of beans that I know from my childhood in upstate New York. I have to adjust to the nominal boundaries, asymmetrical planting and organic organization of African agriculture.

We find the chief in his yam field. At 73, he is an old man wearing a dusty jacket and battered hat. He moves with the reduced motions of age but his eyes twinkle at greeting us. I'm struck by his dignity, a serene restraint in manner and voice. He conducts us to one of several yam storage barns in his fields. It is quite small, maybe 10 feet square, made of a bamboo framework with palm thatch and walls. Its interior is surprisingly cool, and the yams are neatly laced to the framework. The chief drapes a more formal cloth over himself and starts back with us, happily chatting with Eric's father in German. Mr. Kiers learned some German in his native Holland; but the chief learned his from the German colonizers before World War I, before Togo was administered by France! The two elders seem delighted with each other.

We wait in what I take to be an audience chamber while the old man showers. All around us on the walls are photographs of Éwé chiefs in their brilliant *kente* robes, heads circled by figured plaques of gold, fingers heavy with gold rings. There is also an autographed photo of the German president Heinrich Lübke in its bright silver frame. On the table are vases of plastic flowers and a large short-wave radio. The chief returns to eat with us, and we step outside to watch two women pound the yams they have boiled for our meal. They stand on either side of a waist-high wooden mortar and alternately drive large wooden pestles into the cooked yams it contains. They have to be nimble and attuned to each other to maintain the alternation; the mortar is too narrow for more than one pestle at a time. They are amused that we find this common chore so fascinating, and laugh as they build up the tempo, pounding the yams into a bland glossy sticky dish called *fufu,* the basic starch of a Togolese meal. Throughout the chief's compounds, women are filling the evening air with the staccato rhythms of the pestles.

Now Trudi and Luc have to learn a new trick: to swallow without chewing. A portion of *fufu* is taken up with the fingertips, plunged into a highly-flavored sauce (we are eating beef and smoked fish in rich red palm oil), popped into your mouth and just swallowed. No chewing necessary at all, the pestles have done all the work. Eric and I are old hands at this, and laugh when his parents, fighting the instinctual urge to chew, end up with the sauce dribbling down their chins.

Two years earlier, I had come to Palimé with Eric and two good friends from Lomé, LeBon and Bernard, when we saw a puzzling but memorable performance of *Macbeth*. Our friends introduced us to a group of young men who seemed to spend all their time

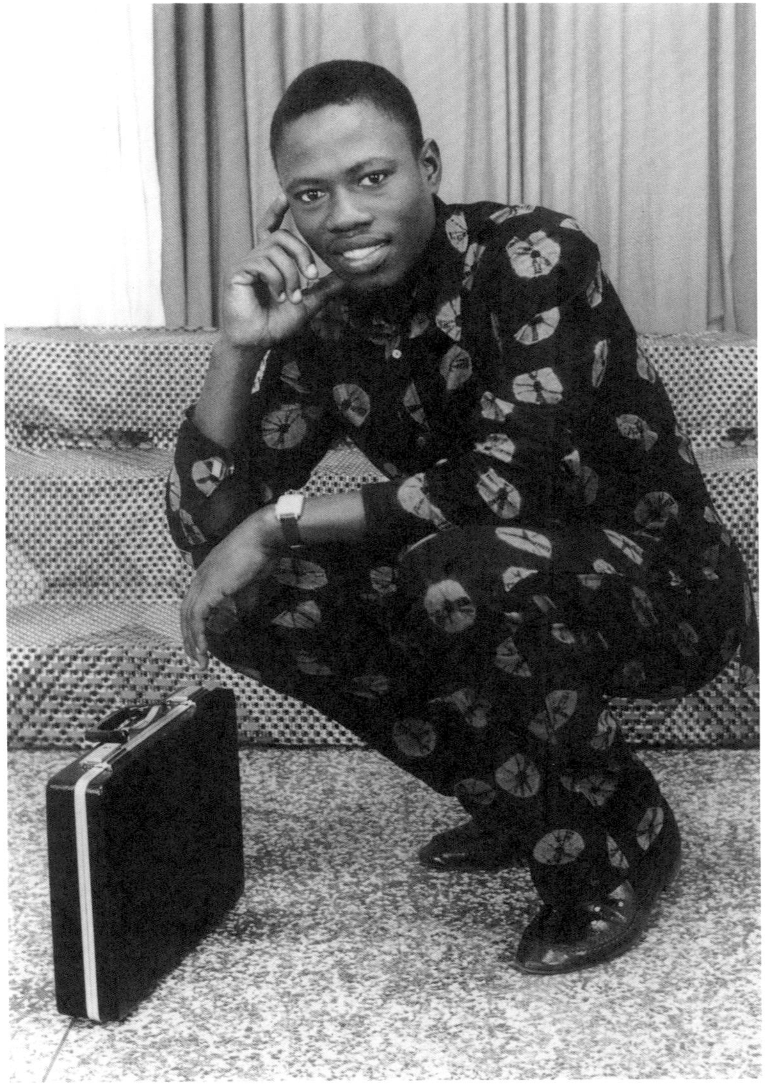

René LeBon, Lomé

dancing. I had brought a hand-held Sony video camera and spent several mornings filming them as they practiced rapid complicated steps to an orchestra of drums; but in the afternoon, they all seemed to disappear together. "They're preparing a performance of *Macbeth*," LeBon explained solemnly, adding that I couldn't see it until it was ready. Several days later, he told me to bring my video camera and follow him. We walked into the fields outside the town and in a clearing of beaten ground under a spreading tree, I found the young men already in the midst of their performance. They were strangely transformed, having exchanged their modish shirts, jeans and sandals for traditional cloth and even grass skirts. Their feet were bare, beads had appeared at their throats and waists and many had painted their faces and torsos white. I recognized them as the boys I knew, but they might as well have been from another world and time. Most of them seemed to be in trance, their eyes rolled back or closed. The drums volleyed compellingly, but the dancers drifted to and fro to their own rhythms. I wondered dimly which ones might be Macbeth and his lady, and raised my camera; the next moment it failed, leaving me with only a few seconds of exposed film. I wonder to this day what power interfered with the Sony. Plainly, what I saw had nothing to do with *Macbeth*. Neither LeBon or Bernard would ever tell me what was really going on—an initiation? some kind of collective *gris-gris*? Now I knew that I would be forever in the dark about some things; and that I couldn't expect too much of my camera in these situations.

The next day, after a warm farewell from Tobui Apetor and his family, we drive north into the land of the Akposso people, where Luc and Trudi have a family they've never met.

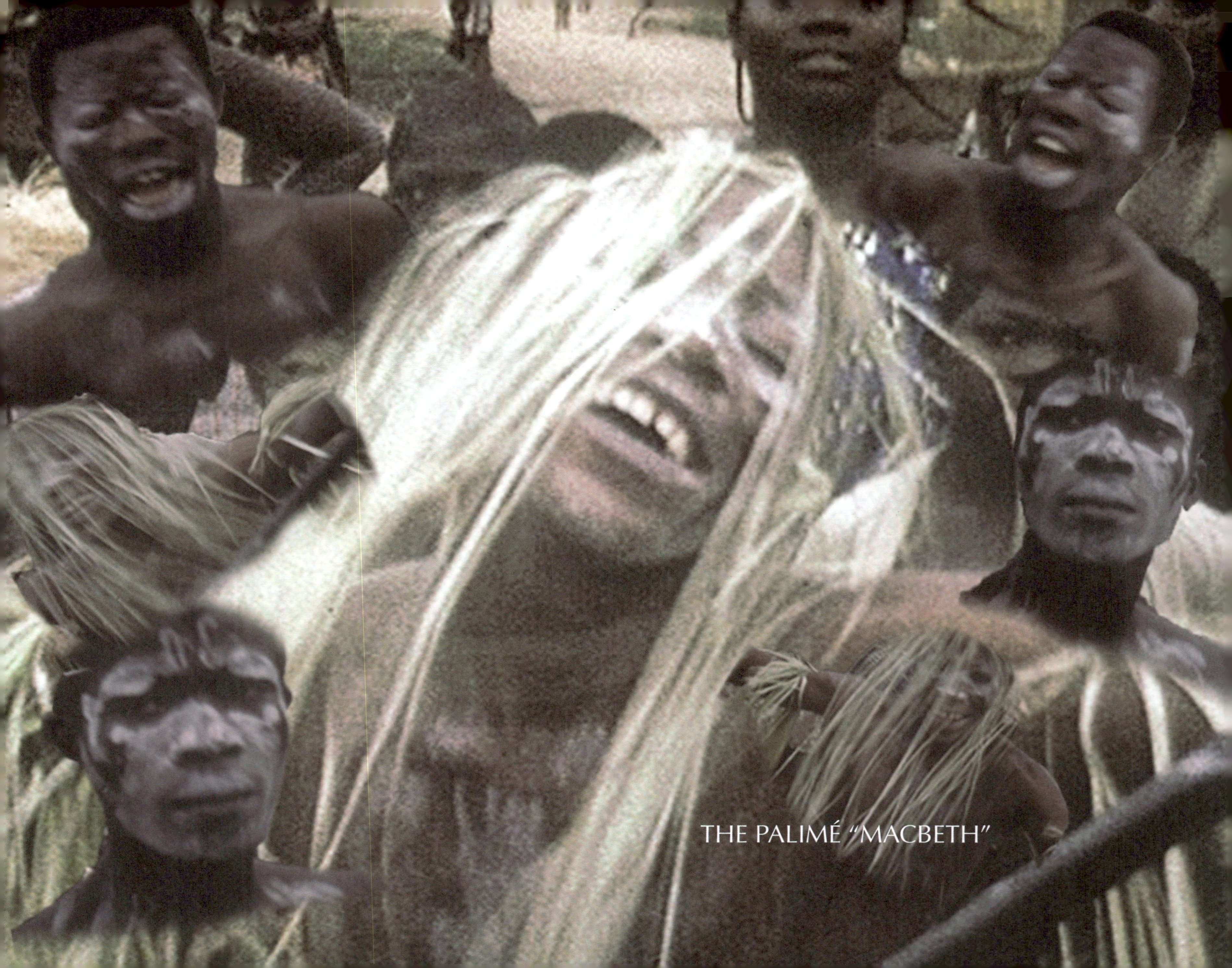

THE PALIMÉ "MACBETH"

ÉLAVAGNON

Eric's brother Lucas had married his sweetheart, Margaret Sharp, in an Akposso village called Élavagnon ("things will get better soon"), north of Palimé. Eric was eager for his parents to meet Paul Wega, the Élavagnon notable who had arranged for the two Californians to be married in a traditional village ceremony.

The wedding was Eric's idea. Lucas had been staying with him in Lomé for several months, traveling and taking photographs. Lucas is a transplanted Dutchman who speaks English through formidable moustaches and rasps his R's from deep in his throat. He dashed around Lomé on a red Honda motorbike, his long blond hair streaming, and the Togolese called him *Dans le Vent*, literally "in the wind", meaning "cool". He and Eric shared a sensitivity to absurdity and injustice in human affairs and the two brothers were often in a fine state of gleeful indignation. Both also loved the beauty in humanity and recognized it in traditional societies. Lucas had trained as a photographer, and spent his time in Togo taking iconic photos in black and white: the sweat on a laborer's back, women doing each other's hair, a young village girl pausing in mid-stride to hearken to a sound we can't hear.

Eric had been introduced by Togolese friends to Paul Wega, a fetish man and herbal healer from Élavagnon , and had invited him to Lomé to stay in Quaker House to perform certain healing ceremonies for the household, where jealousies and a death in the staff had given rise to dissensions. Paul had also alleviated some health problems, and Eric was convinced of his honesty and efficacy. But could he do something more: could he lure Margaret from New York City, where she was employed and enjoying the pleasures of the city, to rural West Africa to get married? This necessitated some major *gris-gris*, and Paul took Lucas and Eric down to the beach at night, where they sacrificed a chicken and launched into the waves an enameled basin full of offerings stuck with candles. They wondered, as the little flames drifted out to sea, whether the influences they had invoked would ever reach the very far away shores of Manhattan Island.

As Margaret tells it, she opened her apartment window early on a workday morning and was astonished to a find a large praying mantis on the windowsill. There was something compelling in its vivid green exquisite organic realness, there on the gritty ledge. It preoccupied her; all day she could think only of the mantis, and Lucas in Togo. Within weeks, she was in Lomé. A few days later, Lucas, Eric, and she were in Élavagnon, where Paul had arranged a four-day traditional wedding. Now, a year or so later, it was time for the village to meet the parents of the groom.

Paul's household was in a state of real excitement at meeting Luc and Trudi. But how did they seem to know when we would arrive? The nearest telephone, after all, was in Atakpamé, a sizable town some distance from the huddle of thatch-roofed adobe compounds that comprises Élavagnon. The car had barely come to a stop at the roadside, however, when cries of "*Bonne arrivée!*" rang out and Paul led his entire compound out to meet us: Paul himself, a slight gentle middle-aged man, smiling now but never without the air of dignity that went with his local notability as a healer and major householder; his wives, Nellie and Patience; Dada, his mother; his elder son's wife, Victorine; a number of children—Héjo, Sept, Bébi among them—and other personalities. There was Stephen, a young man from Ghana who may have been related, and Yéyé ("*Le Fou*," he was

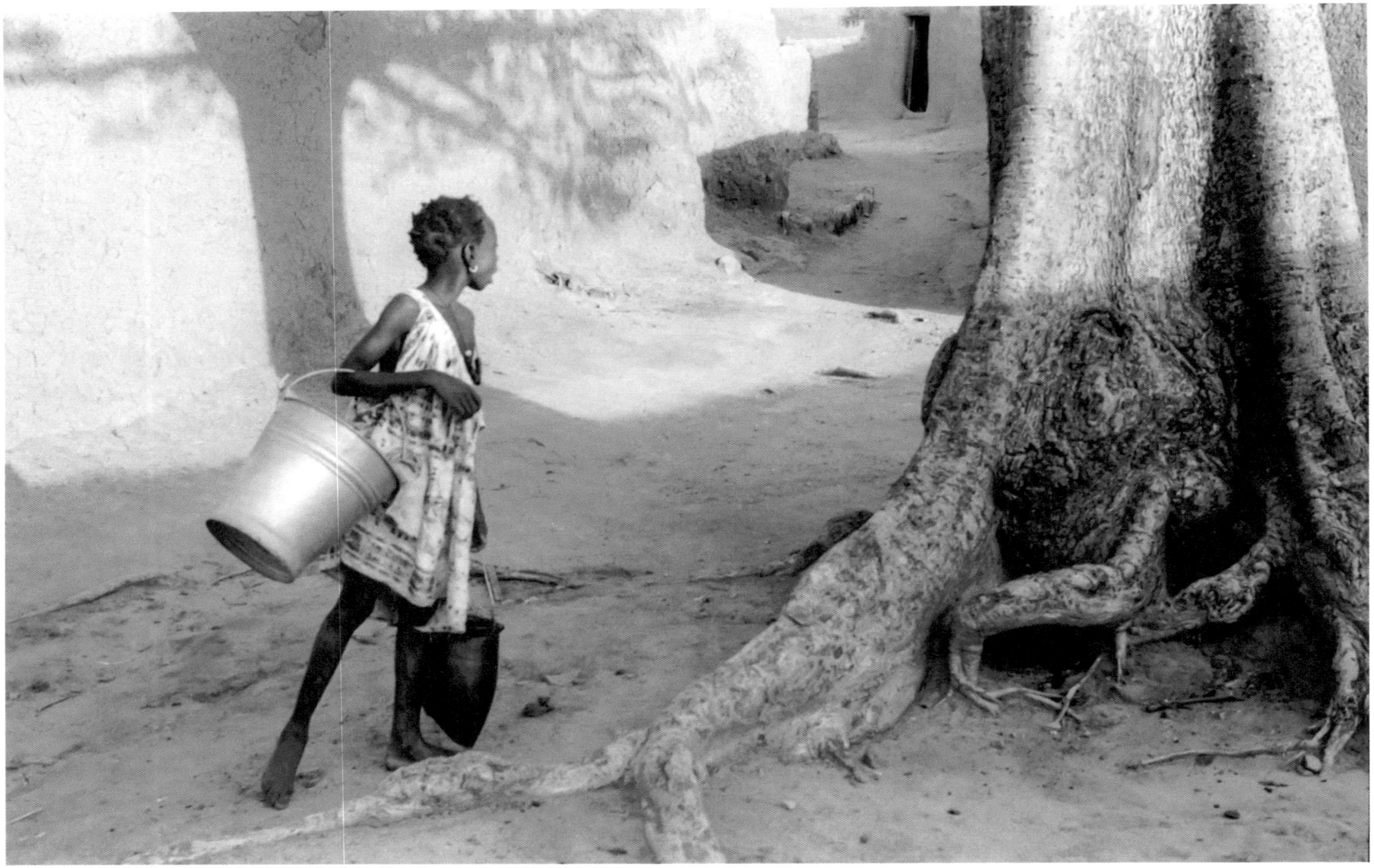

"A young village girl pausing in mid-stride" by Lucas Kiers

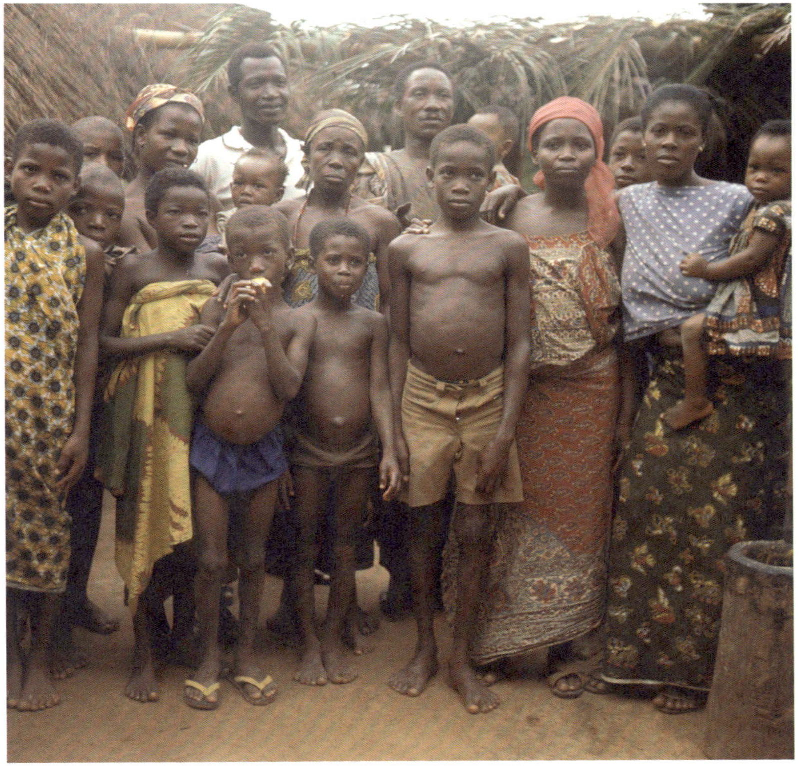

Élavagnon, Togo. Paul Wega's household

called,"the crazy guy") who was in Paul's professional care for epilepsy.

"Bonne arrivée, bonne arrivée!" The children jumped up and down, their elders seemed pleased beyond words as each stepped up in turn to clasp the Kiers' hands in both of theirs in an affectionate lingering African handclasp, with smiles and cries of delight all around. Trudi's eyes were wide with surprise and pleasure. "Oh, oh," she said at each introduction, and Luc, in his hearty way, returned the handclasps with a prolonged pumping motion. The Kiers were good sports, but the drive from Palimé had tired them and before long they had driven off, promising to return in the evening, to the hotel in Atakpamé with its flush toilets and hot-water baths. Eric and I, however, followed the crowd back into the compound, where Patience and Victorine had prepared a quite different kind of welcoming bath for us.

The women took us in charge, leading us one after the other to a small palm-frond enclosure at one side of the compound, where I could hear a stream flowing nearby at the bottom of a steep wooded gully. Once I was inside, the two women, grinning now, tweaked my clothes and urged me to strip. As I stood there in my pale nakedness, they motioned me to step up to a large flat stone at the center of the small enclosure, where Patience immediately threw a bucket of heated water over me. She and Victorine went to work with plenty of soap and some sponges made of coconut husk, turning me this way and that, adding water and soap, laughing and exclaiming as they scrubbed with a will, above, below, between. No part of me was exempted or escaped comment, and although deaf to their Akposso language, I could detect only good-humored amusement in their voices. *"Laver la tête!"* ("Wash your head!") said Pascale, as she poured another bucket over me before working my hair into a lather. A thorough rinse, a meticulous toweling and a clean, pressed cloth to wind around my waist, and I was led back across the compound feeling refreshed and even transformed. My otherness had been scrubbed away, my intimacies revealed and accepted, my membership in this new family, confirmed. There remained only for Victorine to take me indoors, where she dusted me liberally with talcum powder before allowing me, still happily dazed and trailing a cloud of scented powder, to rejoin Eric in our rooms along one side of the compound.[4]

We didn't have long to unpack before Patience put her head around the doorway to insist we follow her to see her *champs* (cultivated fields). Each wife in a household has her own fields; but what should make Patience's so special, we wondered. But Patience is irresistible, a pretty young woman newly married to Paul, perpetually good-humored and known for playing jokes on everyone in the household, and we set out with her across the cultivated land around the village. There is an essential Africa in these fields and in the little paths leading between patches of corn, yam, and beans, interspersed with tall trees and untamed bush, where we are called to by villagers bent double over their short-handled hoes. We stop to rest in the cool shade of a yam barn, and Eric explains that the land is communally owned and assigned to village households according to their ability to cultivate it. A large household like Paul's, with several wives and their children, has a better chance of earning surplus cash from the harvest to buy a radio or start a small business.

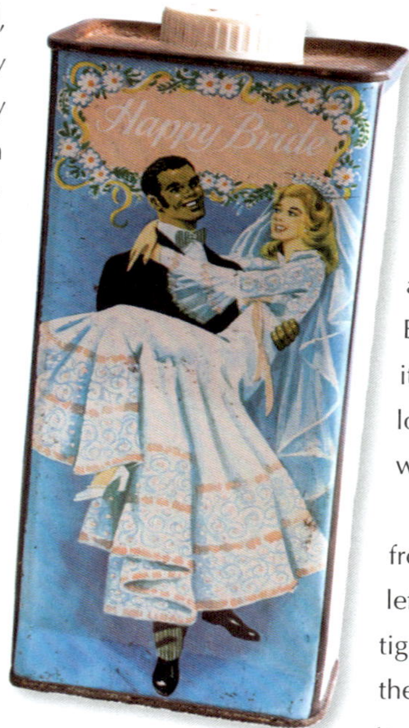

Ghana talcum powder

We've walked on a little further before Patience announces with a grin that we've reached her *champs*, and points to an open place ahead. At first, I have no idea what we're looking at: certainly no cultivations, but a roughly round, sunken area about 20 feet across with a smooth, grayish, curiously organic surface and unidentifiable odor. Patience is laughing heartily at our incomprehension, and positively doubles over when she sees from our faces that we've understood: this is a communal toilet. The logs that line it at intervals allow you to sit and defecate into the pit, and its slightly crawling surface is made of uncounted maggots thriving on the waste. Patience knows that *yovos* are sensitive about this kind of thing, and has brought us here to enjoy our puzzlement and revulsion. On reflection, the pit is quite practical. The maggots keep the waste at manageable levels and reduce the smell. Privacy is not such an issue here—people just look the other way. Patience's merriment is infectious, and we laugh at our own discomfiture. But neither Eric nor I ever actually use the bush toilet; perhaps it's the thought of falling backwards off one of those logs.... at any rate, we drive all the way to Atakpamé when the need arises.

Our rooms in Paul's compound are a wedding gift from the village (along with some yam fields that are left to Paul to cultivate). The two ample rooms are contiguous and form one side of the courtyard, which is further enclosed by another range of rooms at right angles to ours, each with its own doorway, and a larger house for Paul and his wives. In the middle of the courtyard is a thatched, open-sided cooking hearth.

The rooms that were built for Lucas and Margaret have tin roofs and are painted bright yellow inside. The whole compound

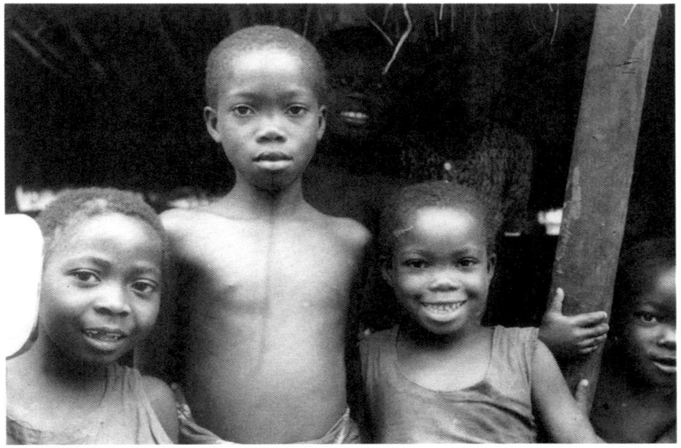

Paul Wega's children, Élavagnon.

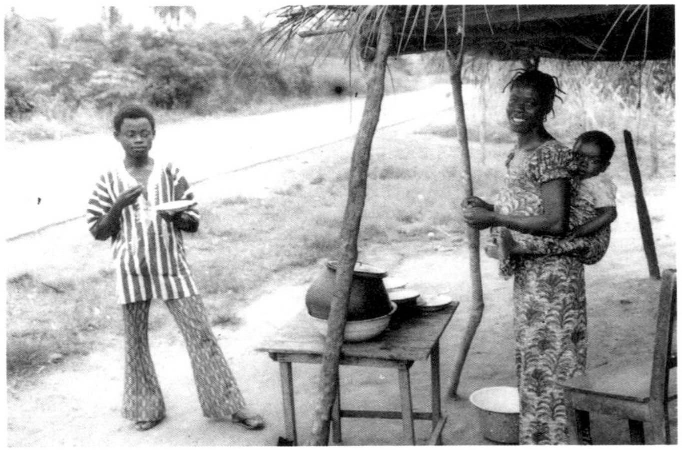

Nellie and Stephen, Élavagnon.

had pitched in to build them, and I still have Paul's meticulous bills for materials: corrugated tin roofing, timbers, nails, paint—along with six bottles of beer and a quantity of palm wine. The children lined up to help us plaster the walls, passing plates of earth mixed with water. Commercial paint brushes proved impossible to find, so Paul soaked the branches of a particular plant until the fibers spread sufficiently to hold paint. I brought the work to a halt by suggesting we paint only the lower wall and leave the beautiful earthy brown of the adobe plaster bare to the ceiling. There were blank looks and puzzled muttering over this, and without Eric's concurrence, the walls would have been painted sunny yellow to the top.

In the evening, Luc and Trudi return from their hotel in Atakpamé, and a feast of welcome is served in the new rooms. Nellie has roasted a chicken with an egg inside and prepared several fiery sauces swimming in red palm oil for the *fufu*. There aren't enough chairs for everyone, the children stand lining the walls. Faces look softer, eyes brighter in the glow of a couple of kerosene lamps. Toasts are drunk in beer: Paul welcomes the Kiers with deeply felt eloquence, to which Luc responds solemnly, his eyes twinkling nevertheless. Then Paul's patient, the crazy Yéyé, asks for a dance and leads me and then Eric around the table, clowning to everyone's huge enjoyment until hilarity rocks the room and at the same time the skies over Élavagnon open in a tremendous downpour. It becomes impossible to be heard over the rain drumming on the tin roof, and it seems as if the house, the party, the whole village must be washed down the road. But then it stops and, in the silence, Stephen, the young Ghanaian, takes up his guitar and sings a song he's written in Pidgin English about his individuality, and maybe about the life of an artist.[5]

Eric and I often spend days at a time at Élavagnon. Before leaving Lomé, we scour Quaker House for books, magazines, tapes, a Walkman and AA batteries to keep us entertained in the unelectrified bush. We rarely make use of these imported pastimes, though, except when Eric puts in earbuds and listens to music on the Walkman. We find that we are quite entirely happy in the immediate present of the compound and its activities.

On a typical morning, at first light, Paul and perhaps one of his wives with fields of her own would take up their short-handled, heavy hoes and go off to the yam fields. The school-age children, Héjo and Sept, walk to school in Hihéatro down the road, leaving the younger children with the women in the compound. Even the very young children are busy minding their juniors. I enjoy watching a three-year old carefully securing a one-year old to her back.

When the boys come home from school in the afternoon, they are instantly put to work carrying water and firewood or running errands; homework waits until evening. Paul appears at the end of the day with yams and onions and peppers from his fields for dinner. The compound courtyard becomes the focus of life. Paul bathes from a pail of cold water and relaxes, waiting for dinner. Eric is supine in a kind of rustic deck chair, listening to Mahler songs and twirling a chicken feather in his ear. Dada has shown him how to strip the feather down to a tuft that tickles the inner ear, an almost erotic pleasure. Dada herself is busy preparing bean fritters to be sold at the roadside tomorrow morning. She has been sorting, grinding and sifting the beans all afternoon. I'm fascinated to watch her skillful, deliberate kind of cooking. Yesterday, she stewed *agouti*, a kind of fat field rodent. The animals had to be skinned and butchered and the meat painstakingly tied with raffia string into neat little bundles before being simmered for hours. Dada's roadside sales provide her with a small independent income.

Nellie, too, is cooking, but for the whole compound. From the thatch of the little cook house, I see her pull a large kitchen knife. The knife, the big kettle and a bottle of palm oil, a few cans of tomato paste and plenty of onions, garlic and red peppers, are her only equipment as far as I can see. She knows I'm watching her, and chuckles to think I find such ordinary things interesting. Tonight, she's using the knife to chop a big yam, fresh from her fields, into small wedges to be deep-fried in palm oil, because she knows how Eric and I dote on the crispy taste. A cauldron of sauce is bubbling next to the palm oil, and Victorine and one of the boys are pounding other yams into *fufu*, skillfully alternating the pestles, concentrated but relaxed. In fact, all these activities seem to happen in a relaxed, deliberate way, with none of the stress we associate with work. No one hurries or makes any more effort than is necessary to each task.

The children find plenty of time to play, despite their chores. Three or four of them are engaged in a terrific game of cards. They bring their card down from high over their heads with a tremendous slap onto the table, rise in protest to challenge the score, dare or accuse each other in violent tones, their eyes bulging; and then everyone collapses in laughter. Others are running back and forth across the compound dragging a variety of toy vehicles. On close inspection, these are ingenious constructions and contain not a single element that isn't recycled or homemade from tin cans and wire, cleverly combined to resemble current models of trucks and automobiles. The children are shy when I take an interest. "What kind of car is this, Sept?" I ask. "It's a ..... a Mercedes," he replies in a barely audible voice, his eyes downcast. One of the youngest girls, Bébi, is bawling her head off unnoticed, as she has been for ten minutes or so. Her older brother finally quiets her by blowing bubbles: that is, he brings a stalk of manioc plant, holds it in front of her, and snaps it in half. Sap flows copiously at the break, and Bébi stops crying. Then he bends the stalk into a loop, allows the sap to collect over it, and blows it into a large opaque bubble which floats away as his sister, fascinated, tries to seize it. I'm marveling at all the manufactured products—plastic bottle, liquid soap, plastic loop—that have just been made unnecessary. I've seen the children make a popgun from a hollow reed and a wad of leaves, and an Erector set from tall grasses.

By now, twilight has fallen. Héjo is washing clothes in a bucket. Yéyé is sweeping his doorway. Nellie steps up to the black pot and dishes portions of *fufu* and sauce into enamel plates. The evening meal is a quiet, even solemn moment; perhaps some people here have known real hunger before. The adults sit together on mats or little chairs around a kerosene lamp. The children eat in various hierarchical groups of their own devising. Over the compound walls, from deeper in the village, comes the sound of the town crier, the *gongoleur*, beating out a rhythm on his double-belled iron gong and announcing in a distant sing-song that—Paul translates for me—a pair of green flip-flops has been found.

There is a deep, pervasive sense of peace in the compound at twilight. It's no wonder we rarely read the books we've brought to make the time pass. We don't seem to experience time as something separate from the activities that swirl and flow around the courtyard all day long. No one has a watch or asks what time it is. Nothing seems to be done compulsively, against the clock or with an idea of efficiency, but rather in its own time, deliberately, without hurry. Time seems generated out of whatever is happening at the moment, the alternating rhythm of the *fufu* mortars or the slow darkening of the sky. Time is present time, and shorn of past and future, chronology and compulsion, is no longer something substantial enough to be hurried or slowed, "killed," or even *passed*.

The children do their homework in the lantern light. We sit around talking quietly, or receive a visitor. The night is soft, the sky powdery with stars. Eventually, everyone says "*Bonsoir, bonsoir,*" goes to their respective doorway, and to bed.

The next morning, we go greeting: that is, we pay a round of visits to several village notables and friends, some of whom may already have stopped by Paul's compound. We approach their doorways calling out "Ago-o-o-o" and clapping hands instead of knocking, as no one shuts their door when they're at home. In Akposso language, the morning greeting exchange goes,

"*Ivoë!*"

"Adié!"

"*Adié!*"

"Avlé!"

"*Eh...........*" (a drawn-out melodious sound.)

After these greetings, chairs appear and everyone has a little glass of *sodabi*, a clear and highly alcoholic distillation that, as the visits succeed each other, leaves us very merry by the time we get back to our compound. Soon after we return, our visits are reciprocated. Our recent hosts show up dressed in their best cloth, and now it's our turn to set out chairs, offer *sodabi*, smile and make inquiries all over again. This kind of thing, I find, can knock you out for a whole day!

No recovery time for me today, though; Paul wants me to drive him to Hihéatro*, where he has been summoned to the bedside of a sick man. Paul insists on "driving" down the bush tracks we follow, sitting on my lap like a child and steering while I manage the gears and pedals. We arrive in the evening light and are taken indoors, where I am given a chair. The darkening room gradually fills with relatives and friends of the patient. The door curtain to the adjoining room is pulled aside and a young man is led in, dressed only in shorts, his skin ashy and his face downcast and set with pain as he holds his side. Paul questions him softly before putting an ear to his stomach and chest and running his hands over them, pressing gently. Then he looks up with an air of decision and calls for a glass of boiling water, to which he adds a handful of herbs. The patient drinks the infusion, then Paul applies the lees as kind of paste to the hollow of his chest and to the corresponding spot on his back. Finally, he stands behind him and draws his hands deliberately all around at his waist, as if he were drawing something out of him and into his cupped hands. Whatever it is, he steps to the window and blows it into the night with a loud breath. He repeats this gesture eight times before the young man is led away. Beer and sweets are brought, and I notice that the young woman who serves us has carefully sorted out the licorice candy just for me. Paul has some words of advice, the crowd melts away and we go back to Élavagnon.

* The name of this village derives from an incident in colonial times, when the Germans were masters of Togo. They seized the village chief for some infraction and beat him before his people. Such a thing had never been seen before, and he turned to the crowd and cried, "Hihéatro!", the world is turning (changing).

Bouncing back over the same road the next morning on a follow-up call, I wonder how to think about Paul's practice: effective herbal remedies? *gris-gris*? power of suggestion? Probably all three. But I'm nevertheless astonished to see that a welcoming crowd has gathered in the road, and at the forefront, grinning broadly, erect and glowing with color, is the young man who had seemed so afflicted last night.

Paul is a healer. There is another sort of fetish worker who specializes in recovering lost objects, and Paul takes me to one of these when my camera is stolen. He feels responsible, because the theft occurs in his compound, while Eric and I are asleep in our rooms. Someone had reached through the window in the night and slid the camera from under my pillow. How was I not wakened? Who could have done this? Eric was as puzzled as I, Paul's brow was dark, and the compound was in an uproar. Enquires in the village proved futile. I was prepared to write the whole thing off, but Paul plainly felt his honor was at stake and took me to the fetish man.

First, I had to purify myself. No sex tonight, I was told, and only white rice to eat. I observed these requirements, and in the morning drove with Paul to a substantial concrete house by the road several miles away. Outside, a tall pole flying a scrap of white cloth showed that fetish services were available.

A dignified elderly man received me courteously. After getting a detailed description of the camera from Paul, he motioned me to come close and pressed an egg to my forehead. He seemed satisfied—Paul told me the egg would have betrayed me if I hadn't followed the purification requirements—and fell into a sort of trance, visualizing the camera and where it might be. He shook his head; it wasn't working. So he called loudly into the back of the house and a young woman appeared, a teenager who seemed apprehensive. She knelt on a mat in the center of the room and wound a piece of cloth in a circle on top of her head, as market women do to cushion a load. But this wasn't for a basket of mangoes or a load of firewood. From the corner of the room, the *fétisheur* took a very old rusty bolt-action rifle and placed it carefully on the girl's head. She closed her eyes and we waited expectantly. With no discernable movement of the girl's, the gun began to turn slowly, hesitantly, swinging in one direction and then another as if seeking a target—which is exactly what it's doing, Paul whispered: it's looking for my camera. The *gris-gris* can work through the girl, he says, because she is a virgin. Nevertheless, this attempt, too, proved fruitless. Paul and the *fétisheur* shook their heads, and soon we were back in the car. As a matter of fact, my camera was never found. The thief had been incredibly deft; maybe his *gris-gris* was very strong, too.

I am running full tilt through the African bush and thinking that I probably shouldn't be. Who knows what's in the high grass I'm running through? Branches of small trees whip my face. I bound over an anthill. We're a bit heady from drinking beer, and it's the promise of drinking palm wine that makes us reckless, running and jumping and hooting as we follow George and his friends to what they call "the cabaret." George is Paul's son and Victorine's husband, a genial, heavy-set young man bent on celebrating his homecoming.

The car has been left behind where the road became impassable. Stepping into the grass, we clapped vigorously to clear the way of snakes. Then we were off to the cabaret, running headlong across Mother Africa, the men ahead shouting at those behind, everyone convulsed with laughter. *"Voilà!"* says George, coming to stop. He laughs at our blank looks. We're standing, panting from the run, in a cleared area thickly planted all around with palm-wine trees. No thatched hut, no colored lights, no barman; this is a cabaret? But very quickly, our friends have gathered a number of palm fronds and stripped them down to their spines. These are folded evenly in three and planted in the ground like staples, in a circle. We sit down facing each other on these improvised stools—*"Nos chaises modiques,"* (our low-cost chairs) someone says. Glancing around, I can see that many of the surrounding palms have been felled so as to allow the sap—the palm wine—to flow into gourds set to capture it. Soon it's been collected in calabash bowls and we regale ourselves with the still-fermenting, sweet, slightly alcoholic wine. The "cabaret" rings with shouts and laughter. Some men working in nearby fields join us, their children standing by solemnly, listening and watching as the calabashes go round and round.

Before leaving, we are responsible for ensuring a fresh supply of wine for the next party. We run through the grove from one felled tree to the next, thrusting a little torch of bound twigs into holes that have been cut to the trees' hearts. We blow on the smoldering twigs through hollow sticks to make them flame, and watch as the sap froths and begins to flow into the gourd beneath before dashing through the spinning grove to the next tree, reeling, breathless, happy with wine and brotherhood.

We return to the clearing for another calabash or two, and a round of snuff. The snuff is made of tobacco mixed with things

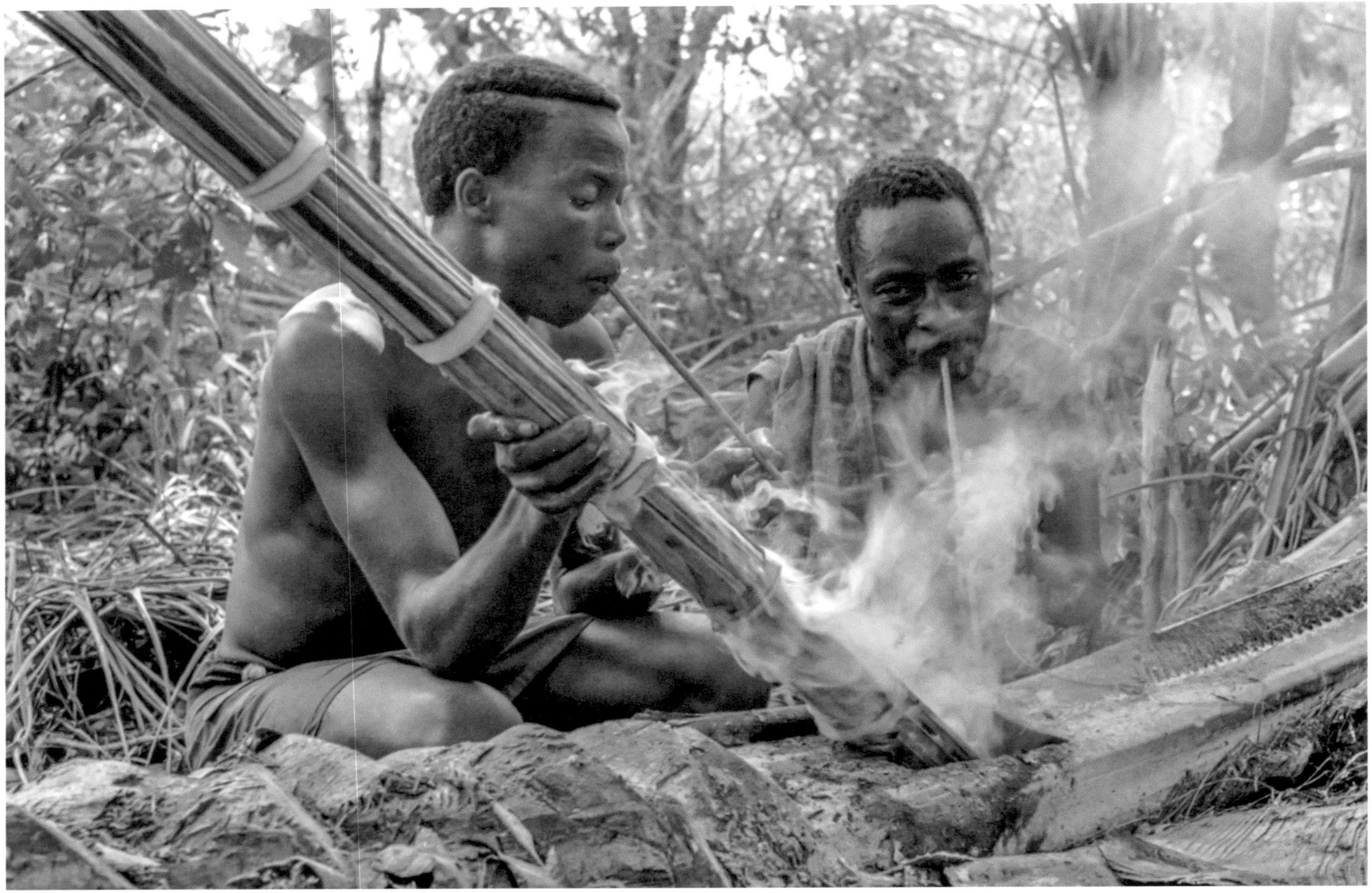

Fanning the palm wine fires, Élavagnon

Photo by Lucas Kiers

no one is able to name in French, products no doubt of the huge, savant African pharmacopeia. We had watched Dada take some, and implored her for a snort. She laughed and said it was for old people. It has a very brief but almost hallucinogenic effect, and we procure our own supply. Its powerful kick has a sobering effect on our little company, and we straggle back to the car, silent now, stepping easily, all of us fast friends in the fraternity of the cabaret.

It's time for Luc and Trudi to start their voyage home to Santa Barbara, and Eric and I are driving them from Élavagnon to the airport in Lomé. Paul and his family have turned out to see them off. According to the proverb, Paul tells them, mountains never meet, but people may well meet again. The Kiers are moved, and Luc in a gravelly voice says that he and Trudi will never forget Élavagnon.

At Lomé airport, we share an emotional parting. The Kiers have been resilient, adventurous and good-humored, and Eric and I are sad to see them go. Luc effectively dispels the mood of regret by leaving Togo with panache. At the gate, he balances his suitcase on his head African-style and carries it thus, grinning, all the way to the gangway. We wave, we wait for a last glimpse of them at a porthole; but instead they appear in the open freight door at the rear of the aircraft, 20 feet above the tarmac, waving until the big door slides shut.

BICYCLING TO COTONOU

Eric can turn his attention now to planning his last Quaker Conference, in Cotonou, Benin. The subject is "Mis-Education in Africa," and he's invited radio talk show hosts, student activists, cabinet ministers, journalists and writers from all over West Africa; also professional translators, so that the statements and debates can be translated simultaneously into English and French. Fifteen or so people have accepted, the translators are on their way from jobs at the United Nations in New York, the program is printed, the hotel booked. Eric has chosen a fancy beach hotel in the capital, the better to encourage the wellbeing and camaraderie of the participants. He's concerned about the hotel, though, and goes to Cotonou to inspect it and speak to the staff. He wants to avoid anything like one of his first conferences, in Liberia, where he reserved the facilities of a splendid hotel outside Monrovia near the Firestone Rubber plantation. Everyone was happy with the rooms, but wondered why their beds were remade three or four times a day. That, and the round-the-clock visitors from Firestone, soon made it plain that the hotel also served as a brothel.

Eric has urged me to attend the conference as a substitute translator, to provide occasional relief to the professionals. My plan, I tell him, is to leave a couple of days early and bicycle the 110 kilometers from Lomé to Cotonou. The coastal roads are level and well populated, and I'll spend the night at Ouidah, where there is a government hotel, or *campement*. Furthermore, I'm eager to take my newly acquired bicycle on the open road. Ben, our African-American friend, has bought a new bike and sold me his old *kéké*, a well-worn English model, black and unadorned as a parson and endearingly used. It has a broken headlight, and with a sense of retrograde triumph, I hang a kerosene lantern over the handlebars. The Togolese universally yearn for a Mobilette or Yamaha, and are amused to be greeted by a *yovo* pedaling such an antique machine. I've given it a Latin name, *Festina Lente*, "Make haste slowly."

Everyone except Eric discourages this ride to Cotonou, shaking their heads and warning me that it's too far, too uncomfortable, too dangerous, too tiring. What would they say, I wonder, if they knew I'd really like to *walk* to Cotonou? I envy the liberty of the old men I see walking along the roadway under big straw hats, a cloth bag over their shoulders and a rough staff to steady them, inching their way with beautiful long strides over great distances.

Justin looks particularly concerned when I tell him my plan. "*Ah, Monsieur Philippe*," he sighs, "*vous aimez à vous gêner*" ("you like to make trouble for yourself."). It makes no impression on him when I point out that he performs feats of endurance far in excess of my little ride. "*Ce n'est pas pour le blanc*" ("It's not for white people"), he says, and that seems to be the general opinion in Quaker House. They insist that at least I should go with Albert the gardener, who is leaving in the morning to visit his brother in Cotonou.

We set off at 6:30 the next morning. Albert, who is in his 20's, has no luggage and wears jeans, a T-shirt and a baseball hat. I'm anticipating something more adventurous, and wear a broad hat and carry a shoulder bag. The kerosene lamp is hung over the handlebars, and I decide to take an enormous striped umbrella, too. This causes a slight delay. The umbrella had been kept in a stand by the door during the dry season and when I opened it, I was startled by an eruption of large flying insects that had been living there—large pale agitated bugs that filled the hallway before fleeing through the open door. "Albino flying cockroaches," Eric says, and the New Yorker in me shuddered and was grateful that this species hadn't yet reached Manhattan.

Linoleum cut by the author

The coast road, swept by breezes from the sea, is still cool at this hour. Today is Togo's Independence Day, and many Lomé residents are out in their best clothes—women in brilliant cloth and kerchiefs, men in traditional *pagnes*—to watch the big fishing dugouts race offshore. We fly down the road past the crowds, the coconut palm groves and fishing villages, the wind at our backs. Albert pedals intently, rapidly, silently; I myself want to shout out loud in exhilaration for this fresh new day and its promise of adventure. We stop at my insistence to watch a group of fishermen working a dugout up from the surf. Instead of pulling it, they swing it in half-circles, moving it up its own length at each swing. Its name is carved along the side: "God Loves Tailless Animal."

Togo is only about 40 kilometers wide at the coast, so we reach the border and cross into Bénin at about 9:30. It's mango season, and we have to dodge the ripe fruit falling spontaneously out of the massy dark green trees. I buy a half-dozen from a girl at the roadside. When the fruit is as ripe as this, you can just squeeze it out of its skin into your mouth, suck it and spit out the pit. I could swear the ones I bought had a slight zing to them, as if they had begun

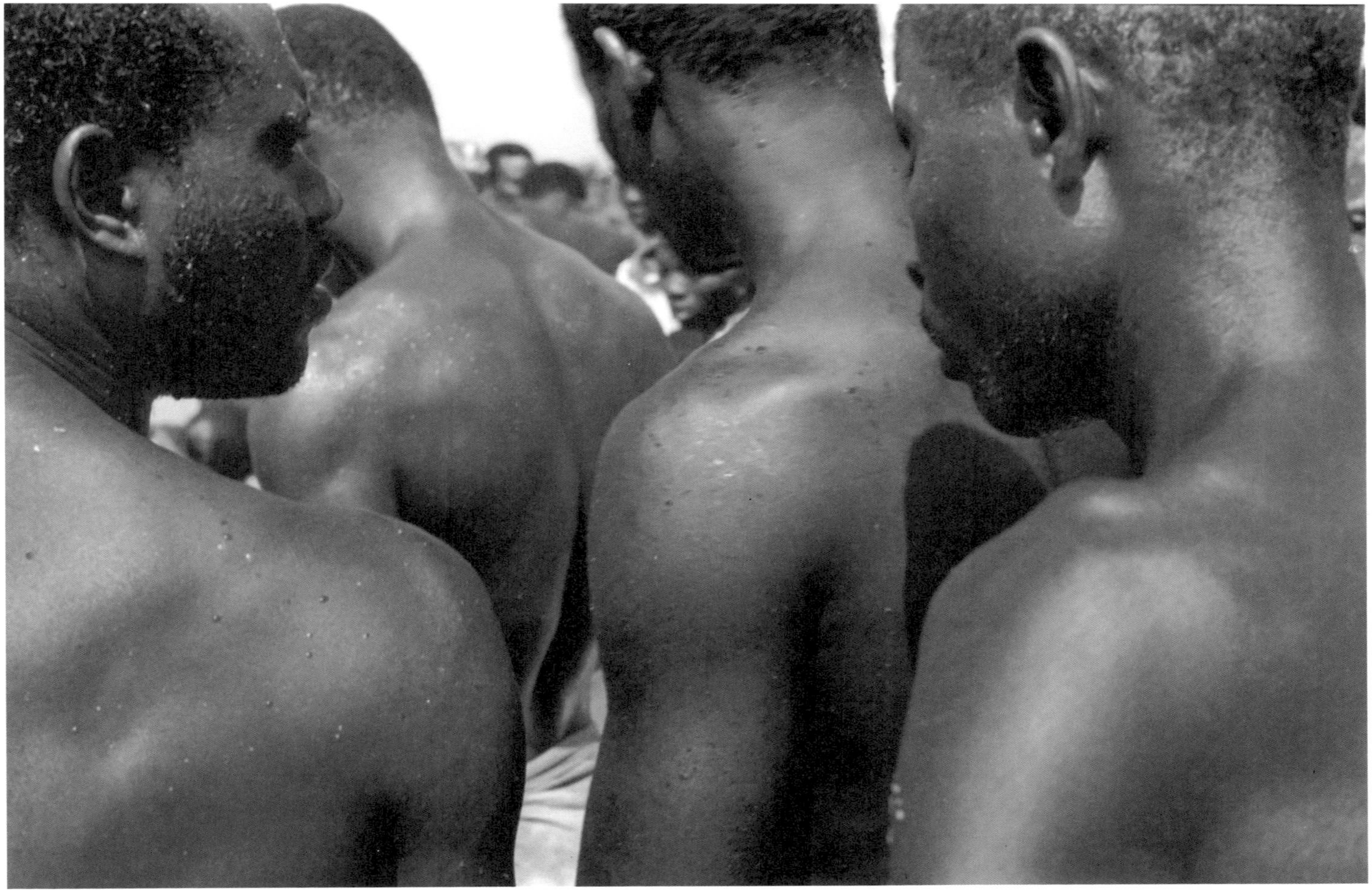

Fishermen on Lomé beach

Photo by Lucas Kiers

to ferment in the sun.

At Grand Popo, where the Mono River runs into the sea and the road forks either inland to Cotonou or continues along the coast to Ouidah, Albert and I part company. He wants to be at his brother's by evening, he says. I'm relieved to think I can set my own pace from now on, and begin by taking some time to explore Grand Popo. Like Ouidah, the town was a major slave port in the 18th and 19th centuries, when millions of captive people were sent to the coast from inland centers like Abomey to be forcibly transported overseas. Many were taken to Brazil, and after slave rebellions in Salvador de Bahia in 1835, the government deported large numbers back to their homeland, where many settled along this coast. Sylvanus Olympio, the first president of independent Togo whose ghost haunts Lomé, was a descendant of one of these Afro-Brazilian returnee families.

I see very little evidence of this tragic and turbulent past. Grand Popo seems to consist of a single long sandy street lined at intervals with modest concrete buildings and ending in wetlands, expansive stretches of sand, swamps and lagoons that I take to be the Mono River delta. The sun is higher now, it's too hot to pedal. I join some people napping under the coco palms. An old man is playing the radio as a recumbent woman, massive and shapely as a Henry Moore statue, sleeps nearby. A dozen children are scattered among them, each dozing on their own little mat of woven palm fronds.

When I wake, the shadows of the coco palms have shifted and lengthened, and I set out for Ouidah. It seems further away than I thought. The paved road throws back the heat, and I quickly grow tired of pedaling; but I persevere, determined to get there before nightfall. My senses, I notice, have grown strangely acute. A tall feathery grass growing along the road looks vividly, quintessentially green. A flock of small black and white birds is singing with penetrating sweetness on the telephone wires, and when they alight on these grasses, their tiny weight bends them double in a swift movement that seems preternaturally clear and somehow significant. Each person I pass I survey and greet out of a great, grave calm born, I suppose, of fatigue. Finally, I get off and walk for a while where the road crosses a vast lagoon. On either side are sparkling stretches of green and blue, water alternating with thick stands of reeds. Wherever there is solid ground, a thatch-roof

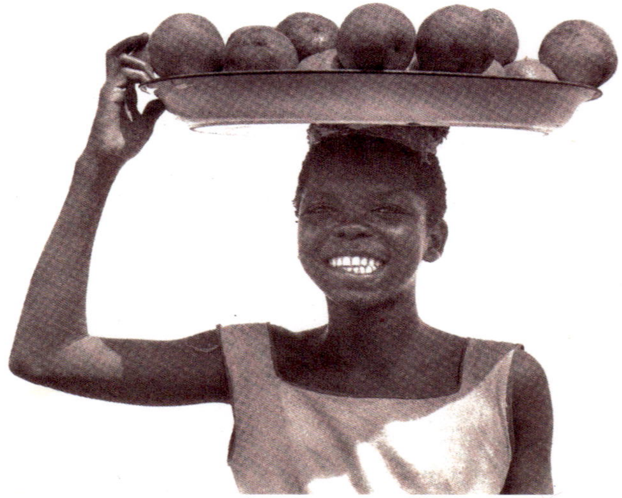

Mango seller

village perches. Dugouts glide among them, and neat alignments of bamboo fish traps impose a surprising order and symmetry on the open, moving water, which is nowhere deeper than a person standing. But then I see heads bobbing in the open water far from the shore, and it looks as though these people live entirely in the water, like fish.

I find my feet are involuntarily stamping the pavement at each step, so accustomed are my legs to pedaling, and force myself to mount again. By the time I reach the outskirts of Ouidah, the sky is suffused with a sunset glow that reduces everything ahead to silhouette. The headless tattered carcass of a chicken, black against the light, is tied across the road overhead between two poles like a warning. Fetish flags abound in front of the dilapidated houses I pass. I've been told that this town is a center of *gris-gris*, with practitioners and ceremonies famous across the region. Many of my Lomé friends lower their voices in speaking of it, and now I see another reason why Albert chose to continue to Cotonou without stopping here.

Night has fallen by the time I find the *campement*. My legs are so stiff that I can't lift them to get off the bicycle! A moment of anxious perplexity, and then I find that by clinging to the lower branches of a small tree in the courtyard, I can hoist myself up sufficiently to let the bike fall from under me. In my state of dehydration, I've become a sponge. The shower I take seems to soak deep into my body instead of just running off. I want to collapse on the iron cot, but hunger drives me into the dark streets to find the night market.

The town seems less sinister now that I've recovered from my fatigue. The night air is cool and sweet, many people are abroad. There are no streetlights, of course, dim figures loom around me and pass with a swish of clothes. A band of children (bands of children seem to take over West African towns in the evening) trots along with me, chanting, *"Yovo, yovo, bonsoir,"* the standard children's greeting for European strangers, whatever the time of day; but then they switch unaccountably to *"Alleluia, Alleluia, Alleluia,"* and escort me into the night market like a chorus of cherubim. Did they mistake me for a missionary?[6]

Before leaving for Cotonou the next day, I visit the voodoo museum, which I'm told was organized under French auspices. Most of the displays are photographs of local rites and iconography, comparing them to their counterparts in the New World. I'm astonished to see how exactly like their originals are the insignia, the deities and the ceremonies of Haitian and Brazilian voodoo, and I'm moved to think that I am in the very place from which so many enslaved West Africans unwillingly left their own land to evolve the strong, restless, creative Afro-American culture I've seen in Haiti and Brazil, and in my own country.

It's about 40 kilometers from Ouidah to Cotonou along the coastal road. It's an unpaved road over red earth and blowing sand, and runs through an unbroken succession of coco palm plantations. Eric had spotted it from the air on a flight into Cotonou airport and urged me to take it. It had looked idyllic to him: no traffic, deep shade and only yards from the beach along most of its length. It had the advantage for the bicyclist of being level all the way.

It was indeed idyllic. I rolled effortlessly along under the carefully tended palm trees. Landward on my left, they massed into a cool impenetrable gloom; on the sea side, where the palms

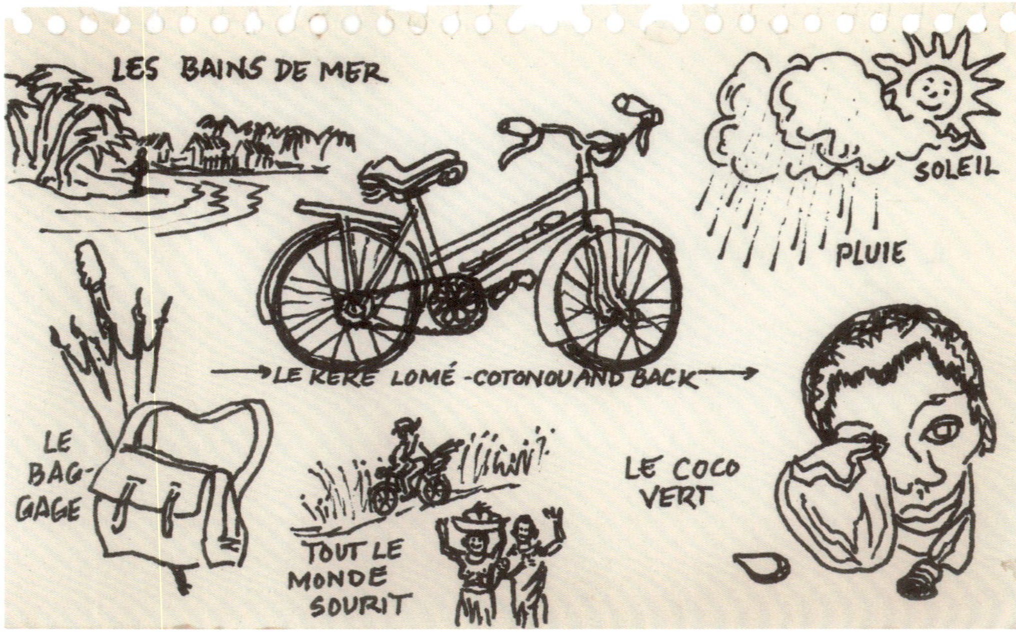

Sketch by the author

were planted in a single closely-spaced row along the road, the blazing sand beach, the sparkling ocean and frequent fishing villages shuttled by between the tree trunks as in a zoetrope. Of the many villages I passed, I saw only the dense woven patterns of their palm frond enclosures, the neat peaks of roofs above and a glimpse of the sea at the end of the sandy footpaths running through them. Everyone seemed to be out fishing. Once, a man thatching a roof called and waved.

Between two of these villages, I stopped for a swim. Sea water never seemed more benign and refreshing, and I swam and sunned and sat in the shade and then swam all over again, and again. A few villagers watched curiously for a while. A young man appeared and plunged in not far from me, then smiled and left as suddenly as he'd come. The conjunction of sea, sun, shore and sky, the adventure of being solitary and the satisfaction of having come this far, combined to penetrate me with wellbeing. Pausing here seemed sufficient for life, and it was only with reluctance that I eventually got back on the bike.

I'd eaten my last mango on the beach, and I was hungry and uncertain how far I still had to go; but I found that I'd developed a kind of optimistic fatalism since arriving in Accra months ago. Something would turn up, I thought, before dark fell. A moment later, a man stepped out from between the palm trees and waved me to a stop. He and his friends, he said, were *"en réunion"* (having a party); would I join them for some green coconut? He led me off the road into a clearing piled with coconuts. Five or six men from a nearby village were sitting on logs. An old man was mending nets while a grandmotherly woman looked after a number of children. My new friend opened four or five coconuts and I drank the cool grateful milky juice. I passed out cigarettes. They wanted to know where I was from, and did not seem especially surprised at my answers. The conversation was intermittent, mostly it seemed that everyone was content to be sitting around drinking coconut milk deep among the trees at the end of the day.

In Cotonou, I developed a terrific sunburn and a high fever, and was bedridden for a day or two. How could I get so burned, I wondered, riding all the way in the shade of the palms? Maybe my moment on the beach; maybe the fierce African sunlight, reflected from the sea onto the road. The Quaker House staff, Justin, Albert, Benoît and others, stood at the foot of my bed, full of concern for my violent complexion, swimming eyes and obvious exhaustion, but unable to resist reaffirming their opinion that bicycling from Lomé to Cotonou is too much for white people: *"Ce n'est pas pour le blanc."*

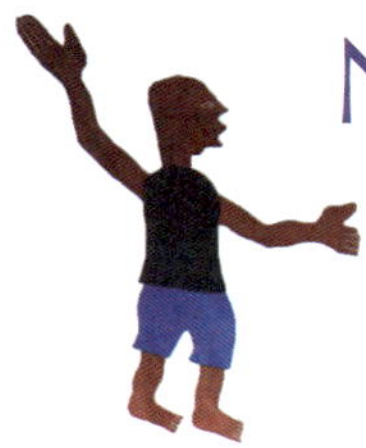

NORTHERN TOGO

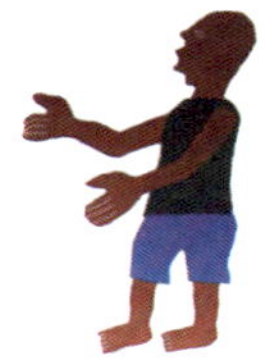

"Mis-Education in Africa" was Eric's last Dialogues conference. When we got back to Lomé from Cotonou, he had to begin winding down his work with the Quakers. He and I had been to northern Togo together two years before, and now I take advantage of an offer from Jerry and Claudine to go back up-country, while Eric stays in Lomé to organize his departure from Quaker House.

Soon, the three of us are driving north in a big white US Embassy pickup truck with official markings, as Jerry is on embassy business. We're headed for Lama Kara, where a measles and smallpox eradication program requires his participation. I myself probably don't add to the official look of the truck, because ever since we left the coast and began our long drive straight up north through the deep green heart of the countryside, I've been standing in the bed of the truck behind the cab, enjoying the rushing air and a commanding view over both sides of the road. The sky is purely blue. Small jaunty white clouds, fleecy, evenly spaced and all blown in the same direction, give the sky a pastoral air. Two years ago when Eric and I took this same road during dry season, the landscape had none of today's exuberant verdancy. The road is paved and perfectly straight but not engineered to be level. It follows the natural contours of the land, and the speeding truck plunges into every hollow and gully in its way. Suddenly we're in deep shade, enormous kapok trees block the sun, all kinds of growth shoulder each other prolifically along the swollen streams down here, the air is cool and heavy with moist vegetable smells; a moment later, we're up the other side into dry hot air, the sun beats down again and the land stretches away on either side. Mango trees with their dense starry dark-green foliage crowd the roadside, and the flame trees are in bloom. Their brilliant orange-red blossoms mass at the top of the trees, incandescent with color. It's an African day, full of open-handed extremes, defying introspection, calling on the blood. Indeed, we flash by a billboard advertising Geritol, an American blood tonic that promises strength and vigor. The manufacturer, I think, has understood that West Africans greatly prize physical vitality— after all, half the products in the fetish markets are aphrodisiacs. But it seems to me that merely surviving the extremes of this climate—desiccating sunlight, torrential rain and a natural world that on a day like this seems unchecked, explosively abounding, high on itself—requires some kind of supplement.

At Élavagnon, we pause to drop off some bags of cement from Eric and to announce the birth of Margaret and Lucas' first child, named Paul after Paul Wega. The effect is electrifying. Patience breaks into a little dance and Dada rushes over to embrace me. Before we leave, Paul brings us an armful of green oranges from his tree—green in color, but ripe to perfection and wonderfully sweet.

As long as the road remains paved, Jerry drives at a high rate of speed, slowing only for long-haul trucks barreling down the middle of the road or for bands of schoolchildren or a herd of goats or the frequent carpets of beans or corn spread out to dry on the macadam. The drying mats are snatched up by men and women who materialize out of the roadside at the approach of the flying truck and wave us happily on. From high on the back of the truck, I discover for myself the joy of waving. When the truck passes people on the road, they look at its shining bulk with expressions of curiosity or puzzlement. A wave, and their faces are instantly transformed by delight. Children shriek and run after the truck, shouting for us to stop. As we pass a group of villagers sitting in the shade of a big tree, they leap up in response, exploding into arms, hands, flashing smiles, laughter. The novelty of being waved at by a *yovo* in a truck must be very great. Some people are too thunderstruck to wave back, some turn and look behind them to see what I'm waving at, and some stare fixedly at the truck speeding away as if they expected it to do something amazing, like turn into something else entirely.

The only human geometry in this rolling countryside is the straight line of the road, the rectangles of occasional concrete buildings or the conical thatch roofs of villages clustered among fields and groves at the end of paths leading from the roadside. I only just glimpse these villages, so screened are they behind trees, their dun natural color so like the prairie grasses surrounding them. Sometimes a waft of woodsmoke-scented air alerts me to them. I try to picture what kind of life goes on under those conical roofs or around the big tree at their center where goats and dogs are asleep, children play in the dust and old men converse. A Westerner might call these villages huddled in the landscape, "close to nature." We like our modern houses to be low to the ground, oriented on natural scenery and lapped in shrubs and flowers. These Togolese villages are certainly inextricably bound to the natural world by agriculture and religion; but they rigorously exclude the landscape. Within the village precincts, very few green things are suffered to grow, perhaps only the great tree at the center. The village environment is totally man-made of adobe bricks and plaster, earth moistened and shaped by hand into walls which rise from the same earth underfoot, beaten hard by passing feet. The walls and ground flow into each other as rain and wear join them in gentle curves. Rather than facing the fields and hills around it, the village turns inward on itself. The outer houses turn their backs on the fields, and family compounds focus on a courtyard. Doors and unglazed windows are small to keep out the elements, and may offer only a chance glimpse of a view. There must be a partly defensive purpose to this plan, to keep out wildlife and outsiders; but when I've stood in the middle of one of these villages, surrounded by the sights and sounds of human life contained within monochrome adobe surfaces flowing organically into each other, curving horizontally and vertically and completely encompassing me, I wonder whether there isn't another purpose to this architecture: to embolden humanity. It seems to be a declaration of the people's powerful creative distinctiveness from nature, and its exclusive inward focus reminds them of their best ultimate resource: each other.

Jerry has pulled over so we can watch the sun set. He and Claudine climb up into the back of the truck with me. It seems suddenly very still after bumping over the now unpaved, bone-breaking road. As the cloud of dust we have raised begins to settle around us, we see we have stopped by an open area, a meadow of long grasses framed by stands of teak trees. Our ears, stunned at first by the sound of the engine, begin to take in the sounds of the place: birdsong from the trees, frogs croaking in the grass. The increasingly horizontal light of the sun is diffused by the settling dust into theatrical beams of light shining between the tree trunks and across the meadow. The air is still and sweet. We too are still, standing together silently, absorbed in the sunset.

At the farthest end of the field, barely visible, a man appears—or rather, his head and shoulders appear above the tall grass. One arm is raised to steady a double gourd on his head. He walks zigzagging along a path we can't see, advancing towards us without haste, getting closer. We watch him, the only thing moving in the twilight scene. At one point, he pauses to turn and look behind him to see what we could be watching. Our anticipation mounts until we finally see him in full as he steps onto the road: a solemn, short, grizzled farmer in earth-stained shorts returning from his fields with his gourd full of palm wine. The world is simple for him: all strangers must be welcomed, even these three oddly silent ones who have unaccountably stopped to stare across his fields at nothing at all. He greets us, *"Ça va?"* (How are you?), takes down the gourd from his head and with grave deliberativeness, pours out a cup of palm wine. He sips it ritually before handing to Claudine, who accepts it with both hands and passes it to each of us in turn. He waits while we drink, then puts the gourd back on his head, takes up the cup, wishes us farewell in his own language and continues down the road. Jerry, Claudine and I watch wordlessly as his figure recedes into the darkening light. It seems that there's nothing to be said after the lovely simplicity of the little ritual with which he has accommodated us into his world. It's dark by now, we get back into the cab of the truck to drive to Sokodé, where we will spend the night.

As we approach the city, a man appears in the headlights and waves us to a stop. He is a Hausa man, happily intoxicated and insisting we need help. He puts his shoulder to the tailgate as if to push the truck himself. Jerry and I get out and try to reason with him, but it's no use and he makes Jerry join him in a kind of jig in the middle of the road while Claudine and I clap the rhythm. His merriment is contagious and we join him, dancing and laughing like fools on the road, in the truck headlights. He runs after us as we finally drive away, shouting *"Bonsoir, bonsoir,"* as Claudine blows kisses from the window.

It's three in the morning. I can't sleep in the heat and humidity of the night, and pad down an exterior corridor of the hotel to an open-air shower stall to cool off. Sokodé is dark and silent. Inadequate streetlamps throw down weak cones of light on dim, still things—a bicycle leaning against a wall, a crushed tin can. I can see nearby the black windowless medieval bulk of Sokodé prison looming against the sky, blotting out the stars. Above me, however, the brighter stars seem to have dilated in the heat, softly pulsing amid a swirl of galaxies. The Big Dipper bestrides the sky along with an alluring, unfamiliar constellation with stars for its eyes, feet and outstretched arms, suggesting the long thin figure in a Navaho sand painting. As I watch, a shooting star flashes across it. The cold shower water seems to go right through me. I'm standing in the jet of water, under the stars, feeling that I'm the only person awake in this hotel, in this whole town, and suddenly, unaccountably, I've left my body and I'm looking down at myself from far above, at the tiny figure in the shower stall in the soft vast starry night.

The next day takes us north through verdant uplands to the town of Bassari. Hills crested with woodlands rise on both sides of the road, with prairies between where big, evenly-spaced trees make the landscape look like a park. Villages poke their pointed roofs above the prairie grass and the slopes of the hills. This is the land of the Kotokoli people; two years ago, Eric and I, taking a different road, had stopped at one of these villages, called Péwa. A remarkable *griot*, a star of the oral tradition, was singing there, a master musician, historian, satirist and comic who made Péwa forever memorable to us.

PÉWA

At that time, we had stopped to visit Jim Miller, a Peace Corpsman engaged in a fish-farming project in the village. Sixteen fish ponds had been excavated and stocked with catfish and Israeli carp to provide the villagers with a valuable supplement to their diet of grains and greens.

You come into Péwa through a kind of gatehouse/gathering place, a large circular thatched building with two doorways placed across from each other. Jim meets us at the road-front doorway and leads us out the other, into the village. We are immediately absorbed into its total adobe environment, following Jim as he leads us among the houses and dodging past their low projecting eaves of thatch. There's nothing you could call a "street," just a succession of more or less open spaces connected to each other in a surprisingly random fashion by the narrow ways between the closely-built houses. There seem to be as many ways to Jim's house as there are houses to wind among, and at times we're completely encircled by their blank walls. We pick our way between two houses and suddenly we're in a lively little plaza where people are stooping in and out of low doorways, children are scrambling around on the ground, someone is drawing water from a well and women sit with their legs straight out in front of them in their cool interiors, nursing babies, smiling and greeting us as we go by.

By the time we get to Jim's house at the edge of the village where the fields start, I feel that I, too, could live here. His house is larger than the others and served as a community guest house until the villagers turned it over to Jim rent-free. Through its small deep-set windows I can look down the rows of maize that grow right up to the house, tall as a man. Above their tassels, beyond the fields, craggy limestone highlands close the view. Anyone setting out or returning from the fields passes this house, and as we sit talking to Jim, someone is always looking in, greeting him, stopping to chat.

Jim Miller wears a cotton Yuroba-style cap, conical with a top that flops down. He is tall with blondish hair and mustache and a prominent nose. He tells us that he graduated from a technical college in Chattanooga, Tennessee, with a degree in fisheries. He's been in Péwa three years now, having renewed his

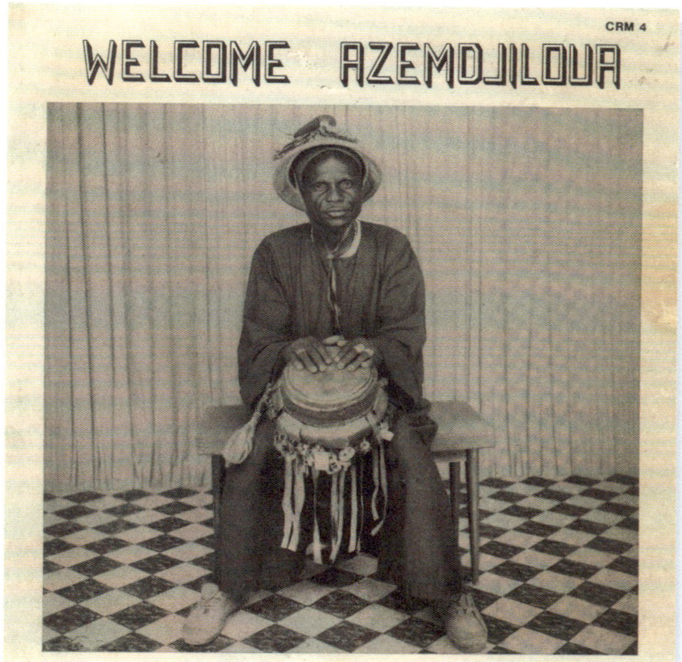

The Péwa griot (record cover)

two-year contract with the Peace Corps. When he first went home for Christmas, he says, "I couldn't stand it." His friends and family didn't know what to say about fish culture or Togo. "How's Africa?" he was asked—"Now what kind of a dumbbell question is *that*?" His buddies wanted to know if he'd slept with a Togolese girl, and to tell him about the women they'd had or the money they were making. "Couldn't *stand* it," he tells us, and came right back to Péwa.

He gives us lunch, hotdog stew and an apple pie with a crust made of millet flour and a filling of canned apples from China. We listen to recordings he's made at village dances, the drumming and singing barely audible above the rain that begins to fall outside, a serious rainy-season downpour that we watch through his doorway. It falls straight down in torrents and turns his thatch eaves into cataracts. Two women from the fields have come in to shelter under the eaves. The older has close-cropped white hair, the younger has a baby on her back. As we watch, they begin to dance to Jim's recordings, knees bent, heads down in seeming concentration on their feet, which shuffle to the music in tiny expressive steps. The recorded drums quicken and they throw their heads back and jerk their shoulders rapidly back and forth, grinning to see how much we enjoy their dance. The rain stops as suddenly as it began. The two women stoop from under the cascading thatch and go back to the fields.

Jim says we're lucky to be in Péwa today, as we can join the whole village for a kind of memorial service for the father of a local notable. The master of ceremonies, he tells us, is a famous itinerant *griot*, or minstrel, from Benin, Maman Azemdjiloua, come to Péwa especially for this occasion.

Our friend Julien Koumako from Palimé, the medical student, has joined us by the time the memorial ceremony begins in mid-afternoon, when the weather has cleared. Around a clearing under some enormous kapok trees, the chief of Péwa has taken up an honorary position in an armchair, flanked by his wives and counselors and the whole village, adults and children, standing three or four deep in a big circle. Perhaps he's expecting another shower, because the chief is wearing a long gray raincoat. A brightly embroidered cap proclaims his importance, along with dark glasses and trousers of a heavy cotton cloth dyed brown with kola nut and sumptuously embroidered around the cuffs, from which a pair of tennis shoes protrude. Opposite the chief on the other side of the big circle, the *griot* and his band are waiting to begin. One man taps a hand drum impatiently, another tunes a two-string guitar, a third tries out some crackling rhythms on castanets of coconut shell. The *griot* himself is easy to spot among his accompanists. He is a short, dark-skinned man in a striped West African poncho and a tightly-woven pointed Fulani straw hat decoratively inset with colored leather. But it's not his clothing that draws our attention, it's his manner: he radiates a quiet charisma made of self-confidence, humanity and wit. As we watch, he's giving instructions to two small boys, and Eric and I glance at each other, marveling at the kindliness and total lack of condescension he displays, and at the twinkle in his eye.

We have been given chairs and seated next to the chief and a tall dignitary in a long white Muslim robe who is the son of the deceased man we are honoring. They greet us formally in Kotokoli language and motion us to sit on their right, between them and their wives. There are seven or so women, one or two older and others quite young. One of these, richly wrapped in Nigerian cloth and holding a baby in tiny European clothes, has such a dark, luminous complexion and such pure curves in her cheekbones, forehead and neck, that I have to look away, afraid of staring at her.

The *griot*, strumming the two-string guitar, steps into the circle and throws out a spoken phrase. The band takes it up, making it into a chant that they embellish with staccato volleys on the coconut shells and the deep, rounder sound of the drum. As they chant, he weaves in other lines as he moves around the big circle of villagers. He pauses to address the chief, the family of the deceased, and even us, hailing Julien as the medicine man from Dakar with "big testicles" and deploring good-humoredly the white men's ignorance of his language. He moves on, stopping before different groups of villagers to praise and exhort them, evoking village traditions and Kotokoli proverbs. His audience is delighted, the people break into whoops and gales of laughter or shake their heads in disbelief at his audacity. Now he pauses to consider his next riff while the band continues, building intricate, blood-quickening ramifications of song and rhythm that seem to rise and circle over our heads. The *griot* starts, wheels, and he's off again, gesticulating, haranguing the crowd, delivering prolonged tirades that leave his audience howling, weak with laughter. There's little melodic line or vocal range in what's he's saying; but it's more than just speech—it's more cadenced, and accompanied by this galvanic music. And everything is improvised from moment to moment out of everyday language! The Péwa minstrel seems to me like Homer himself, like a sublimely stoned rapper, like an inspired auctioneer whose patter presents an entire culture. He's a street crier to the whole world.

The afternoon becomes evening and evening night. Pressure lamps are set out around the big circle. It never stops: when the *griot* takes a break, dancers step into the lamp light— men and women from the village, singly, by twos, in little groups one after the other, dancing like the two women we had watched in Jim's doorway. First, they pause for a moment before the chief and drop to one knee; he raises his fist to his lips to signify assent. Then they move off, dancing slowly over the beaten earth to the rhythm of the hand drum. No stamping the ground, no waving the arms or jumping, no vocals—just that same concentration on the feet, a strong rapid shuffling in the dust, full of constrained energy that makes the whole foot, toes to heel, surprisingly expressive. The dancers stay close to the ground, bending at the knees and waist, shoulders hunched over, the upper body immobile, drifting over the ground on a little cloud of dust raised by their animated expressive feet. Hands float, hinting at gestures, making half-formed passes in the air like a mute encouraging commentary. Then all at once, the drum breaks into a louder, faster rhythm and the dancers bring the whole top of their bodies into brief, violent motion. The knees are still bent but the head snaps back and shoulders pump vigorously back and forth so that for a moment it looks as if their torsos are divorced from their waists. High pitched trills of appreciation rise on every side, and the host in his robe or one of the chief's wives approaches the dancers, circles them slowly, smiling, and then with a graceful deliberate gesture, places coins on their perspiring foreheads. The dancers receive this tribute head back, eyes closed, feet still working the dust. The coins cling for a moment before falling off, to be immediately retrieved by small boys who dart out of the crowd, collect them, and present them to the *griot* and his band. So this is not a competition, I think; the men and women who dance are honored not for their individual skill but for their contribution to the entertainment of the entire community.

I step through the ranks of villagers and walk down the road to stretch my legs. Instantly, the glare and hubbub behind me is snuffed out by the mute towering darkness of this African night. The music seems suddenly muffled, distant. The villagers are reduced to a picket of shadows silhouetted against the hot white light of the lamps, which glows on the lower branches of the surrounding kapok trees. High overhead, however, the treetops are part of the night sky itself, black against a million stars and tossing in a gust of wind from far beyond the Kotokoli uplands, blowing elementally and obliviously over the people and their celebration. No wonder they pump up the pressure lamps, turn their backs to the night and stand shoulder to shoulder to dance and sing and assert their story against the darkness out here! They don't have to feel what I'm feeling now, awe and vulnerability before the tremendous parallel reality of nature and darkness all around me. I suddenly wish I had come with a flashlight, and hasten back to my seat in the circle of light. The *griot* is still wheeling and singing tirelessly, raising gusts of laughter from the crowd. An elder sitting near me engages him in a shouted tit for tat. Babies are crying, women are trilling, the music never stops. Then the dignified robed man who is the son of the deceased steps forward with two elders and approaches the singer. They drape a magnificently embroidered white robe over his head and tug it down to his knees. Eric leans over to say that it looks like he's getting an honorary degree. The *griot* looks noble now, no longer the itinerant minstrel in trousers and flip-flops, but a resplendent kind of holy man, a *marabout*. He accepts the gift and the compliment, but he's not, I can see, a man to let this kind of thing go to his head. He's an artist—he's already got everything he needs. In a moment, he's on the move again, circling and haranguing and singing, quickening our humanity with the abundance of his own.

BASSARI

Now, two years after the remarkable ceremony in Péwa, the embassy truck by-passes the village because Jerry has official contacts to make in Bassari, further to the west. This town is the capital of the Bassari people and a government administrative center as well, but quite unpretentious for all that. The tin-roofed houses straggle up unpaved streets to the high green sacred mountain behind the town. While Jerry and Claudine are visiting Brian and Sarah, Peace Corps friends who work here, I climb the mountain with two young Bassari students, Tchien and Élie. They take me up the winding streets and onto the slopes. We pass through an abandoned village of crumbling mud walls and disused grinding stones. From the mountainside, we can see all the way to the Ghana border, where banks of clouds gather around more mountains. From a village below, a drum is beating out a message. "An elder has died," Tchien translates. I've heard that before, and wonder whether the boys are reluctant to tell me more.

On our way down, my companions express their admiration for the West and pepper me with questions about life in New York City. I tell them that everyone on the street there is afraid of each other. We walk on in silence as they think about that; but they insist that Togo needs *aide technique*, foreign experts, to help it modernize. So I propose that Westerners, too, need foreign experts from West Africa who can teach us what we've forgotten: how to live with each other in communities like Bassari or Élavagnon. The boys are wise enough not to take me too seriously, but maybe they wonder at my detachment from my homeland, when they are so attached to theirs. I feel I've been talking too much.

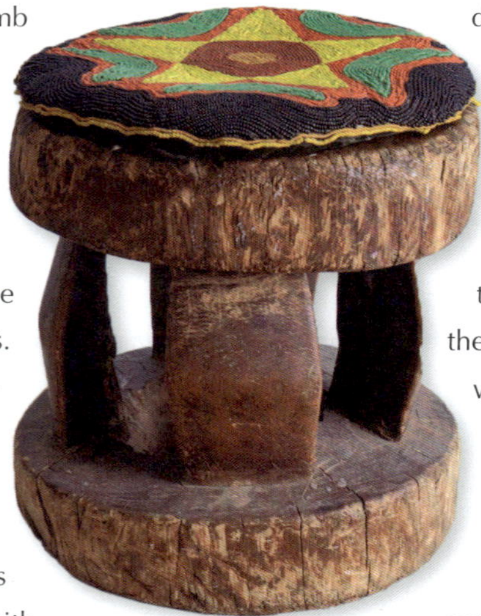

The stool from Bassari market.

We stop in the town market. The people here look leaner than they do in Lomé or Élavagnon, and imported goods are fewer. I see a lot of Fulani, fine-boned nomadic tribesmen who drive their cattle all over the north, trade in every market and weave a close white cotton cloth that Eric prizes. I watch as a young Fulani man drops to one knee and begins a long greeting with an older woman he has just encountered. "What's your news? Are you well? Your family—village—cattle—goats?" To each of these ritual questions, she answers with a grunt; but during the whole exchange, they are facing *away* from each other, turning their backs on each other and speaking into the air! Then suddenly they go their separate ways without a glance. Élie explains that the woman is the young man's mother-in-law, and this greeting with eyes avoided is part of the great deference he owes her.

I am wondering whether to try to buy one of the carved wooden stools the market women are sitting on. They are made from a single section of tree trunk hollowed out between the seat and the base into flexed supports like little legs, bowed under the weight they bear—especially that of these big women, under whom the little stools practically disappear. I make an offer to a grandmotherly woman selling cassava. I remember with contrition her confusion and reluctance, overcome by her more cash-minded sisters shouting for her to sell. She was looking for something else to sit on as I walked away with her stool.

Some pillowcases embroidered with messages in French caught my eye. I bought one that read *"Je t'aime"*; but what to make of another that said, *"Je vis parmi eux mais ils ne m'aiment pas"* (I live among them but they love me not)? Wives leave these pillows on the bed, says Élie, to let their husbands know how they feel.

Jerry and Claudine and I will stay in Brian's house tonight while he is away. Claudine and Sarah Bond, their other Peace Corps friend, prepare dinner. Jerry and I sit in the courtyard with Ama, the landlord's wife, and her children. The house is in a small village outside Bassari, and is really three houses, three adjoining round, thatched-roof houses with geometric designs painted in black on the walls and ceramic plates embedded in the adobe around the doorway. Ama and her husband live on the other side of the compound, which is cozily walled away from the neighboring houses.

We are waiting for dinner and watching Ama and her children. The little girl laughs and laughs at her infant brother. Where Jerry and I are from, waiting implies frustration, impatience, and wasted time; here, it seems like a kind of contentment.

A number of villagers, singly and in small groups, begin to arrive through the gate of the compound. They sit, talking and laughing quietly in the growing dark, in a semi-circle against the wall. They are all men, some quite elderly. Could this be a kind of a council, or just a habitual evening gathering at Brian's place? Some kind of greeting is in order, I think, and walk over to clasp hands with the older men. After a while, they hobble over to return my greeting in their few words of French. *"Ça va?"* they ask, smiling and shaking hands repeatedly to make up for our lack of a common language. Their palsied movements might be comical except for their dignity and sincerity. I want to send them a round of *tchacpalo*, a local beer made from sorghum, but Ama doesn't understand and sends for a high school student in the village to translate. It's quite dark by now and there are only a few kerosene lamps to light the courtyard, so I can't really see the person who arrives and sits down beside me without a word. His French is good, spoken gravely in a soft voice. His name is Dana, and he brings a jug of beer and a cup which he fills and hands to me with the same measured gravity in his motions as in his voice. For a moment, as in the women's bath in Élavagnon, I'm back in ancient Greece, a guest in the house for whom my host's son pours a cup of wine.

The jug goes around among the old men. Dana and I sit companionably side by side in the dark. From over the wall, over the whole thatched back of the village, a distant *gongoleur* beats his iron bells and makes a long sing-song announcement. Someone has been bitten by a scorpion, Dana explains.

Later on, when everyone has left and we've had dinner, we carry Brian's cushions outdoors and lie in the center of the circular courtyard to observe the night sky, as if we were in a planetarium; but the void overhead is deep and real and blazes with actual constellations that palpitate with starlight and are crisscrossed by live shooting stars.

It's not until morning that I can really see Brian's three little houses. He's arranged separate spaces inside to sit, to work and to sleep, and filled them with simple, serviceable furniture. The air of purposeful organization about his interior is confirmed by a visit to his neat model fields and chicken coop. I admire his style of life and the work he's doing, and wish we could meet. I wonder, however, whether his houses, the privacy and space they afford him and his evident self-sufficiency, might not isolate him from the villagers. Their life is dictated by the precarious economy of subsistence farming: everything is shared, interdependence is a necessity, privacy is unknown, material acquisitions are scarce and a genial physical promiscuity is the norm. Brian presumably requires a little distance, like anyone brought up in the modern West, to live and work happily for the Peace Corps. As a man of possessions and personal space, I imagine that his lot among the traditional villagers is to be comparatively alone.

Jerry has business in Lama-Kara, a large town to the east of Bassari and the capital of the Kabré people. He proposes we take a shortcut, an unpaved road that shows only faintly on the map and runs east and west for about 30 kilometers between the larger, paved *routes nationales* running north and south. Once we're on this road, we soon realize that it's little more than a bush track, with tall grass growing down the middle and closely on both sides. No road cuts, no bridges. When we cross a stream, we have no choice but to plunge unhesitatingly into the water, bumping over rocks and emerging muddied on the other side. But the truck rolls on bravely, clawing its way up stony slopes and speeding along the more favorable stretches with the lush grass whipping its sides and undercarriage. I've climbed up to stand in the back of the truck again, and I can see we're crossing wide rolling green land with groves of trees on the hills. Occasionally, villages appear as clusters of thatched houses among fields of millet. The sky is a fine flying blue with towering white cumulus clouds sailing across it all the way to the horizon. It looks grand and peaceful and utopian, like a lost unchanging land forgotten by time and the charging traffic on the *nationales*.

Suddenly, a human figure steps out of the roadside grasses ahead, a woman who gestures energetically for us to stop. She has several pots and baskets and large enamel basins full of produce with her and wants a ride to Lama-Kara for market day. We urge her to hop in, but she points ahead to where another half-dozen women are waiting with their babies and market goods. Where have they all materialized from in this sparsely settled landscape? But there's room for all, and we help the ladies settle themselves and their clanging enamelware in the back of the truck. No one hurries, everyone is in good humor and, eventually everything is stowed and we creep gingerly on, the ladies cradling the children while their basins slide around with loud metallic noises. I congratulate myself: we are no longer just an official vehicle with only three Westerners aboard. Now we are an African ark bristling with humanity, noisy with women chattering and babies wailing, top heavy and rolling like a ship down the uneven road.

At Lama-Kara, we stop at the big market to discharge our passengers. A small crowd gathers to watch as we help them get their baskets and pans down from the truck. Then, as we resume our seats in the cab, the women come up one by one, each one thanking us with downcast eyes, some low words, and a traditional genuflection. Their diffidence is so endearing, their thanks so sincere. I wonder how they will get home.

TCHARÉ

We've made good time, and decide to continue northwards to the remarkable market at Tcharé. We drive towards Niamtougou and pass President Eyadema's house at Pia. A little beyond, at a large tree by the roadside, we turn off onto a track leading to the market. Jerry and Claudine leave me at a rustic stand selling *tchoucoùtou,*

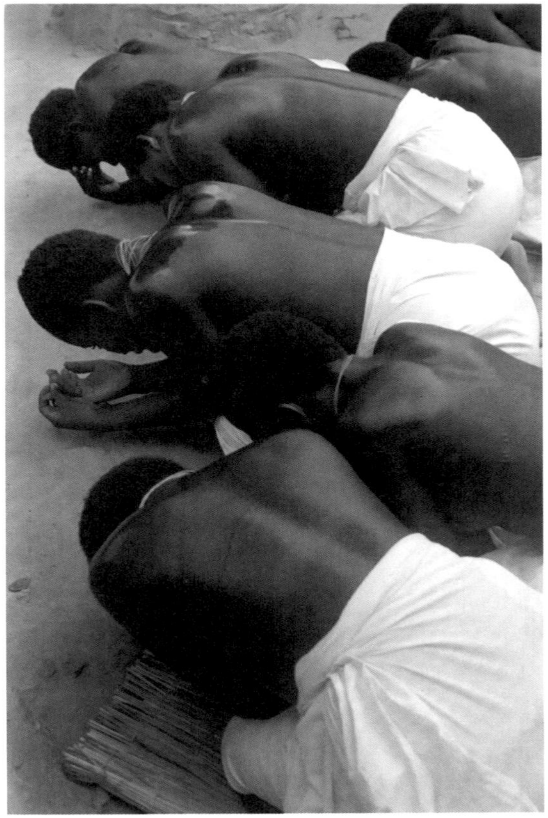

Young fetish women Photo by Lucas Kiers

the millet beer of the Kabré people, while they continue on in the truck. I've been here before with Eric and want to retrace our steps along the footpaths that thread the forested slopes and deep gullies down to the market.

I join the people all headed in the same direction. At a bend in the path, a file of young women is coming through the trees. They stop still in surprise at seeing a lone *yovo* on foot and stare at me openly, expressionlessly and a little uneasily. But I can't be as marvelous to them as they appear to me. They are, for one thing, quite completely naked and wear only a string of beads at the waist. Their breasts are just budding and their hair closely cropped; they look as virginal as the new day. We're standing not ten feet from each other, staring in mutual astonishment, I in my layers of clothing and Western self-consciousness, they in their ritual nudity. Their identical look and strict array, enforced by two elderly women at either end of their line, certainly has something solemn and ritualized about it, and I later learn they are undergoing an initiation into adulthood and the fetish arts. They live apart, naked, silent, and forbidden anything not strictly traditional. After a moment, their escorts have broken the spell between us and moved them on, still in silent single file, through the woods.

In the ensuing pause, I become aware of a sound somewhere ahead, rising from below through the trees, an unidentifiable sound made of many sounds commingled. I thought it must be rapids or a waterfall when I first heard it. "No, that's the market," Eric had said, and not long afterwards, the trees thinned and we had found ourselves looking down, as I do now, on a sea of heads, a crowd milling thickly through a large open area below, eddying around big trees and thatched stalls, calling and contesting and

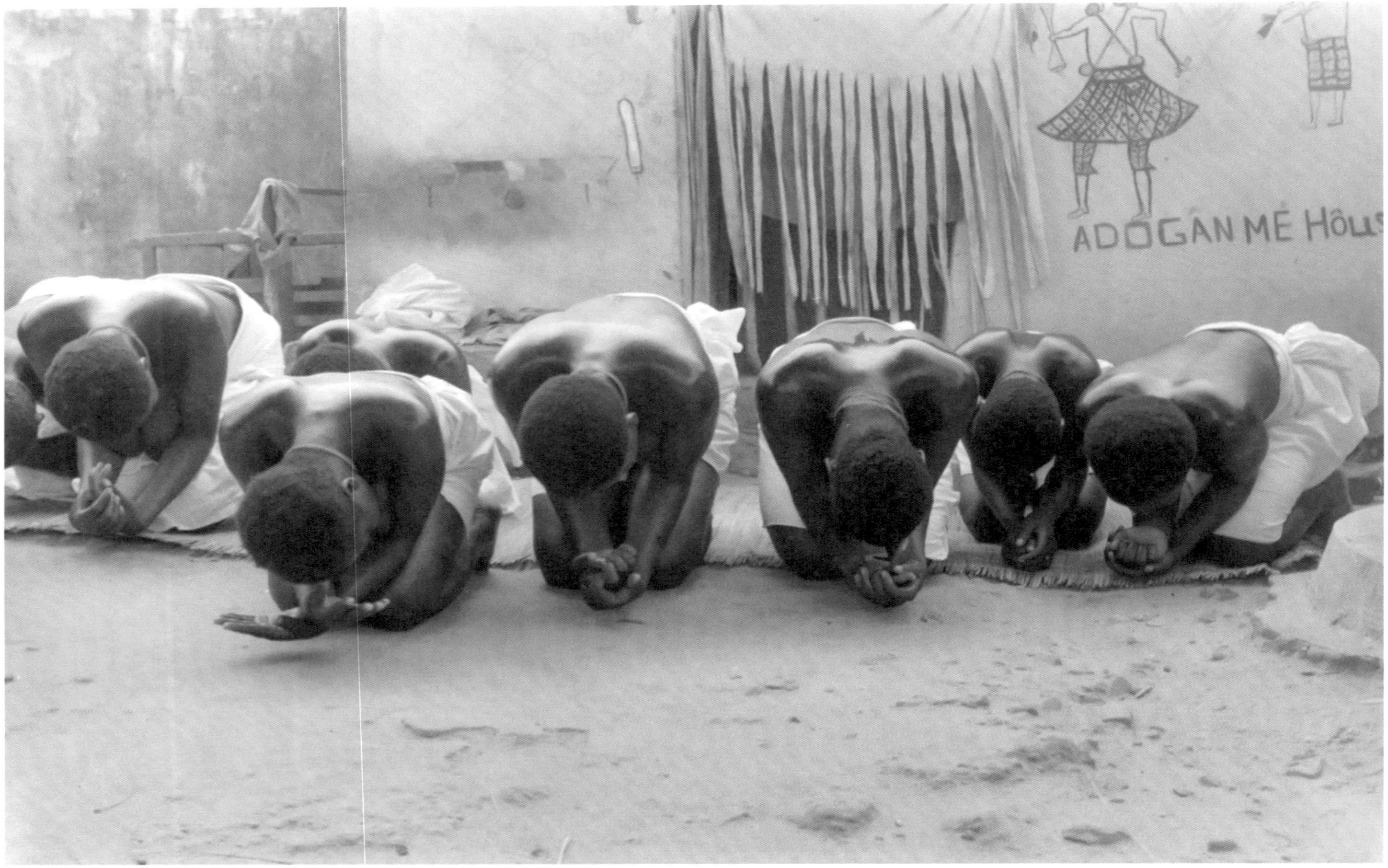

Young fetish women. Photo by Lucas Kiers

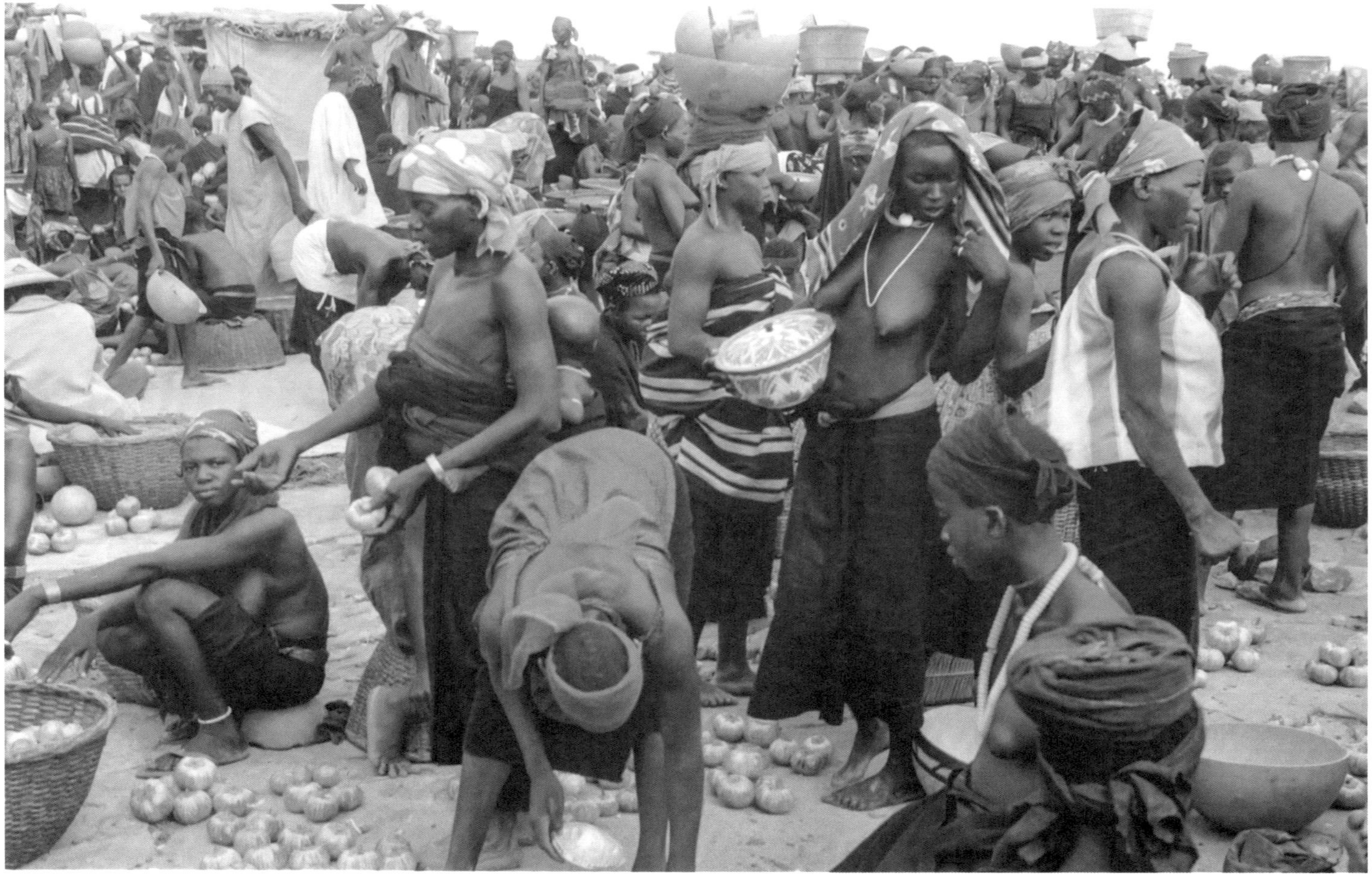

A northern market. Photo by Lucas Kiers

bargaining under streamers of wood smoke that rise to me along with that leathery smell of humanity: Tcharé market.

Soon I'm in the thick of the crowd, where eventually I find Jerry and Claudine. This is not a rich coastal market like Lomé's, where goods from all over West Africa, the East and the West are abundant. Here you can buy agricultural produce, foodstuffs, batteries, cheap cosmetics, fetish articles and *tchoucoutou*—not much cloth or other artisanal products. The economic divide between north and south Togo is evident in the patched clothing, ubiquitous goiters and maybe the short stature of these northerners. There are, however, wealthy shoppers here, too, like the tall, glossy women walking disdainfully through the crowd, wrapped in European damask overprinted with stenciled African designs, leading children dressed in shoes, shorts, and immaculate little white shirts.

It starts to rain and everyone, rich and poor, takes shelter together under a hangar with a tin roof. The downpour makes a terrific noise on the tin and it's impossible to speak or be heard. I can look at people more closely and I'm scrutinized in turn. Stares turn easily to smiles and nodding of heads, and there's a companionable unity in our enforced silence and inactivity as we wait out this downpour all together.

The rain lets up abruptly, the sun comes out, the commotion of market day resumes. I encounter a *fou* (crazy person). There's always a *fou* in West African markets. They can be as unkempt as a New York City street person, and stark naked to boot. Like the village idiot in Western tradition, they are suffered, sheltered, and fed, and wend their peculiar way through the heedless markets, talking loudly to vendors, shoppers or themselves.

The Tcharé market *fou* seems to have method in his madness. Under an old raincoat and a straw hat, he is dressed in an assortment of Western clothes cut up and then sewn or patched back together. There's a kind of satire of the European in his outfit. He radiates good humor from a gnome-like face with quick, small eyes and a fleeting expression of mockery. The watches on his wrist are made of bottle caps held together with raffia. He holds them up to my ear to hear them "tick". There's a camera around his neck assembled from small metal parts and bristling with knobs and buttons. When I admire it, he offers to take my picture. He clears the crowd from around me, backs up to get the whole subject in the picture, squints appraisingly at the light, peers through the viewfinder, looks up with a frown to adjust a knob or two, then snaps the picture with a flourish.....and rewinds the film! All this he performs in perfect imitation of the self-conscious, preoccupied manner of a real photographer. I'm delighted, and give him some change. By this time, a curious crowd surrounds us, and everyone has something to say about how he should spend the money. A man speaking French complains that since the *fou* lives at public expense, he should buy himself something decent to wear. (Maybe this man was schooled by missionaries, I think.) At any rate, the *fou* confounds us all by spending my change at a little table covered with tins of talcum powder, bottles of hair grease and vials of brightly colored nail polish, where he's paying the market girl to paint his fingernails bright green. The public-minded onlookers are volubly indignant, I'm applauding, while my crazy friend wanders off into the crowd, admiring his fingernails.

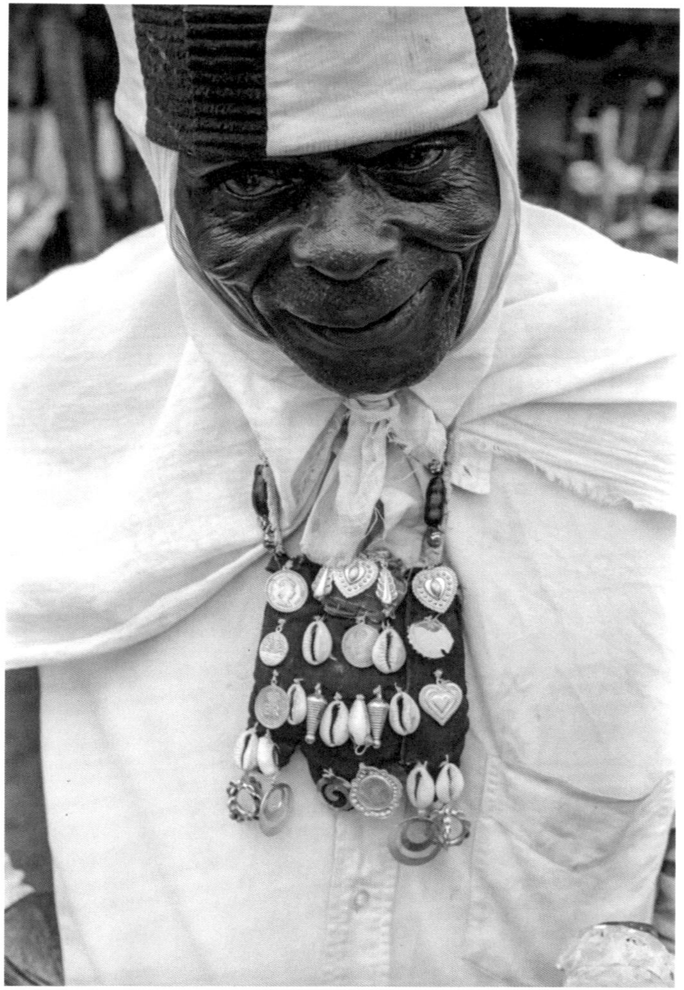

A market madman. Photo by Lucas Kiers

YADÉ

I have bought some dried fish and tobacco in the Tcharé market as a gift for my hosts at Yadé, a village outside of Lama-Kara, where Jerry and Claudine drop me off before continuing into town. I'm staying in Yadé with Jérôme and his wife Dada. Eric and I have stayed there several times in the past and it's almost as familiar as Élavagnon. When Dada sees the dried fish, she claps her hands and does a little dance for joy. I saw her do this same thing two years ago on Easter morning, when the neighbor's wife gave birth in the adjoining compound. The mother just squatted down in the courtyard while Dada caught the newborn in a big banana leaf. Then she did that little dance of joy, elbows out, head up, hopping strongly from foot to foot.

Jérome is an *ancien combatant*, a veteran of the French army. Once, when Eric and I were here in the dry season, he took us across the fields to a neighboring village to return a visit we had received and to drink *tchoucoutou*. In the stony countryside around Lama-Kara, where there is no rainfall for months at a time and the sun bakes dry the fallow terraces edged with volcanic pumice stone, there's not much to survive on except millet beer. In the villages, the households take turns serving it a week at a time to all comers. On our way to one of these villages, a Kabré farmer hailed us from the far side of his field and came running with evident delight to meet us at the stone wall. We stopped to greet him and were stunned by his reply: he opened his mouth and a live toad popped out—or most of a toad, head and bulging eyes and a forefoot. He swallowed it back and scampered away, crowing with satisfaction in a strangled kind of way. Was this a dry season pleasantry among the idle farmers, or performed

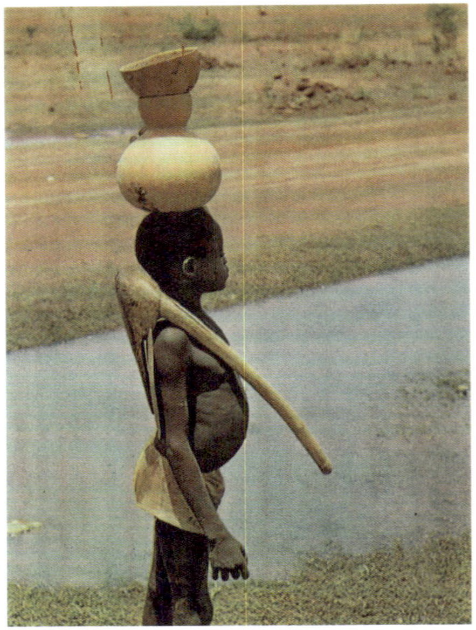

Kabré child, back from the fields

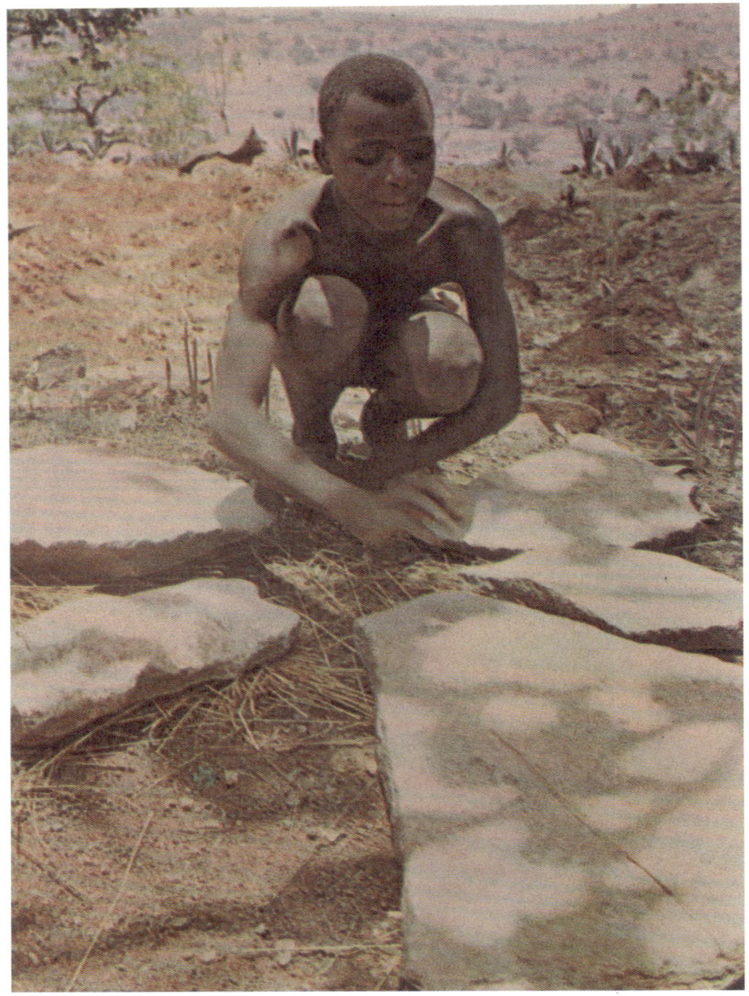

Making music with stones, Kabré country

especially for the passing *yovo*, who is so easily spooked? No one could say. Dry season seems to have its own heady culture among the Kabré. They drink a lot of *tchoucoutou* and make music on stone keyboards: flat stones are selected out of the rocky earth for their differing sonorities, arranged in a circle and played by the musician with yet another stone. Maybe toad-swallowing is just one more dry season entertainment among the sly, humorous, slightly inebriated Kabré villagers.

We follow the pumice walls over the dry land. Every hill we skirt is crowned by what seems to be a tiny medieval village with

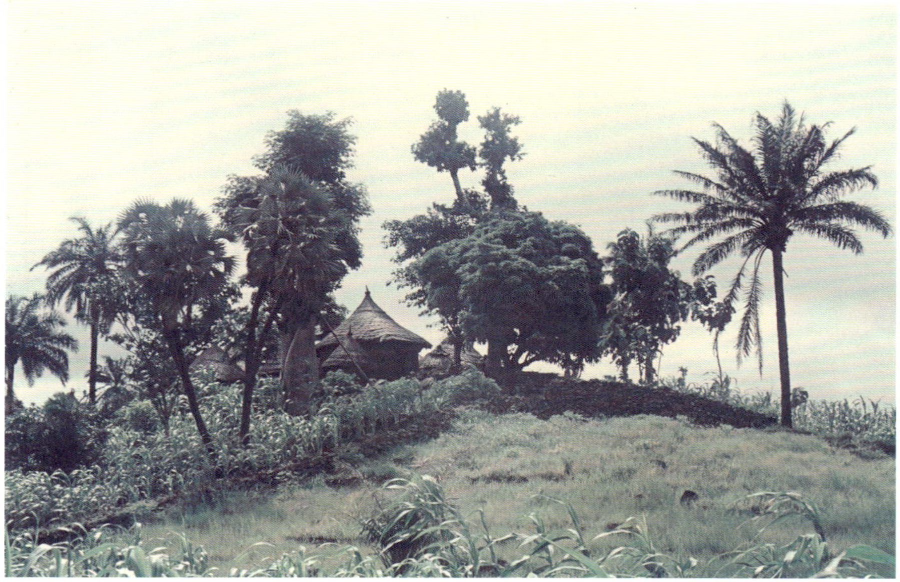

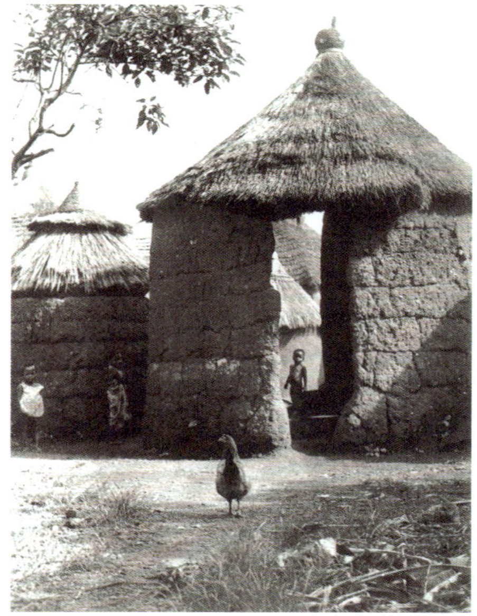

Kabré compound

walls and gates and towers, but is really a Kabré household made of a number of round, conical-roofed houses of different sizes, each with its own purpose, bound together by an encircling wall. There's a house for each wife, one in which guests are received, a shelter for a goat or a pig, a storehouse for millet....

We follow Jérôme into the village and duck under the thatch eaves into the cool, dark, circular interior of this week's *tchou-coutou* pub. The light from the low doorway shows that a dozen villagers are here before us. In the egalitarian way of northerners, they move over without ceremony to make room for us on a rough bench. I'm grateful not to be offered a chair. A woman approaches with a calabash of beer for each of us. The surface is still bubbling and swirling with active fermentation, and I brush away the bees, who want some too. As she gives me the calabash, the woman's hand passes lingeringly along my own in a ritual welcoming way.

The *tchoucoutou* had a sour taste, but its slightly heady effect and the pleasure of being cool indoors with these people who seemed to accept us and who chuckled and spoke in low tones a language I don't understand, filled me with contentment.

Now, two years later, I'm here in the rainy season. Claudine and Jerry are wise to stay in Lama-Kara, as Jérôme's compound is full of family and guests. His sons Émmanuel and Isoffa are home, and a family from Sokoto in Nigeria seems to have moved in as well. The wife is a good-natured Kabré lady with an infant child. Her husband is a tall Nigerian with refined features and the strong aura of a person of influence. In his long Muslim robe he makes a striking figure. He's come to Yadé at Jérôme's invitation to pray and work magic that will help Émmanuel pass his exams, for the man from Sokoto is an eminent fetish-worker and soothsayer in his own land. Will he do a reading for me, I ask? His response is unexpected: come back in a day or two, he says. The spirits he works with, his familiars, only travel by foot, and he came by bus. When they catch up with him, he can help me. Somehow it seems plausible that spiritual beings might adhere to traditional ways and shun modern transportation, so I agree to wait.

A few days later, Isoffa comes to tell me to follow him to the soothsayer's room. Before leaving, I look out my window and see with unusual clarity, in saturated colors, a lone tree standing on a hillock in the fields and embraced by the furrows of young millet curving around it. In the distance, twilight is falling over the mountains. Isoffa is urging me to come.

The fetish man's room is unlit but I can see as I enter that his wife and baby are there, and Émmanuel, who will translate. I sit down on a mat facing a heap of cowrie shells, old coins and an iron ring. The soothsayer is standing before a small altar on the wall. I can't see it, it's veiled behind a handkerchief. I hear his murmured prayer, and smell frankincense.

Now he begins a long incantation as he runs his hands through the cowries, swirling them around, lifting handfuls and letting them fall. I'm invited to put my hands, too, into the shells, and to focus on the questions I want answered: should I stay and try to find a job in Togo? If I go back to the U.S., what kind of career awaits me there? I'm trying to project my questions into the cowries as intently as I can. Then the reading begins. I take up a handful of the shells at his request and put them down before him. He begins to sort through them. Another handful, and another. Each one provokes a chuckle or two, a shaking of the head and the word *"anasara, anasara"*, spoken under his breath in a tone of puzzled amusement. I know this word, it's the northerner's equivalent of *yovo*. He seems to be struggling with the alien peculiarities with which I've injected the shells. He shakes his head, he goes "tsk, tsk" with his tongue, and I begin to feel like a really hopeless case. Finally, after consulting a book in Arabic, he answers my questions—or rather, he tells his wife, who translates into Kabré for Émmanuel, who translates into French for me. Meanwhile, the baby is bawling so that I can hardly hear; but I gather I'm to go back to my own people, where I will tell them all I know about Togo. He also says that I shouldn't quarrel with my traveling companions, and stop spending a lot of money without knowing where it goes.

These suggestions seem to me practical enough, if not especially prescient—although, as I write all this down more than 40 years later, I wonder whether there wasn't, after all, a prophecy there. He tells me further that I can assure a fortunate outcome to my concerns with a personal ceremony. I must buy a variety of white things in the market: a white goat, a white chicken, three meters of white cloth, three kola nuts and fifteen francs in coin, and give all this away to the first needy person I encounter—but not to someone who asks. These measures, on the other hand, seem highly impractical, and my hesitation must have shown, because he says he can make a charm instead, which need only be thrown into the Kara river at twilight from the bridge in the middle of the town.

The charm is an impressive production. It involves a small leather album about two inches square holding manuscript leaves in Arabic, to which Emmanuel and I add some prayers on slips of paper. Then the soothsayer has me put in a sewing needle and some thread before taking it over to the altar, where he speaks in low, intimate tones to the mystery behind the handkerchief. He seems to implore it on our behalf and gestures back to me (*"anasara"*) and to Émmanuel. He makes several passes over our heads with the little album before finally opening the covers. The needle and thread have done their work and unaccountably disappeared. The slips of prayer have been neatly sewn into a bundle, a charm that he gives me to throw into the river.

The next day, I am standing on the Lama-Kara bridge in the evening. The daylight has faded, the Kara river is a dark half-seen torrent below. People are passing back and forth behind me in the twilight. I lean out and toss the soothsayer's charm into the water and as I straighten up, a young man almost collides with me. I catch a frightened look on his face before he apologizes, mumbling that it's surprising to see a white man out after dark. I think he understood perfectly what I was doing, and his fright is at seeing me on the bridge in the twilight throwing what could only be a charm into the river: a *yovo* doing *gris-gris*.

The embassy truck barrels without stopping through Péwa and Élavagnon on our way home to Lomé. Jerry has to report on his northern vaccination project, and I'm eager to rejoin Eric for a long trip we've planned through Nigeria, Niger and Mali. We pass a line of cars parked along the roadside. Some of the passengers, I see, are picnicking on the grass. A little further down the line, people are dancing to a radio placed on the hood of a car. Doors are flung wide, I see people lounging on the seats or gathered just to talk. And then I see why: we pass the lead car, where a half-dozen men are helping the driver change a flat tire. So a flat tire in Togo seems to be the occasion for an impromptu party, a chance for everyone to enjoy being sociable, instead of the vexatious delay it represents back home.

When we're still an hour or two from the city, we arrive on the scene of a road accident. It's hard to see what has happened, a crowd of people is in the road and there seems to be no police at all. Jerry pulls the truck over and jumps out, trying to warn everyone to clear the way for oncoming traffic. No one pays attention to him, and in the general hubbub and confusion he climbs back behind the wheel and we drive on. Could we have helped? Our instincts urged us to intervene, but something tells me that even purely humanitarian actions might be seen as misplaced, overbearing or even coercive in the unsettled conditions of post-colonial Togo, and I'm glad we didn't try to impose ourselves further on the confused situation.

Darkness falls, and the road descends from the hills onto the coast, where Lomé appears as an expanse of electric streetlights, startlingly bright after the darkness and oil lamps we've become used to in the north. Suddenly there is a barrier across the road ahead and armed soldiers surround the truck. They shout hoarsely, they level their firearms at us, they give every appearance of agitated hostility as they shine flashlights through the windshield and thrust angry faces against the windows. Claudine and I sit very still and avoid eye contact while Jerry talks to them quietly, explaining our mission and pointing to the official embassy vaccination logo on the truck door. Their hostility subsides, they lower their guns and wave us through the barrier.

"Some kind of checkpoint", Jerry says. I'm reminded we're not in the villages anymore, but back in the capital where differing regional and ethnic identities translate into strong political tensions.

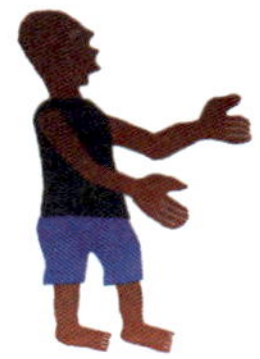

NIGERIA and the SAHEL

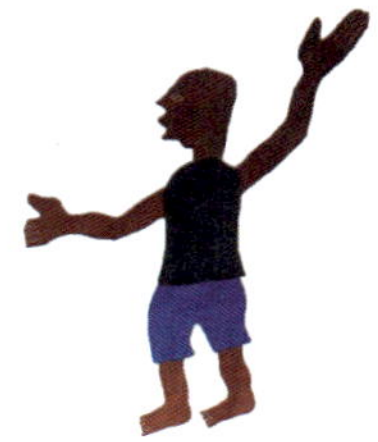

LAGOS

Two weeks after my return to Lomé, Eric and I have set out on our long trip into Nigeria and the Sahel. We arrive in Lagos on a truck called "Little Drops of Water." This kind of vehicle, which is the basic unit of long-range transport throughout West Africa, is a cross between a bus and a truck. A heavy-duty truck chassis is topped with rows of wooden benches that stretch clear across, without an aisle, under an open-sided roof. There are three kinds of seating: on the benches, where everyone is packed in and sheer proximity keeps you wedged upright and padded against the sideway lurching of the vehicle; up front with the driver, where the soft seats accommodate two or three higher-paying passengers who have only to worry about dodging the sudden wide quadrilateral shifts of the powerfully vibrating gear stick in the floor; or finally, on the roof, which commands a view of the countryside but is usually too crowded with baggage and livestock—chickens, a trussed goat—to admit passengers.

The buses gather on teeming, dusty parking lots on the outskirts of major cities. They arrive and depart according to an African idea of scheduling. Eric and I had gotten up early to catch a 7 a.m. truck to Cotonou on the first leg of our trip, and were gratified to find we were the first ones there. The truck is called *"Le Retour des Titans"* ("Return of the Titans"), presumably the driver's favorite movie. He's nowhere in sight, however, so we take choice seats on the outside of a bench and wait. By 8:30 or so, a few more passengers have arrived and happily seat themselves to eat the breakfast they have bought from the food stalls that line the bus park. Still no sign of the driver. Eric becomes impatient and grumbles about irresponsibility and lax attitudes, and when the driver finally appears, demands to know when we will be getting underway. The driver's answer is incontrovertible: when the bus is full, he says with a sunny smile. I think triumphantly, Humanity rules! Chronological time seems to have only a spotty hold on West Africa, and far more consideration is given to the people's actual coming and going.[7] I don't think we left Lomé that morning, picking our way through the melee of the bus park, every seat taken, top-heavy with baggage, everyone chattering excitedly except for a dozen babies at their mothers' breasts, until after 11 a.m.

We changed buses several times, from "The Lord is My Shepherd I Don't Know Why" to "Poor No Friend", where signs inside read "Keep Your Load" and "No Smoking No Fighting." Buses passing us in the opposite direction, I noted, were called "Good Night

Sleep Well" and "Had I Known", along with "Love Those Who Love You" and "Sea Never Dry". So here we are, finally, in "Little Drops of Water", driving through the outskirts of Lagos as evening falls. Several of our fellow passengers have contrived to fall fast asleep, sideways onto the shoulders of their seatmates or forward, pillowed on an arm over the back of the bench in front of them. I'm exhausted from these many hours on hard seats, I yearn to acquire the ability to sleep like this, anywhere, anyhow. There's too much excitement, though, in my first experience of Lagos for me to think of sleeping. It's taking us hours to crawl into the city through this unimaginably dense and confused traffic. There doesn't seem to be any space at all between the vehicles that jam the streets, and we proceed by literally scraping by each other, often under the energetic direction of the assistant driver, who descends from the truck, voluble and gesticulating, to guide our progress inch by inch.

The fumes, the noise and above all the lights, confirm that we're not in Lomé anymore. Togo has nowhere near this apparent abundance of electricity, and I feel like an up-country bumpkin, gaping at the endless open stalls we crawl by, each blazing with light. Most of this light comes from red, green or blue colored neon tubes. We pass a hardware store whose serried metallic wares make a blinding display of bright scarlet pots and pans. There's a profusion of stalls selling music, each blaring the latest Congolese or Nigerian or reggae or American pop tunes, drowning each other out in succession as we pass. From one of these, a perfect aquarium of green neon, floats an old Everly Brothers hit, "Devoted to You." Eric joins me in taking up the song as it fades behind us, singing it in perfect thirds, tunefully, tenderly, down the length of the garish noisy indifferent street.

The "Joy Advanced Cafeteria" goes by and further on, the "Wisdom Advanced Laundry" and the "I Believe in God Watchworks". Young men are having their hair cut in stalls hung with hand-painted wooden boards showing the latest styles. And what, I wonder, can be behind the puzzling stall sign advertising a "Guinea Love Nap Office"?

The crowds of people in the street bewilder us. I see tall Yuroba women swathed in golden fabric from head to foot stalking grandly through the press. Their golden head cloths are intricately tied so that the ends finish like tongues of fire on their heads. Nor are the men to be outdone. They wear matching outfits: cap, tunic and trousers of the same brilliant tie-die or print, the cloth often perforated in patterns or lavish with gold embroidery. Then there are those ensembles that don't match at all, vivid colorful cloth from all over West Africa in clashing colors and patterns, laid on carelessly or perhaps by design, which make of the teeming street a spinning kaleidoscope of fashion.

After checking into a hotel in Old Lagos and recovering a sense of stasis lying on our beds under the slow hypnotic ceiling fan, we take a walk in the surrounding streets. Everyone seems to be outdoors in the warm night full of people lounging or striding, of shouts and murmured conversation and bicycles speeding by with no lamps but ceaselessly ringing bells. We stop to peer over the shoulders of a silent knot of men gathered under a streetlight. They are watching a game of checkers. The two players stare fixedly at the pieces on the board. Suddenly, one of them half-rises and seizes a piece, raises it arm's length above his head and slams it down hard on a different square. Without hesitation his opponent takes up one of his own checkers and skips it across the

WEST AFRICAN FASHION

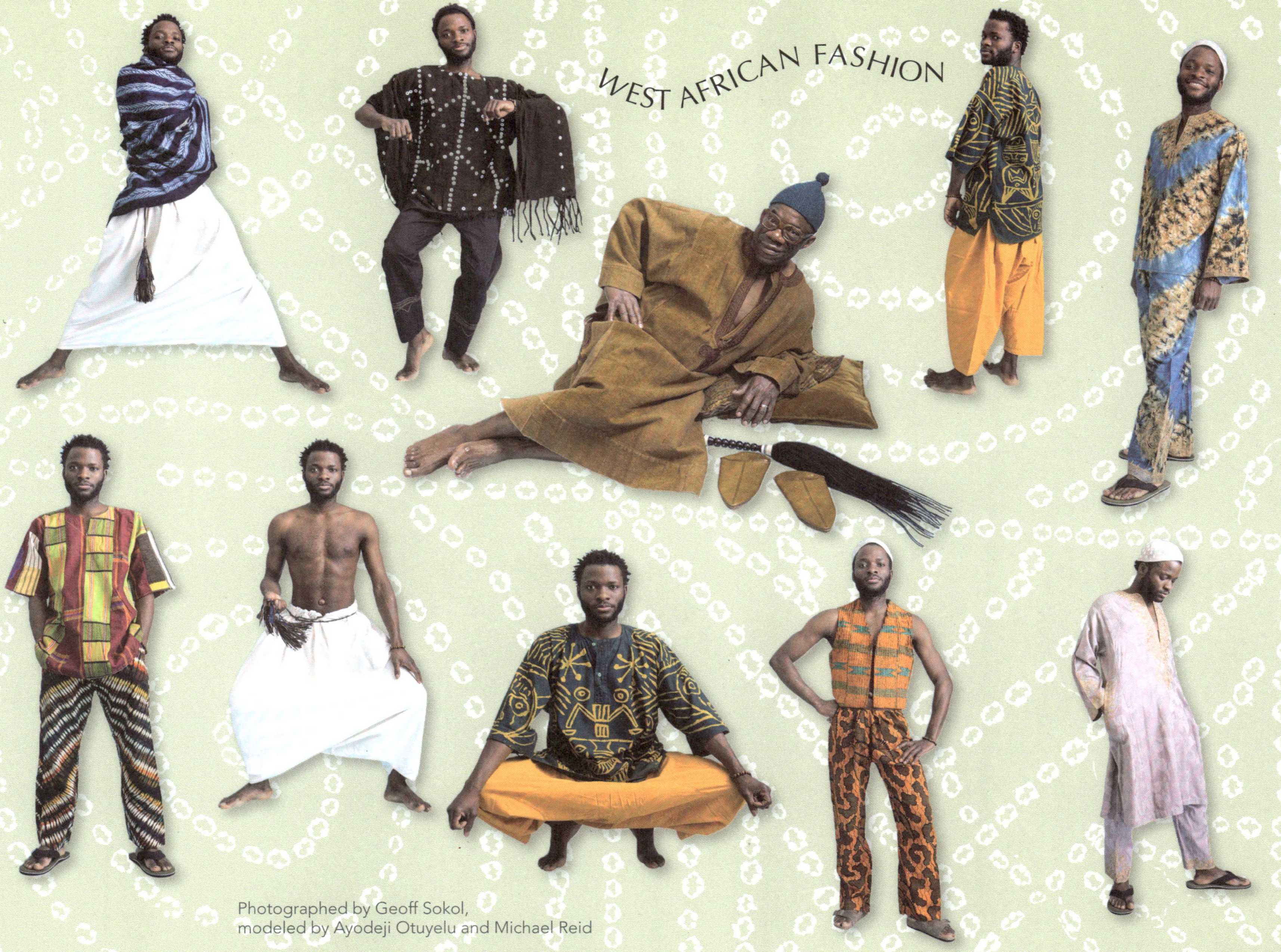

Photographed by Geoff Sokol,
modeled by Ayodeji Otuyelu and Michael Reid

board, banging it down violently each time and sweeping away a number of the enemy. Not a word is spoken. Everyone starts staring at the board again. We walk on, feeling a little dazed by the rapid alternation of stillness and extreme movement.

The architecture is on a tiny scale in this older part of town. Houses are mostly one-story buildings painted pastel colors below rusty tin roofs, their facades ornamented with cock-eyed classical details. I love their cheerful naïve look. Every once in a while, they go high rise—not like a conventional multi-story building, but more like a child's stack of toy blocks: a piled-up tower of cubes, each one a room I suppose, precariously poised one on the other and held up, it seems, by nothing except the exterior staircases that zigzag to and fro across from landing to landing to end finally at the doorsill of a room that radiates neon-green or red or blue light and teeters, barely balancing, at the top of the stack.

We are standing under a ground-floor window peering through the shutters at an interior eerily bathed in red neon light. The shutters open and a young man, laughing at our curiosity, says his name is Christopher and invites us in. A moment later we are in Christopher's apartment introducing ourselves and looking around at the almanacs on the walls, a couple of chairs and a little desk, a curtained doorway to a bedroom—all permeated with red light. Christopher calls down the hallway and a small boy appears, makes a little obeisance—a quick bended knee— and is sent out for Cokes. Somehow our host's friends learn that he's receiving, the room fills with people and the bedroom takes up the overflow. There is talk of work, of traveling, about Nigerian friends in New York and California. Addresses are exchanged, promises are made to write soon. Someone tells us to look him up in Kano when we're there in a couple of weeks. Then everyone walks us to the corner and we are all calling and waving goodbye.

ABEOKUTA

The Lishabi Hotel in Abeokuta, where Eric and I have taken a room on the top floor, is built at the top of one of the hills that characterize the town, so we have a fine view from the balcony. It's late afternoon and we're eager, even after the long bus ride from Lagos, to explore the town. Where should we start? Below us spreads a smoky, clamorous landscape of tin roofs which flow like a rusty unstoppable tide up and down the many steep hills, drowning their natural contours, except here and there where enormous tall outcrops of smooth naked rock rise abruptly out of the urban tangle and bring everything to a sudden stop at the bottom of their impossibly sheer vertical faces. These stupendous monoliths are sacred to the Egba people, and I can see why: their polished irreducible bulk looks godly in contrast to the dwarfish, tinny world of mankind lapping at their feet. They speak of ancient duration and seem toweringly aloof, communing only with other elemental phenomena like the present late evening sun, whose daylong heat they radiate and golden light reflect.

We decide to watch the sunset from the top of one of these rocks. On the way up, at the Oba's palace, we stop and read the inscription on a memorial cannon, souvenir of a 19th century conflict between the Egba of Abeokuta and the slave-dealing kings of Abomey. An elderly citizen is reciting the city's history, explaining that, in its day, it was surrounded by walls 18 kilometers long. A crowd of children has gathered to stare with a finger in their mouths at the strangers who listen so attentively. We're eager not to miss the sunset, however, and point to the top of a nearby outcrop. The children understand at once and a dozen or so of them set off with us, showing us the best way to climb. We must look like two Pied Pipers in the midst of the children, except that it's they who lead us. Finally, we have clambered up to where we have a clear view of the city on its hills. The eastern slopes are already in shadow, their crests still in the light. Diverging ranks of tin roofs mark the thoroughfares, a pall of fumes, the din of traffic and faint human voices rise up to us.

Eric and I settle down for the sunset. The children, unsure but curious to see what we're waiting for, sit at a distance behind us, talking and laughing quietly. The sun slowly approaches the horizon of hills opposite. The ragged silhouette of roofs on their crests begins to take on a surreal intensity, so clear in the increasing backlight that we have a feeling of visual intimacy with those distant houses, as if we had bent down to see them up close in a picture book. The disk of the sinking sun begins to accelerate and becomes a duller and duller red until it plunges altogether behind the hills from where, like a sleeper pulling up the covers, it draws all the evening light swiftly after it.

The lights of the town have gradually come on. Abeokuta reappears in vivid points of colored neon lights and in warmer pools of lamplight on street corners here and there. The children have long since fallen silent and crept away. We come out of our trance to climb down and find our way back to the hotel.

Yuroba cloth is famous throughout West Africa. Eric displays as many textiles as he can on the walls of his living room in Lomé, where he juxtaposes large silk *kente* cloths from Ghana, broad and splendid and intended to swath a king, with humble cotton fabric covered with indigo stencils or tie-dye patterns, naïve and spirited. He is always adding to this collection, so in the morning, we seek out the Abeokuta cloth market, following along constricted alleyways and apparently random footpaths as casual as in a village, until we find a hanger full of ladies selling cloth. We wander around in a desultory way and find nothing to buy until Eric discovers a large indigo with stencils of a coronation, showing a seated chieftain wearing a ballooning kind of European crown, with his name and date of investiture. As the market lady opens the folded cloth in the uncertain light, the lighter blue of the stencil seems to undulate and shuttle over the dark true indigo background, and I know that Eric must have it, and that when we get back to Lomé, we'll take it down to the beach together and spread it in the surf to fix the unstable indigo dye in salt water.

IFE-OSHOGBO

When the beautiful naturalistic "Ife bronzes" were first seen by Europeans, they couldn't believe these sculptures came out of Africa, and one German anthropologist ascribed them to a lost colony of ancient Greeks! Much of African statuary is made of wood, after all, and seems to be portraits of spiritual, not human, beings. The Ife heads, on the other hand, represent rulers and ancestors in a masterly stylized naturalism, and it was difficult to call them "primitive." They must be, it was concluded, somehow Western. The bronzes we see at the Ife museum strike me as having a puzzling Asiatic look. The Ife carvers and casters depict eyes with the upper eyelid over the lower, like an Asian eye.

We are staying nearby in Oshogbo, where most of the time it rains. Out of a leaden sky comes an all-day all-night rainy season downpour that turns the town's streets to mud and confines us to our ground-floor room in the Long Life Hotel, where we watch from our beds as curtains of rain turn the courtyard into a morass. A clammy dampness makes the concrete walls and floor even less hospitable; the very sheets and mattresses on our unsprung iron beds are damp. Sleep is long in coming. I try to picture the beautiful Ife faces we've seen, but I still can't dispel the gloomy discomfort of the rain or a growing conviction that Oshogbo and Nigeria and the whole African continent are very far from home.

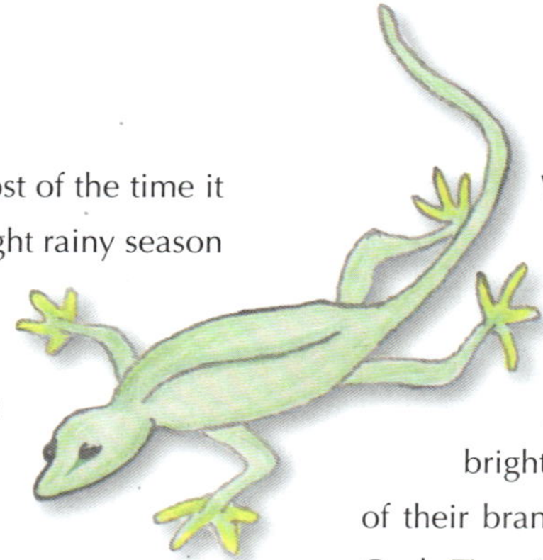

To pass the time, I am watching the circular blur of the ceiling fan. By fixing my eye on just one blade and following it around, I can deconstruct the blur into its several blades; but this soon becomes an effort, so I watch the geckos instead. There are six or seven of these small companionable lizards frozen at various angles at the edge of the ceiling and along the tops of the walls, their long thin tails making delicate curves. I watch to see when one will dart forward to snap up a bug or defend its territory; but mostly they just wait, upside-down, unblinking, immobile except for the rapid palpitation of their throats.

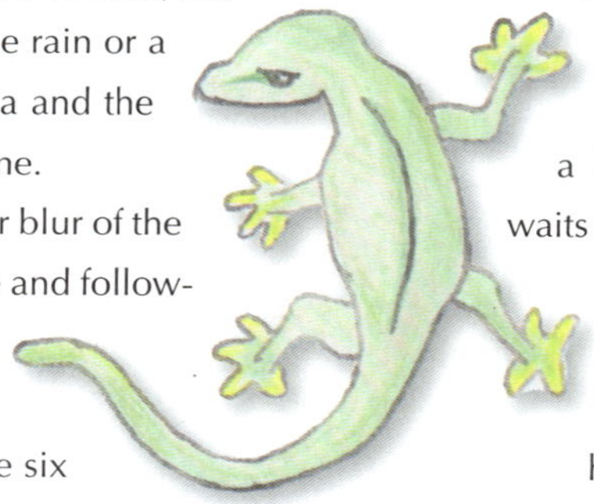

The humid air from the ceiling fan descends upon me gently, evenly, and the lazy deliberate beat of the blades becomes hypnotic. They seem to be pulling in and winding up together the damp air in the room, the geckos on the ceiling, the room itself with Eric and me on our beds, and beyond us the whole dark wet West African night, winding us up together and spinning us gently off to sleep.

Something wakes me a little later. In the semi-darkness, I can see Eric lighting mosquito coils. These are Chinese products and come in flat, brightly colored boxes with big characters and a picture of their brand: Mountain Cat, Double Rabbit, Turtle, Three Star, Cock, Tiger. Within the box, each coil, flattened into a tight spiral, comes in a thin paper envelope of its own. The coils are easily broken, and Eric is easing each one out of its envelope and carefully impaling its very center onto the little tin stand that is included. I watch, half-asleep, as he holds a lighted match to the end of the coil, waits for it to flame and then blows it out. His face, inclined in concentration, lit softly from below by the match that gives his hand a translucent glow, is for a moment like a religious portrait in chiaroscuro, iconic and beautiful.

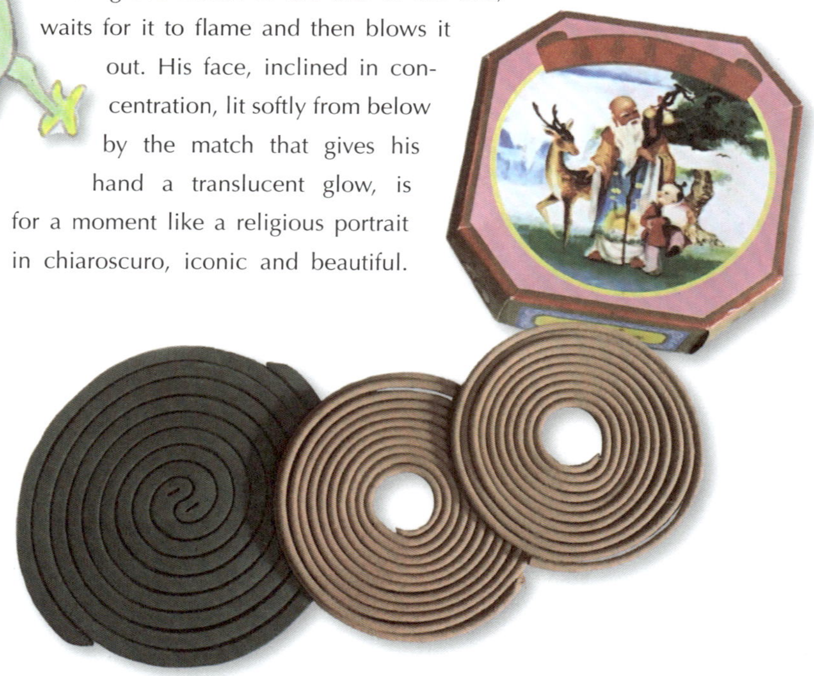

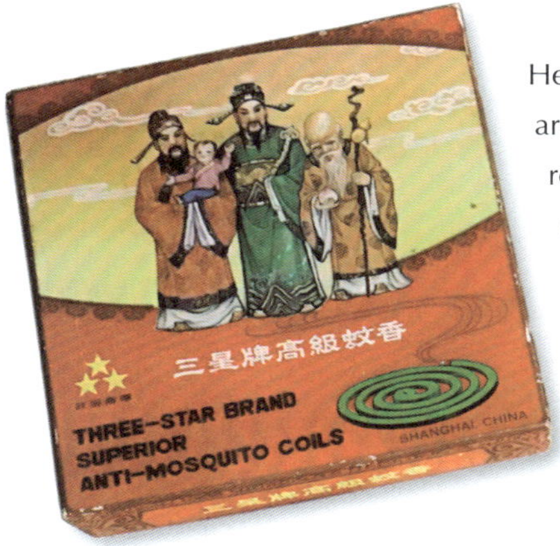

He places the coils on the floor around our beds, and then the room is really dark except for the deep red glow of each coil consuming itself around and around all night long. If I should wake again, I can guess from these friendly spiraling fires how much time has passed, or watch a mosquito dodge and dive to avoid the fragrant repellent smoke. We wake up next morning to a clear, dry new day, the geckos have retired and each coil has left us a token of the long unconscious night: an exact ghostly facsimile of itself on the concrete floor, a perfect spiral of fine fallen ash around each tin stand.

BIDA

We're on the train to Kaduna, a major city of northeastern Nigeria. We'll stop at Bida, a small town on the rail line, to "return the visit" of a participant in one of the Quaker conferences. The train is marvelously antique, with a wood-fired barrel-chested locomotive of uncertain powers and a string of passenger cars with bare wooden seats. We are the only Europeans aboard. Sleeping on those hard seats, we find, takes some getting used to. Everyone else seems accustomed to them, and sprawls or curls up or leans on each other and seems to sleep quite soundly. Eric passes the time by recounting a train trip he took in India, where the crowds were so dense in the carriage that he took refuge in the luggage rack and stayed there for two days, eating food that was passed up to him and peeing into tin cans.

Everyone has brought something to eat, and we share our hotel sandwiches and receive some interesting fritters and sauces in return. As foreigners, we are permitted the run of the train by the conductor, until he warns us against sitting on the iron steps at the ends of each carriage, which are permanently lowered to the track. He's concerned for our safety, and urges us to go back to our seats. But it's too fine a way to travel, right above the tracks that spin by under our feet, exposed to the cool rushing air and all the scents and sights of the green cultivated land we are crossing; we politely decline to move. Stops are frequent, often at simple unmarked areas of beaten ground by the track, where country people have gathered to sell food and milk out of gourds beautifully decorated with designs carved and highlighted in white, rather than the black designs we've seen in the south. These calabashes of milk and the fine-featured women who are offering them make it plain that, somewhere north of Oshogbo, we've left the land of the brilliant urban Yuroba culture and entered the world of the pastoral Fulani.

The Fulani lead their herds across most of West and Central Africa. They are a numerous people of reputed North African origin, the first Muslim Africans, empire-builders in the history of the region and preeminent herders of cattle. They greatly value personal beauty, and some Fulani hold beauty contests in which young men, elaborately groomed and dressed, vie to be chosen by shy, all-powerful maidens. Some West Africans will tell you that a Fulani child born ugly will be exposed and left for dead; but I think they're jealous and trying to account for the ubiquity of the

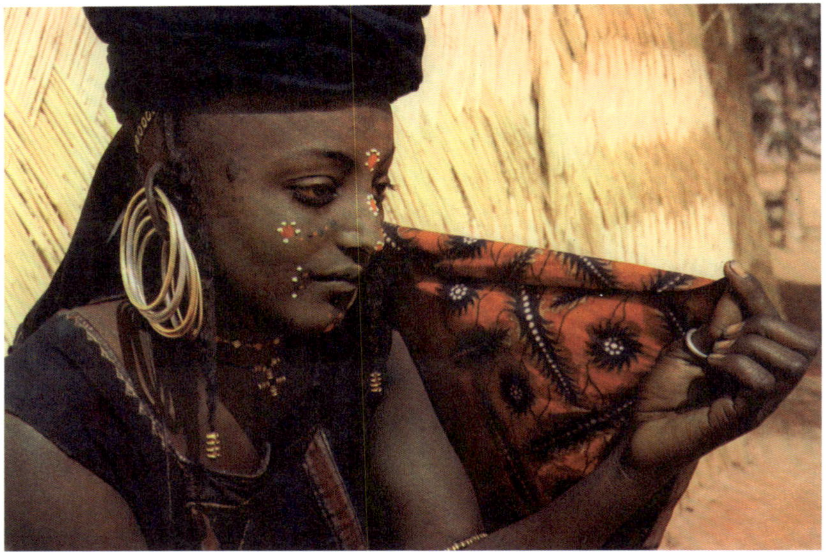

Fulani woman; RIGHT: Fulani youth dressed for a beauty contest.

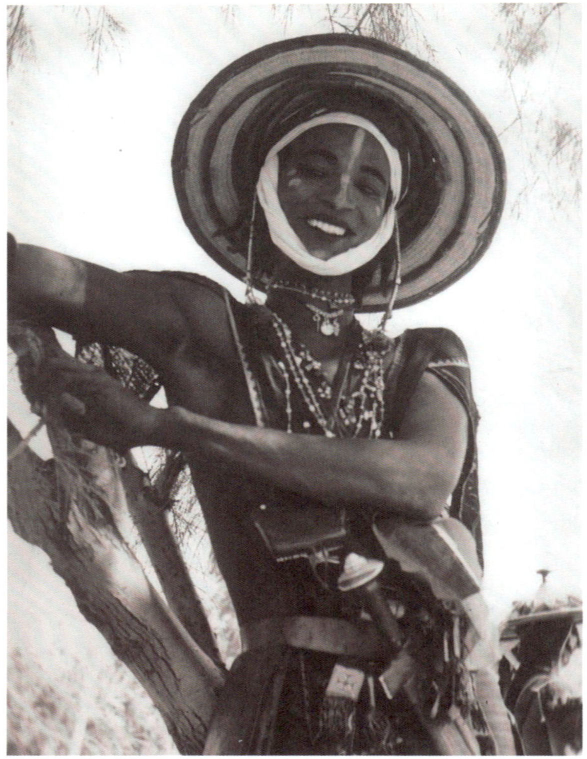

beautiful long nose, flawless skin, and fine figure of many Fulani I saw in Nigeria and the Sahel.

Bida is a Fulani town; our train is nearing the vast grazing lands they roam with their herds, and their traditional craftsmanship is evident in the young women we see from the train. The women are delicately tattooed and wear a textured white cotton cloth of their own weaving, sometimes with vivid black, green and red geometrical embroidery. At one of our stops, a young man in tunic and trousers of this white cloth, eyes us with openly amused curiosity, as we do him and his conical hat of finely-worked straw inter-woven with brilliant leather ornaments, perched over a little turban, and his elegant staff carved with a phallus at the top. Our eyes meet, we greet each other and he trots after the train, grinning and waving his staff as we pull slowly away, the engine chugging hugely and laying a thick black plume of smoke over the green fields. The train is painfully slow and labors to get over the slightest rise. After a while, I lay my head on a bare wooden armrest as I've seen my fellow passengers do, and fall asleep. A little later, Eric shakes me awake, declaring that the locomotive had exploded, the whole train slid backwards down a slope and everyone had got out to lighten it while repeated attempts were made to get it going again; and I slept through everything! I'm pleased: I've learned to sleep like an African, anywhere, anyhow.

Our host in Bida is a "settled Fulani" and his house is a conventional concrete structure with cool tile floors and glass louvers in the windows. We eat with his family in chairs at a round table, and the conversation is in English. I'm reminded we're among a pastoral people by the large bowl of melted butter in the middle of the table. Everything we eat, meat or grain, is first dipped in butter.

Afterwards, we go to the market, shaded by kapok trees with thick tall canopies and massive smooth trunks that rise out of a maze of above-ground roots. The roots snake over each other, interlacing and creating deep hollows between them. It's still and cool there, and I get a shave from a barber who's set up shop under the trees. I lie between two embracing roots, lay my head on a third, and look up into the vertical depth of the canopy. Birds call and fly between the branches. Butterflies spiral among them. A fine uneven rain of pollen and debris falls continuously. The sun sends an occasional ray that spotlights some foliage or the length of a branch, and I can focus far into the pyramidal gloom. At one point, I think I see a monkey swinging through the tops, but I can't be sure, and settle back to enjoy the slow, exquisite ministrations of the barber. He dabs a bit of fragrant oil on my skin and then shaves it with a shiny little homemade knife sharpened to a razor's edge. A dab at a time, cheeks, jaws, neck, then inside my ears and finally my nostrils are meticulously pared with an array of little knives. Onlookers gather to stare, chuckle and move on. The barber never says a word and works in utter concentration. All around in the sunlight outside the shade of the trees, Fulani women are selling milk, moving in a white animated blur of dust and sunlight, movement and chatter.

KANO

We stay a couple of days in Kaduna, an uninteresting city built by the British colonizers as an administrative center. We both have colds, and are grateful to take a break from travel with our host, Shima Gyoh, a Quaker conference alumnus. We are still 170 miles from the mythical city of Kano, and are stirred to see Hausa and Tuareg people here in the bland, ahistorical streets of Kaduna. The Tuareg men are veiled and robed in indigo, with medieval-looking swords in leatherwork scabbards always at their side; and the Hausa horsemen canter down the streets, white robes streaming, black turbaned faces smiling at our admiration.

Our bus comes into Kano at dusk. A man walking through a ploughed field is sowing seed broadcast, a beautiful wide gesture as old as agriculture. Another is praying in the middle of his cultivations, all alone talking to God, his work finished for the day. We pass a truck coming the other way, I remember the words blazoned over the cab: "DO GOOD TAKE IT EASY". I take it as a mantra.

We stayed in Kano almost a week, "returning visits" with Quaker alumni and seeing French friends of Eric. But mostly we just walked endlessly along the adobe streets and alleys of Old Kano, which radiate from a great plaza in front of the Emir's palace. At sunset, the whole city goes to prayer and the streets and

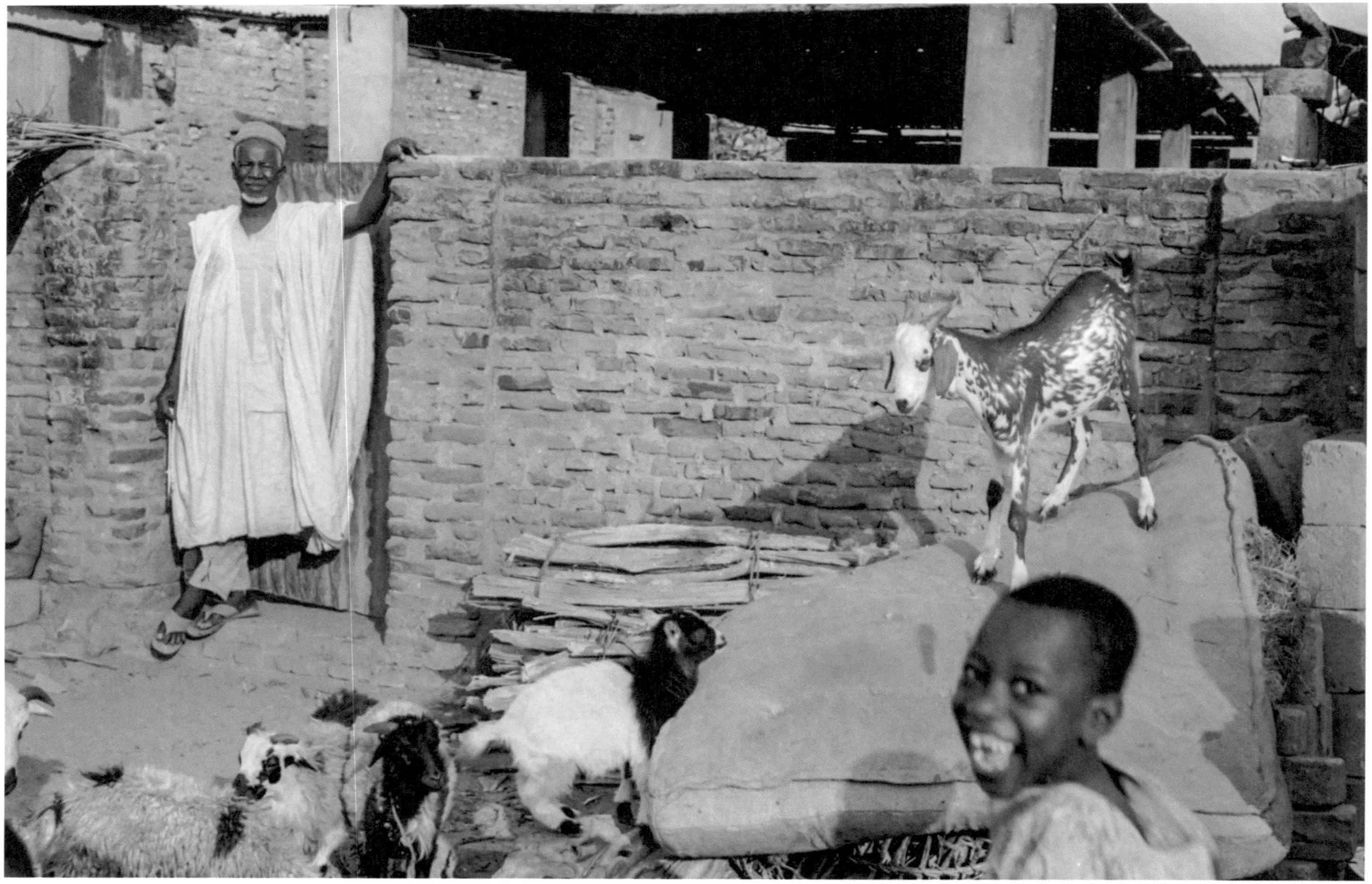

Back street, Kano

Photo by Lucas Kiers

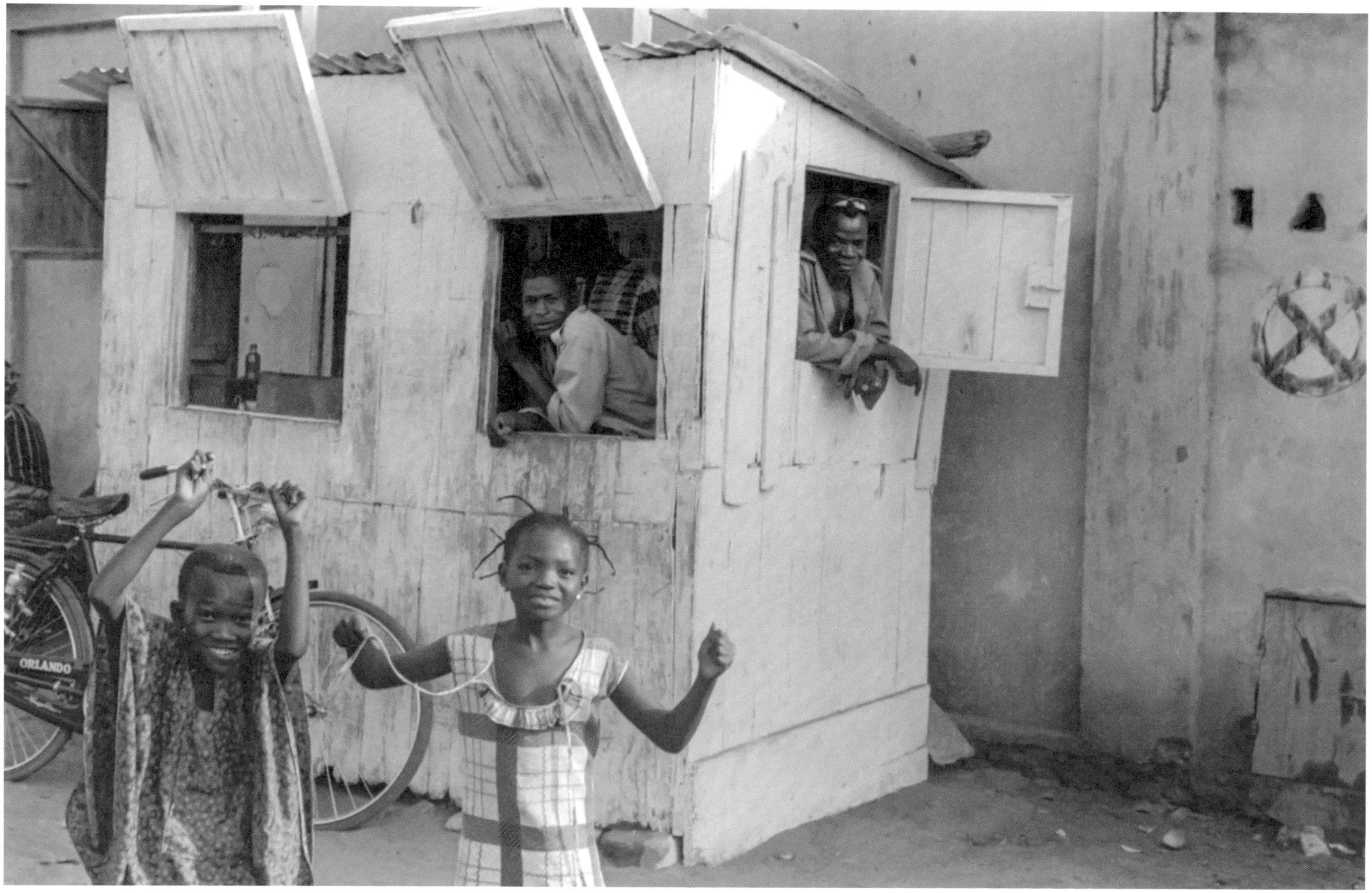

Back street

Photo by Lucas Kiers

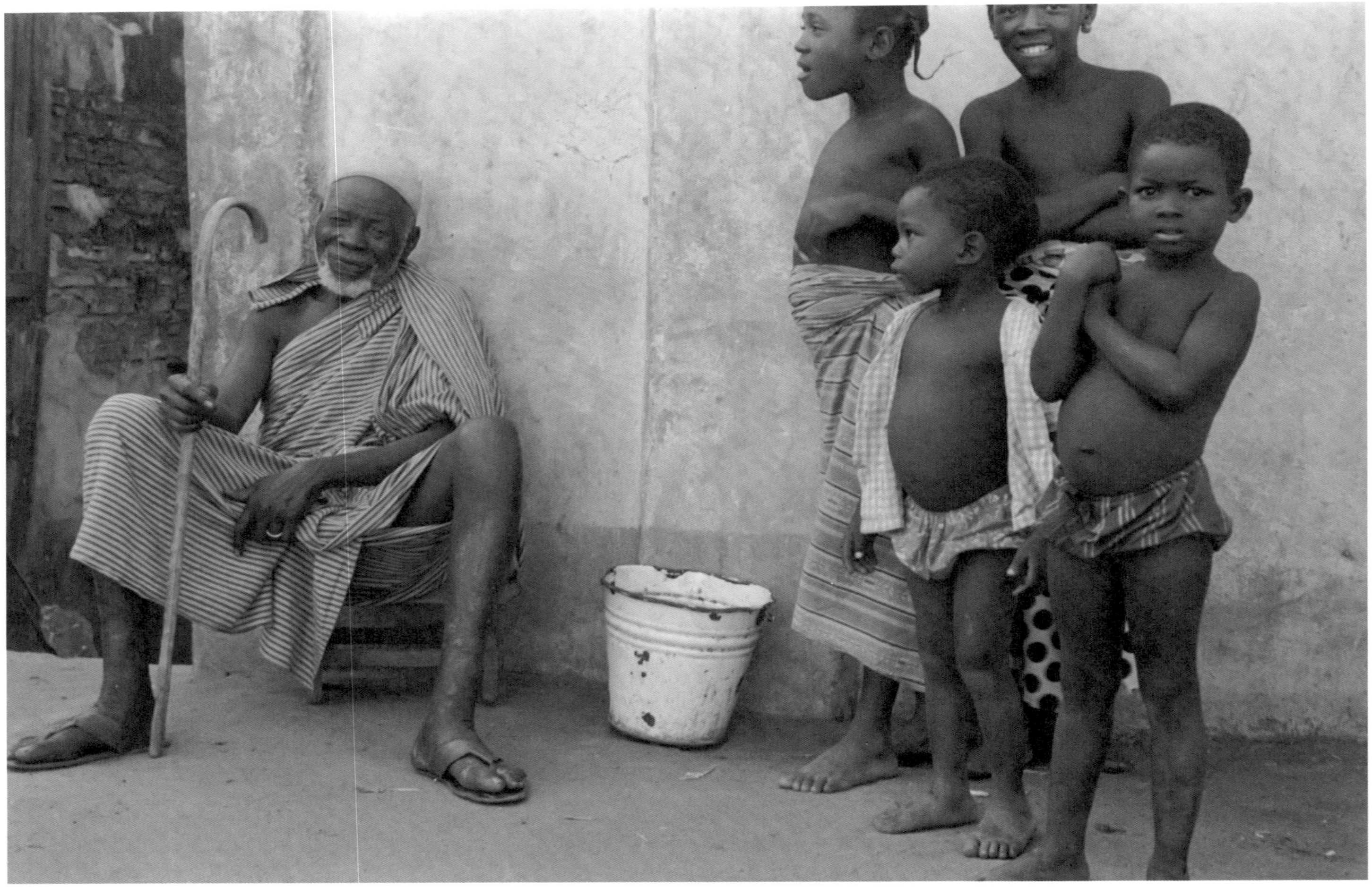

Back street

Photo by Lucas Kiers

squares are full of men in spotless white robes lined up in ranks to pray and recite the Koran. Their bicycles, uniformly finished in silvery chrome, are parked in their own shiny alignments. When prayers are over and everyone remounts, the silver bicycles fly away down the streets in every direction bearing tall, thin, deeply black men whose white robes billow out behind them.

The streets of the Old City are unpaved and the buildings made of adobe, so that their golden desert colors surround us in every direction and underfoot. Many doorways are decorated with softly molded geometric bas-reliefs, and the facade of one house we pass is covered with handprints, the impressions of hundreds of hands pressed into the adobe when it was drying. We follow along aimlessly as the streets widen or narrow unexpectedly to end in small plazas where someone is grilling brochettes on a little fire, watched by children sitting in a ring. A larger square is occupied by vats of indigo dye, deserted now in the dusk. In a tiny triangular plaza, a group of Hausa men invites us to sit with them on woven straw mats and share their meal of meat stew. Their hospitality is quick and egalitarian. They have the northerner's reserve, however, a formal dignity unlike the pervasive good humor of the people of Lomé and the coast.

The Kano Museum is opposite the Emir's palace in a fine old traditional building. On display are ancient prototypes of things we've seen in our walks through the city: calabashes, woven cloth, metal and ceramic vessels. A steel spear point is delicately engraved with a star-like pattern; a child's Koranic writing board has a carved wood frame and flowing Arabic script. We emerge from the museum with a sensation of timelessness. These are not displays of objects from a remote and irretrievable past, or quaint things of obscure use. These things can still be found in the market. Time has hardly changed them, it seems; nor, perhaps, has it much changed the way of life that produced them, itself evolved in the unvarying sunshine and heat and the elemental landscape of the Sahel.

We visited the Wari's house, a sprawling maze of mud buildings and courtyards enclosing large halls with vaulted ceilings, curving stairways of softly molded adobe steps, inexplicable small blind grottos in the thick walls and sudden, brilliant, arcaded courtyards. Nothing I saw was symmetrical, nothing was at true right angles or in a straight line. The genius of the Kano style seemed to reach its pitch in a hall of ribbed walls covered with molded and painted red and silver forms, great clashing jostling forms interspersed with bas-reliefs — firearms, a teapot — and complex geometrical patterns.[8]

Through the intensely urban maze of Kano, the Tuareg stalk like haughty forces of nature. The men, enveloped in long, dark robes of deep indigo, are invariably armed and habitually veiled across the lower face, and lead the noisy, fractious camels they have ridden from far away in the Sahel. As Eric and I walk by a group of them seated in a circle on the ground brewing tea, they wave us over and make place for us. Each man has put his weapons behind him, swords sheathed and spears stuck in the sand. The steel point of one of these spears is engraved with the same star-like pattern I saw in the museum. None of them speaks French or English. They smile and ignore us and carry on their conversation as they drink dark tea from little glasses, lifting their veils each time to sip. One man seems to be the designated tea-brewer. He has a small aluminum teapot and raises it far over his

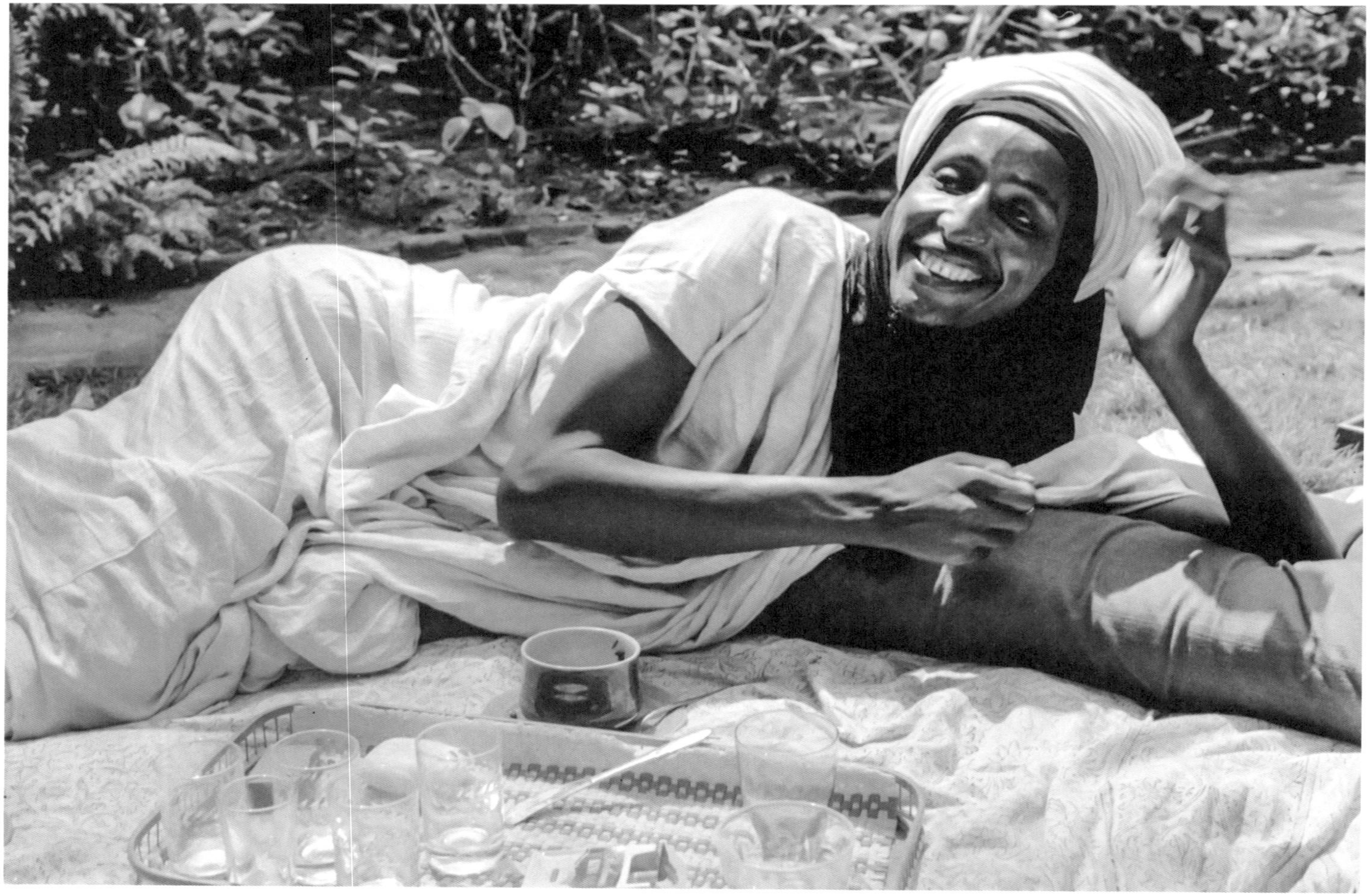

Tuareg tea

Photo by Lucas Kiers

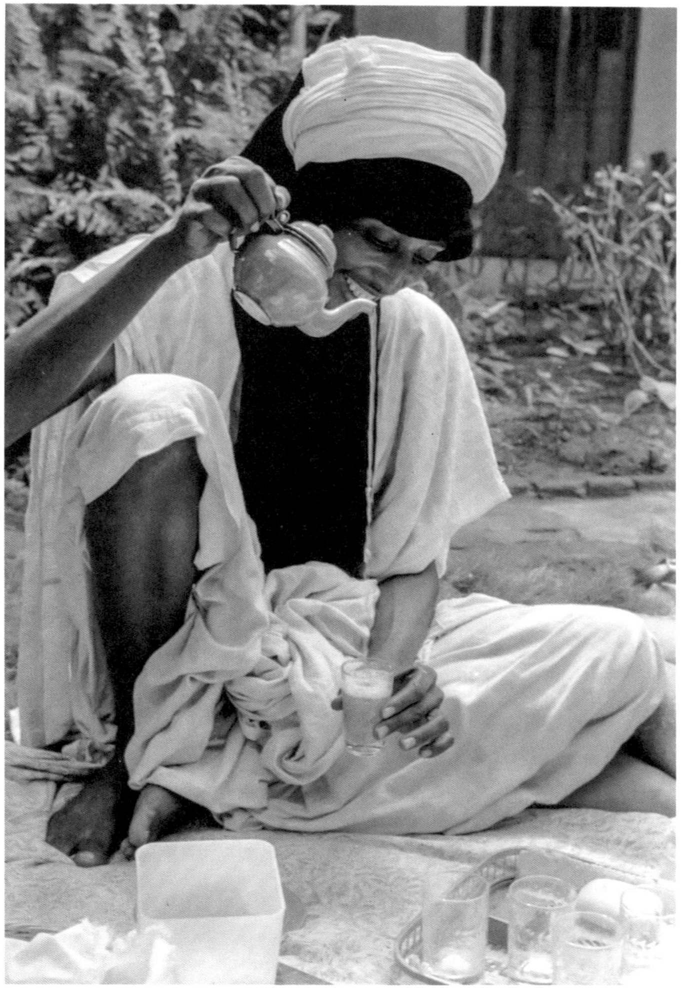
Tuareg tea Photo by Lucas Kiers

head, arm extended, to pour hot tea in a thin unerring stream into two little glasses, one for me and one for Eric. I give him an appreciative glance and take a sip. I start, tears sting my eyes and I recall those fairytale potions that turn you into a wolf or an owl. It doesn't taste bad, really, just very intense, a brew of strong tea, lots of sugar, and some hot pepper. The conversation goes on quite naturally. The men's long brown tattooed arms, extending from the rolled-up sleeves of their robes, move widely to emphasize what they are saying; or their fingers, covered with iron and aluminum rings, sift the sand idly as they talk. After a while, Eric and I get up and express our thanks. Our Tuareg hosts smile and seem to return our warmth.

ZINDER

We are at the Nigerian border with Niger, waiting for our passports to be stamped. Among the people gathered around the checkpoint are a group of Wolof men from Senegal, three young men and their father. During the long wait, I have time to watch how they move and hold themselves. Their bearing seems completely without tension. From narrow waists their broad shoulders spread like wings. Long, long arms rise and fall, fold at the elbow or sweep the air as they talk, and their hands move like powerful tethered animals with an expressive life of their own. This is a kind of personal beauty I'm unfamiliar with, not of form or feature but of pure articulation, unselfconscious, unornamented and like the strokes of that butterfly's wings, rippling away across time and space from this desert spot to have consequences elsewhere.

Our bus left Kano early in the morning and is crossing a

spring-like, rainy-season landscape of trees in leaf and fields of viridian green. Tiny bright yellow birds abound and white herons pace through sheets of standing water, listening for frogs. The bus lumbers past walled adobe towns and an occasional round hut made of reeds, new-built against the rains. Horsemen share the road, and long files of laden camels. Zinder is 150 miles north of Kano, and even with many stops to take on passengers or unload cargo, we're in the city by nightfall.

"Wait until you see the camel park," Eric says at breakfast the next morning. Zinder market is very large, befitting an ancient center of trade from all over the Sahel. Supplying the market is still done by camel caravan, and hundreds of the animals have arrived, been unloaded and "parked" by their owners in a flat area outside the lanes of stalls that comprise the market itself. We watch as a Tuareg trader drives two laden camels between the rows and rows of kneeling beasts, finds a couple of empty spots, hobbles his animals and makes them kneel. These two grunt and roar in protest as they come down off their height and are unloaded. The whole park resounds with protesting camels; they seem unhappy to be left alone with their own kind under the growing heat of the sun. We walk on towards the market stalls and pass the mules, parked in equal number but silent, even meek as they eye us going by; and then ranks of more spirited horses.

The morning cool is dissipating, the desert sun ascends and seems to bleach out every color except white and the purple-blue indigo that are so widely worn. There's a pervasive golden haze in the air; the sand underfoot and the straw-roofed market stalls we're approaching are golden, too. The stalls are neatly aligned along wide ways that go straight up and then down the other side

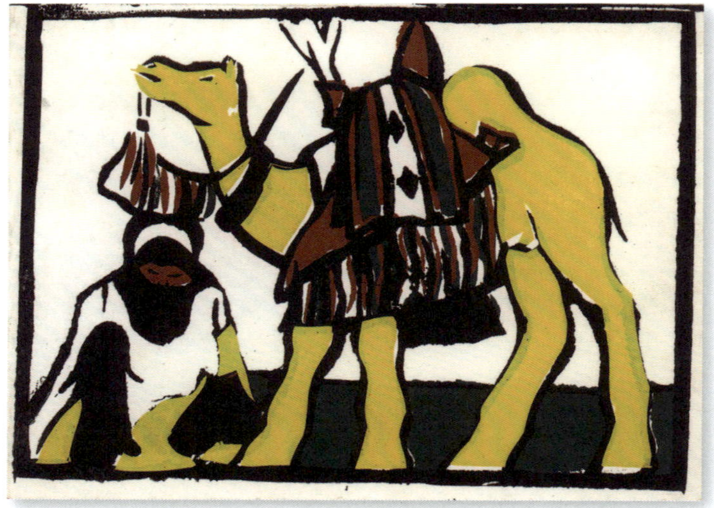

of a sandy rise. A few trees offer shade. The blacksmith stalls are all around us and the heavy breathing of bellows and the ringing of hammers fill the air. The smiths are transforming automobile parts into more practical objects, beating and soldering them into hoe blades or silvery, artfully engraved ladles. No visible boundaries intervene, but suddenly we're among the mat makers. They work in silent concentration, plaiting and weaving fine, pliable, differently toned reeds, interwoven with brightly dyed wool and leather strips, to make mats that are as complex and decorative as rugs.

Potters have their own precinct, next to the gourd makers. Their vessels, piled up in the sand in front of the stalls, dark in color and with swelling shapes, have a cooling effect in the increasingly hot white light, as do the massed water gourds and calabashes, which are intricately incised with black geometric designs and stained a deep, reposeful red.

The jewelers also are set apart, as much by their distinctive sour expressions as by their profession. They trade in gold and silver, after all, the ultimate commerce; so in the generally genial atmosphere of the market, full of greetings and easy smiles, they glower and look straight ahead. A large woman trader, swathed in gauze, sits grandly under a tree with her rings and bangles, pendants and coins displayed on a velvet cloth at her feet. The gold at her ears, throat, and wrists looks impressively massy and gleams splendidly on her dark glossy skin. We stop to bargain in our best Lomé fashion for some small ornaments and a nicely worked copper box, trying to purchase the lot for one price. But she is unsmiling and inflexible, and we finally bow to the small reduction she allows.

Around the other side of the tree, a taciturn old man is selling coins. I'm astonished to see his ample stock of Austrian imperial *thalers* with the portrait of Empress Maria-Theresa and the date, 1768. Eric surprises me further by telling me the *thaler* is still in use as currency throughout the Sahel.

We've walked up the hill and down the other side through a crowd of Hausa, Tuareg and Fulani dressed variously in long white robes and turbans, long indigo robes and veils, goatskins and wide straw hats or tunics of hand-loomed striped cloth. Very few people are wearing Western dress; there seem to be no other Europeans here than us.

Zinder is a busy, important market, dense with people; but no one moves at anything but a measured, deliberate pace, hands clasped behind the back, head high. Everyone is friendly (or at least forbearing) when we stop to talk to them or admire their dress or ornaments. They themselves are only mildly curious about us. At that moment, a man steps out of the press and greets us. He is Tuareg, but not of the long-robed camel-riding kind. He's dressed in a goatskin tunic, like a herdsman. A cascade of tin and leather amulets covers his chest, and there's a sword on his belt. His head is wound in a long black cloth drawn across his chin. Under the wide straw hat he's wearing, his eyes are lively over a long aquiline Tuareg nose.

We "chat"; that is, he speaks his language, we speak French. "Where are you from?" he seems to ask, so we introduce ourselves and ask about him. I am watching him as we converse, wondering how this traditional goatherd dressed in skins and hung with amulets, could be as poised as any man of the world and radiate such dignified self-assurance. His manner is frank, his eyes meet mine openly, we laugh together. Then he seems to say something in farewell and walks back into the crowd. There is something so admirable in his matter-of-fact composure, that I feel suddenly rueful and slightly bewildered as I watch him go, like the Greek traveler who meets one of the gods in disguise and realizes it, too late.

We stop to buy Tuareg veils—long, narrow black cloths of thin cotton. The tradesmen are themselves veiled, and are at pains to show us how to wind it properly. Starting at the back of the neck and moving with Islamic respect for the head, so carefully that their fingers hardly seem to touch him, they deftly wind a turban on Eric. The long, loose end is led across his nose and tucked in. He turns to look at me. The effect is startling. Eric, my habitual Eric, has been eclipsed and transformed by the veil, become a stranger, more like them.

We came to the market early, with the camels. It's evening by now and we are leaving when we're hailed by the same group of Tuareg men who made us tea in Kano only yesterday. Everyone is talking excitedly, smiling with his hand to his chest, saying something about Agadez. Will we all meet again in Agadez?

AGADEZ

The bus to Agadez is a real bus, not a converted truck, with upholstered seats and no name. There's little to be said for the road, though. The bus plows along barely discernible tracks obscured by drifting sand that sends it sliding from side to side. During the two breakdowns we suffer, the passengers descend to wait in the middle of the wide, inhospitable bush. Even here, people go by: shepherds with their goats, women carrying water in large gourds on their heads, traders leading a string of camels or mules. They seem fragile, with nothing but prayers and amulets between them and thirst, fatigue, and predators. It takes us 14 hours to cover the 293 miles between Zinder and Agadez.

We decide to go to the movies. An area of sand near the hotel has been enclosed with a reed fence and veiled men are selling tickets and taking firearms from their customers. Nobody seems to speak French, so we don't ask what the program is, we just find an empty spot in the crowd and sit down on the sand. I look around: no women, of course, and our immediate neighbors smile and welcome us. They may have checked some of their armament at the entrance, but I can see that they have retained swords and daggers in the elaborately stitched colored leather scabbards at their sides. Several have bandoliers of cartridges across their chests; maybe they have side arms under their robes. I hope they don't get carried away by the movie, like the volatile audience at the Rex in Lomé.

The movie appears on the open-air screen as some in the audience are still walking around looking for their friends, calling greetings or talking animatedly. It takes a while for attention to focus on the screen, where agitated figures in black are splashing around in a swamp, fleeing through miasmal mists from a man in a cape, whom Eric and I recognize from his plucked eyebrows, exposed teeth and pointed ears as a vampire—a Spanish vampire, since all the characters are shouting in Spanish. There are no subtitles, but it's easy enough for us to follow the familiar plot as maidens in filmy nightgowns are bitten and the vampire clambers up and down sheer battlements… I'm keeping an eye on the men around me in case they find the nightgowns too provocative or the vampire's impunity too galling and want to join the action. But these northerners remain seated and concentrated on the movie, which must nevertheless have seemed puzzling to them.

The Grand Mosque of Agadez has to be admired from outside, as unbelievers are barred from entering. Its appearance is typical of the mosques of the Sahel: dun-colored walls enclose a large hall of worship dominated here by a high square tapering minaret which bristles with protruding palm tree logs set horizontally at close intervals into the adobe. Once a year, the townspeople ascend the minaret on these logs to replaster it and repair the damage it suffers from seasonal rainfall. The ensemble puts me in mind of ancient Babylon as it might be depicted in an illustrated Old Testament.

As we cross an expansive square, a robed man motions us to enter a high, long building that seems to form one entire side of

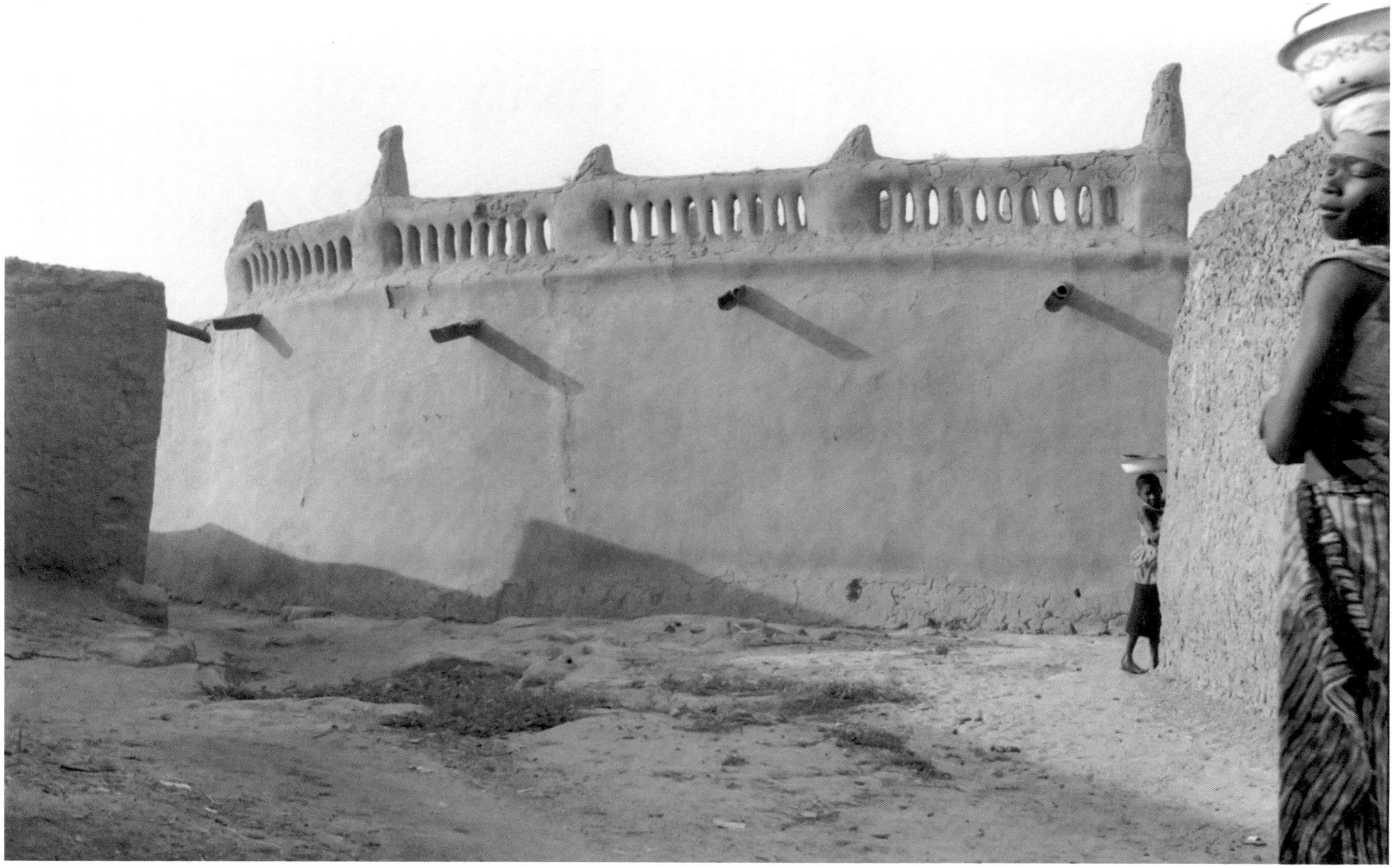

Town in the Sahel

Photo by Lucas Kiers

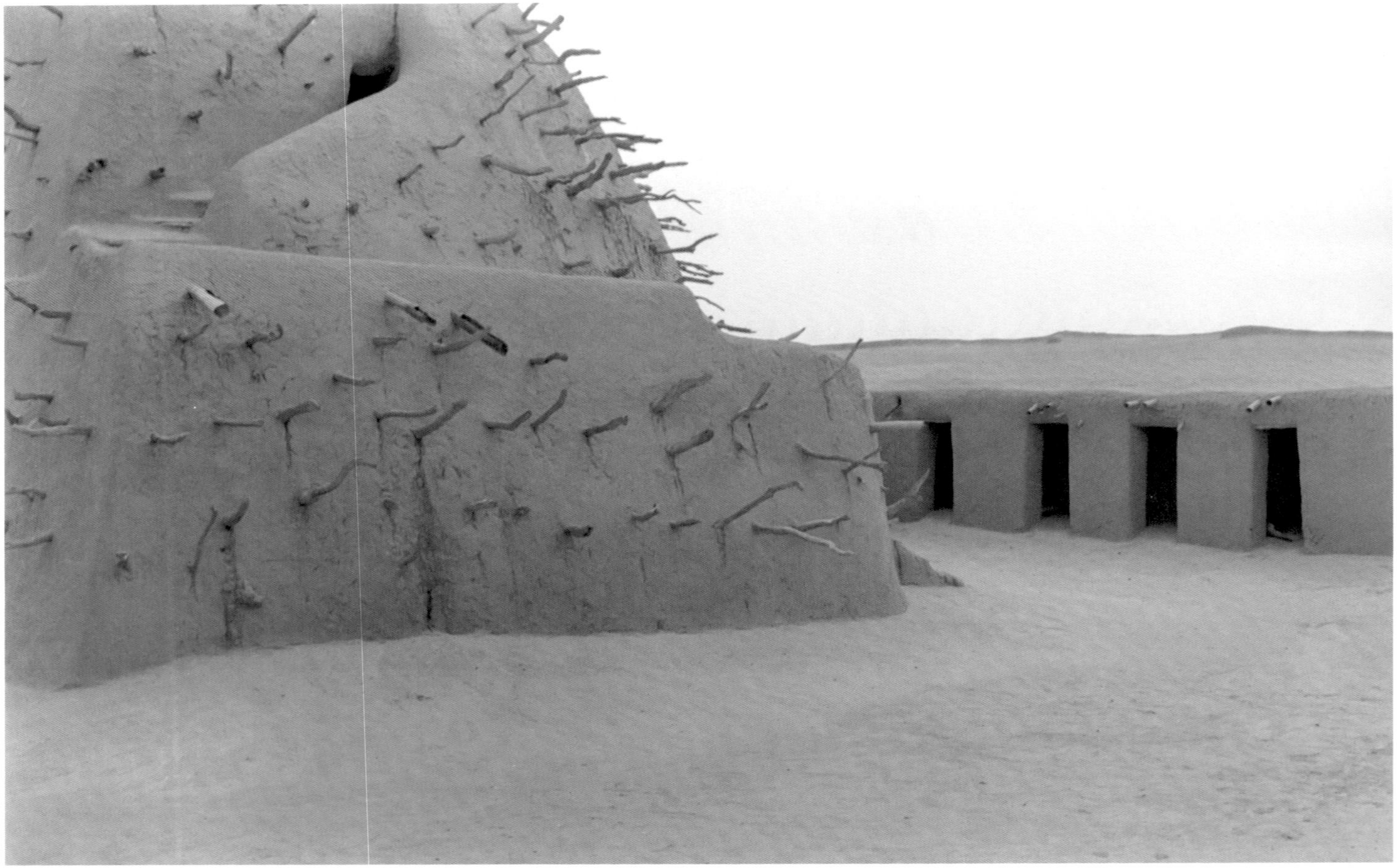

Adobe mosque in the Sahel

Photo by Lucas Kiers

the plaza. It's hard to judge from the outside what this building is. I don't see any windows in its smooth two-story masses that flow into each other seamlessly. No tower, no inscriptions, just the tall wide doorway through which we are ushered by the guardian, who welcomes us to *"la maison du marabout"* (the house of a Muslim holy man). We step across the threshold and immediately our way is blocked by an enormous round pillar that rises from the floor to the ceiling of a small anteroom, occupying it so completely that we're obliged to sidle around it, walking sideways between its bulk and the walls which embrace it so closely. We can hardly help but notice that the surface of the pillar is stained with the clotted blood and feathers of sacrificed fowl. This is the mother-pillar, our guide explains, holding up the whole vast adobe structure and therefore deserving of veneration. He leads us past the anteroom, and we're reminded of the Wari's palace in Kano: large rooms overpoweringly alive with patterned moldings, inexplicable hollows in the thick walls, mud plaster bas-reliefs of airplanes and firearms and astonishing free-standing bulbous columns made all the more evocative in these windowless, shadowy interiors. I saw every kind of architectural element: balconies, arcades, stairways, halls and corridors, ornamented vaults and arches, a blindingly bright courtyard open to the sky and overlooked by a gallery of arches from the second floor… everything molded, poured, built up, carved, pinched and patted out of mud. A potter Genie must have made this place, throwing it down in a lump and shaping it from the inside. "Gaudi!", Eric exclaims.

That night, we slept on the roof of the hotel under crystalline stars that went right down to the horizon. The dawn light woke us in time to get to the bus park for the long trip to Niamey.

NIAMEY

We spent our first night in Niamey in a luxury hotel with hot showers, spring mattresses and air conditioning. The bill was paid out of a gift from my uncle, Philip Hofer, who admonished me to use it only for "necessary extravagances." The hotel's comforts seemed necessary indeed, after the rigors of our bus ride from Agadez, a jolting three-day trip across the Sahel. We left on Monday morning and arrived in the Nigerien capital on Wednesday night after long bumpy stages on desert roads frequently interrupted by breakdowns, prayers at the roadside, exchange of passengers at stops where the bus's cargo was unloaded, traded and loaded again, and unexplained delays during which we dozed in our seats. We ate what came to hand: tea with a bowl of rice at breakfast; at lunchtime, a can of Romanian vegetables in sunflower oil with pilchards, small unfamiliar fish from Holland; sardines with bread for dinner. In between, coconuts, bananas and beef jerky. The first night at our luxury hotel, we ordered chocolate ice-cream sundaes.

It rained a lot, and we both had a touch of malaria. Fortunately, Eric's friends Mireille and Jean-René Ménard took us in and made this otherwise charmless city more hospitable. We each bought a cheap hooded waterproof poncho of a thin transparent material. Eric's was red, mine was blue; Mireille said we looked like *"deux grands bonbons"* (two big cellophane-wrapped candies) as we wandered disconsolately through the drab market under the unrelieved overcast.

I saw the Niger River for the first time. At Niamey, its prodigious 2600-mile course becomes a wide, slow-moving expanse of water with the city on its eastern shore. In the morning, washermen go down to the banks to wash clothes in the shallows and spread them to dry on the grass, where they lie like huge colorful quilts. The men bend low over their work, legs apart, knees slightly bent, spines hardly curved at all as they fold themselves at the waist like hinges to soap and knead, rub and wring the cloth, straightening finally to slap it powerfully on a rock. Their silhouettes against the water look as angular and active as stick men in a Saharan rock painting.

At sunset, Eric, Jean-René and I walk past the museum on the way to the river. On the bright green lawn, a pure-white Brahman bull is grazing, his splendid horns aglow with the late light. We walk along streets planted neatly with rows of trees as in a French city. I can hear radios blaring, an armorer's silvery blows as he beats out a sword blade, loud contentious card games and the call to evening prayer. By the time we reach the riverbank, the sun is a dense orange-red color and sinking into a low cloudbank. The moon is rising behind us, glowing through wisps of pink clouds. The river turns a soft luminous gray. On the gravel flats, a bareback rider is trying to control his restless mount, who snorts and paws the shallows. The horseman drops the reins and they gallop off, swift and watery and one with each other. Jean-René and I are resolved to swim in the Niger as we might in the Ganges, hoping for a blessing. He and I immerse ourselves ritually as Eric looks on. The moon has sprung up from behind the pink sunset clouds and shines out with its pure rightful light.

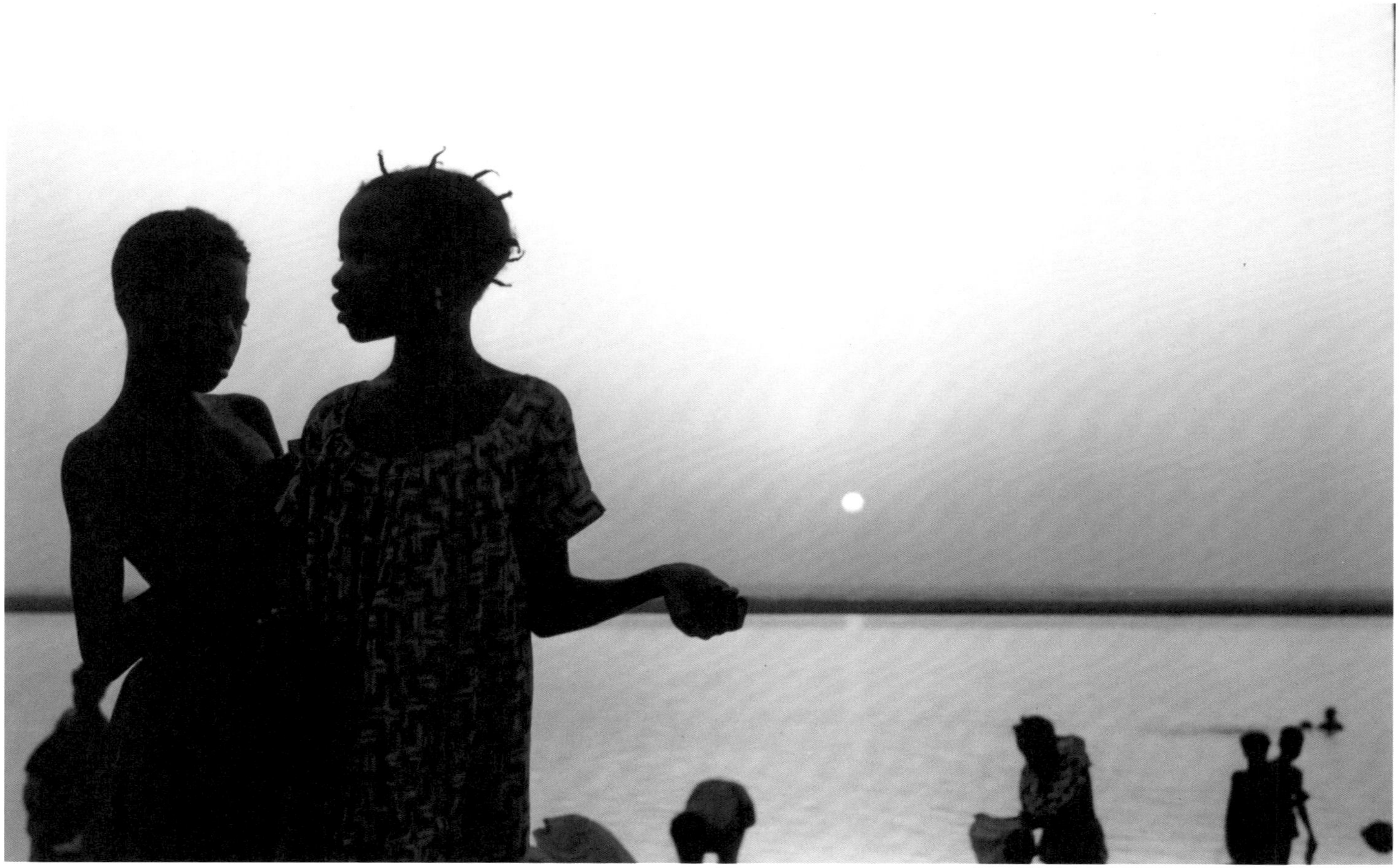

Sunset on Niger River at Niamey

Photo by Lucas Kiers

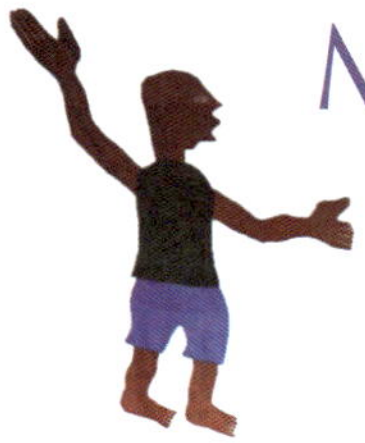

MOPTI and the LAND of the DOGON

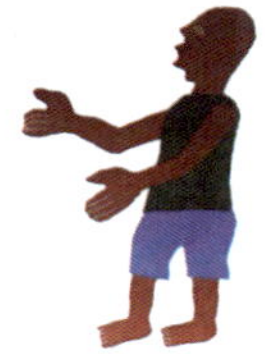

"Russian air-conditioning": that's what Eric calls the icy water dripping on our heads from the overhead ventilators. We're in a Tupolev aircraft on an Air Mali (expats call it "Air Maybe") flight to Mopti. The cabin is mostly empty, so we can change seats at will to get out of the frigid drip or to look out either side of the plane. The earth below looks about the same from both sides: flat to the horizon, the low sun reflecting off lakes and backwaters and off the surface of an inexhaustible serpentine river in flood, the Niger or one of its tributaries. This is the season when the rivers overflow and cover the land with sheets of shallow water. There are villages down there, too, close clusters of rectilinear dwellings in a web of radiating footpaths, no roads at all. They look like humanity's first towns, settlements of the sons of Ham. Even the sun looks antediluvian, an orange-red orb on the horizon, strangely diffuse in the desert haze.

Mopti is a lively town thriving on a riverine commerce of rice, fish and salt. Its port on the Bani River is chock-a-block at this season with cargo and passenger vessels taking advantage of the Inland Delta formed by the floodwaters. The moon, too, is at its full and rises grandly over the minaret and buttresses of the mosque, silvering their rounded adobe surfaces.

After dinner at a sidewalk table at the Bar du Mali, we watch a band of children marching through the busy evening streets. They thread their way through the crowd, chanting something that sounds like MA-DE-MOI-SELLE and banging rhythmically on pots. They seem so free and so cheekily assertive, I ask the waiter what they're doing. *"Ils manifestent,"* they're demonstrating, he says. They're happy, *"Ils sont contents, ils manifestent."*

A student participant in a recent Quaker conference invites us to a party in the evening. We all sit in a circle of low wooden armchairs while one man is disc jockey and another brews endless pots of strong heavily sweetened tea. The records succeed each other, French and American pop tunes, Congolese dance numbers, and Sory Kandia Kouyate, a Guinean griot with a golden voice like Nat King Cole's, singing long breathless lines in praise of bygone heroes and accompanying himself on that harp of harps, the twenty-one stringed *kora*. Conversation flows easily and the young men are well informed about world politics. We drink glass after glass of tea until it's time to go back to the hotel. All that tea has made us sleepless. Our room has only one bed, with a broad but deeply sagging mattress. We cling, wide-eyed, each to his side of the spavined mattress until a moment of sleep sends one or both of us tumbling into the trough and into our protesting selves.

In the morning, we go to the National Tourist Office to rent a car and driver to go to Dogon country—another "necessary extravagance" made possible by Philip Hofer. Bandiagara, the principal town in the area, is only 66km from Mopti and accessible by bus; but we have resolved to try to visit some off-road Dogon communities on the way. Before dawn the next day, we take possession of a rugged Land Rover with Daouda, an experienced guide, at the wheel.

The Dogon are unusual for having resisted the wide-spread Islamization of the Sahel that began in the eighth century. They were also one of the last people to come under French rule in the nineteenth century. Although Islam and modernity have made inroads since then, the authenticity of Dogon sculpture in wood, their architecture and their spiritual dance were still relatively undisturbed until the 1960s. To protect this authenticity, the Malian authorities have tried to regulate tourism and placed some villages off-limits altogether. It's soon apparent to us that our driver is willing to interpret these restrictions liberally. When he stops 20 minutes from Mopti to clear the Rover's blocked fuel line in a gray pre-dawn light full of birdsong choruses, he proposes to take us to several of these closed sites if we agree not to tell the tourist office. Daouda has found the perfect co-conspirators in Eric and me, and we climb back into the car with a light-hearted sense of clandestine adventure ahead.

Out first stop is the village of Songo. Daouda turns off the road onto a track that crosses some millet fields. We bump along past Dogon farmers bent over their hoes towards two salient rock outcrops that rise abruptly above the fields like the prows of ocean liners. Between them, on the heaps of gigantic stone debris at their feet, the people have built their village. Square houses with flat roofs, little granaries with pointed thatch roofs and walled compounds cluster on or between the blocks of rock and step up under the overhanging cliffs like a pueblo of the American Southwest.

Leaving the car behind and climbing up among the houses to meet the village chief, we're struck by the small scale of everything here. The courtyards are tiny, the houses seem toy-like, the jaunty, windowless little granaries have carved wooden doors with totem images of crocodile and buffalo. Level areas are few; so are the villagers, who must be in the fields. In fact, all we see of the inhabitants are the old chief and, above a compound wall, pestles rising and falling over an unseen mortar.

We follow the chief up through the village, twisting around boulders and between structures to a high rock platform under the beetling overhang of the cliffs. There on a rock face are hundreds of linear glyphs in overlapping rows. Many of them look freshly painted, red and black strongly outlined in white. This is where the boys of each new generation come to be circumcised, sitting on the smooth stones arranged to face the glyphs. The stones are black with old blood. The chief is looking over the glyphs and says he usually only sees them once a year at the ceremony. He points out some that stand for village families; one, Daouda tells me, represents evil. There are small shallow grottos in the rock face full of sacred pots, one for each circumcision year; if ever they were disturbed, the chief says, all the pregnant women in the village would abort. He leads us a little higher, from where we have an expansive view of the village roofs immediately below, cultivated fields beyond, and the far horizon of the Bandiagara plateau. The sounds of the village float up to us: bursts of laughter, the rhythmic pounding of pestles, voices calling. A troop of white goats is winding through the dun-colored houses on their way to pasture.

Daouda's next stop is at the tomb of a saint, El Hadji Omar. It's increasingly clear that our Muslim guide, in addition to showing us Dogon culture, is making a pious pilgrimage of his own. Omar's tomb is low and round and clings like a wasp's nest to the big rock it's built on—the very rock, Daouda says, into which the saint miraculously disappeared. The door to the tomb is closed with a wooden Dogon lock carved with human figures standing guard. There are more of these wooden locks in the next village we visit, Nyoh-Konah. They secure the elaborately carved doors of granaries and storehouses and depict figures of ancestors and totemic animals. These carvings are prized by collectors and widely exhibited in Western museums. There's a keen satisfaction in seeing them as the Dogon intended: utilitarian objects with a family brand.

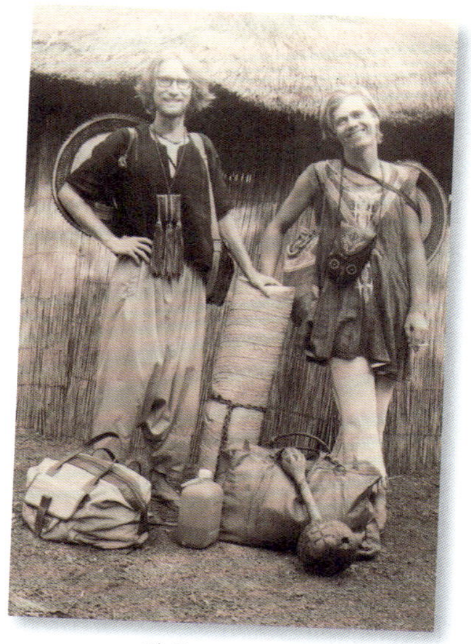

Philip and Eric

Nyoh-Konah seems to include three clusters of houses nestled within a massive u-shaped rock ridge. We have crossed through fields and walked up through a wall of broken stone to the village, which is silent and seems deserted. Then a tiny shuttered window opens unexpectedly and an old man greets us, comes to his door and invites us in. The room, too, is diminutive and pleasantly cool. The man takes up an umbrella and leads us out into the village. His long robe and skullcap mark him as Muslim; the umbrella must be a status symbol. Our tour is brief. We see more lavishly carved doors and locks, ladders and pestles as we scramble up and down rock-strewn passageways between the houses. Never another villager. At a stone staircase, we thank our host and go back down to the car.

Pagan carving, however, is not what Daouda really wants to see. His true objective is the mosque in a closed village called Nando. As the Rover lurches along a track through cultivated fields, raising a plume of dust, he explains that this mosque was built by angels overnight and receives many pilgrims who value its intercessory powers. He's never been there, and intends to pray for himself and his family.

The villagers have seen us coming and a group of people is waiting to greet us as we draw up in the village square. They are very curious about Eric and me and we wonder whether they might enforce the customary ban against non-Muslims in mosques. But we are dressed in our usual comfortable clothes picked up along the way, loose hand-loomed poncho-like shirts and full-cut drawstring trousers.* The villagers seem to decide we're just exotic co-religionists and invite us into the mosque. It's a low unprepossessing adobe building in a mud-walled enclosure. The narrow doorway barely admits us. Inside, we can make out curious

* Sometimes in our travels, young people in blue jeans and shirts would ask us, why are you wearing our clothes? We just said, why are you wearing ours?

molded geometric symbols overhead representing, Daouda says, various paths through life, the doors to Heaven, Paradise itself. He steps up to a rounded protuberance like a breast on the eastern wall and places his hands on either side, shuts his eyes and prays long and earnestly. He motions to each of us in turn to take his place. I hesitate, feeling that I'm here under false pretenses; but Allah, I know, is all-merciful, even to a lapsed Episcopalian in disguise, so I, too, pray at the wall.

We come back out into the heat and sunlight. A long file of people is climbing the flank of a nearby hill, following silently behind a coffin. They are bearing the remains of an elderly woman to the burial ground.

The villages we've seen so far have all been on the Bandiagara Plateau. The heart of Dogon country, however, is at the eastern edge of the plateau where it drops off sharply down to the plains below. The formidable cliffs of the Bandiagara Escarpment are 90 miles long and 1600 feet high in places. The Dogon built their villages below and all along the cliffs, where they were protected from above by the sheer rock faces and from where they could easily spot incursions across the plains by jihadists or slavers. In this relative security the Dogon, since their first settlements in the 14th century, evolved a culture and religion unaffected by Islam or Christianity and undocumented until French anthropologists visited them in the 20th century.

Daouda and the Rover have dropped us off at Sangha, a town on the plateau that overlooks a number of villages at the foot of the escarpment. The next morning, Eric and I set out on the Long Walk, a largely unaccompanied seven-mile hike that will take us down the cliff into the villages, out onto the cultivated plain and up the cliff again at a different point.

I have never felt so much like an outsider as I do among the Dogon. The guide has led us down the cliff face to a village at its foot. No one is in sight as we thread through the houses, until we see a woman on one of the flat roofs. She looks too big up there, out of scale with her tiny house. She doesn't return our greeting. Everywhere we look, we see rock: the cliff faces in the background, smooth bare ledges underfoot, rock rubble in the steep little streets and enormous free-standing blocks with adobe structures built all over and against them. One of these monoliths has an astonishing kind of shelter built on its summit: a very thick flat roof supported by wooden pillars and beams over a shadowy low space underneath, open on all four sides. The roof appears to be several times taller than the interior, and as we approach, I can see that it's made of millet stalks thickly bundled and laid in three courses. The guide scrambles inside and motions us to enter. The overhead beams are very low and we are bent over in the sudden darkness, straining to see. Two elderly men dressed darkly in indigo, one with a close white beard along his jaw line and the other smoking a pipe, are the only other people here. They ignore us. I feel like an interloper in this deeply authentic place—a *toguna*, the guide explains, a lodge where the men meet to debate and make decisions for the community. The low beams are intended to discourage stand-up confrontations.

We sit down on the rock floor in the cool shadows. Minutes go by. The two elders continue their conversation as if they were alone. Their tobacco smoke wreathes through the still air, their voices rise and fall without meaning for me. Their indifference and impenetrability make me feel like an invisible time traveler who

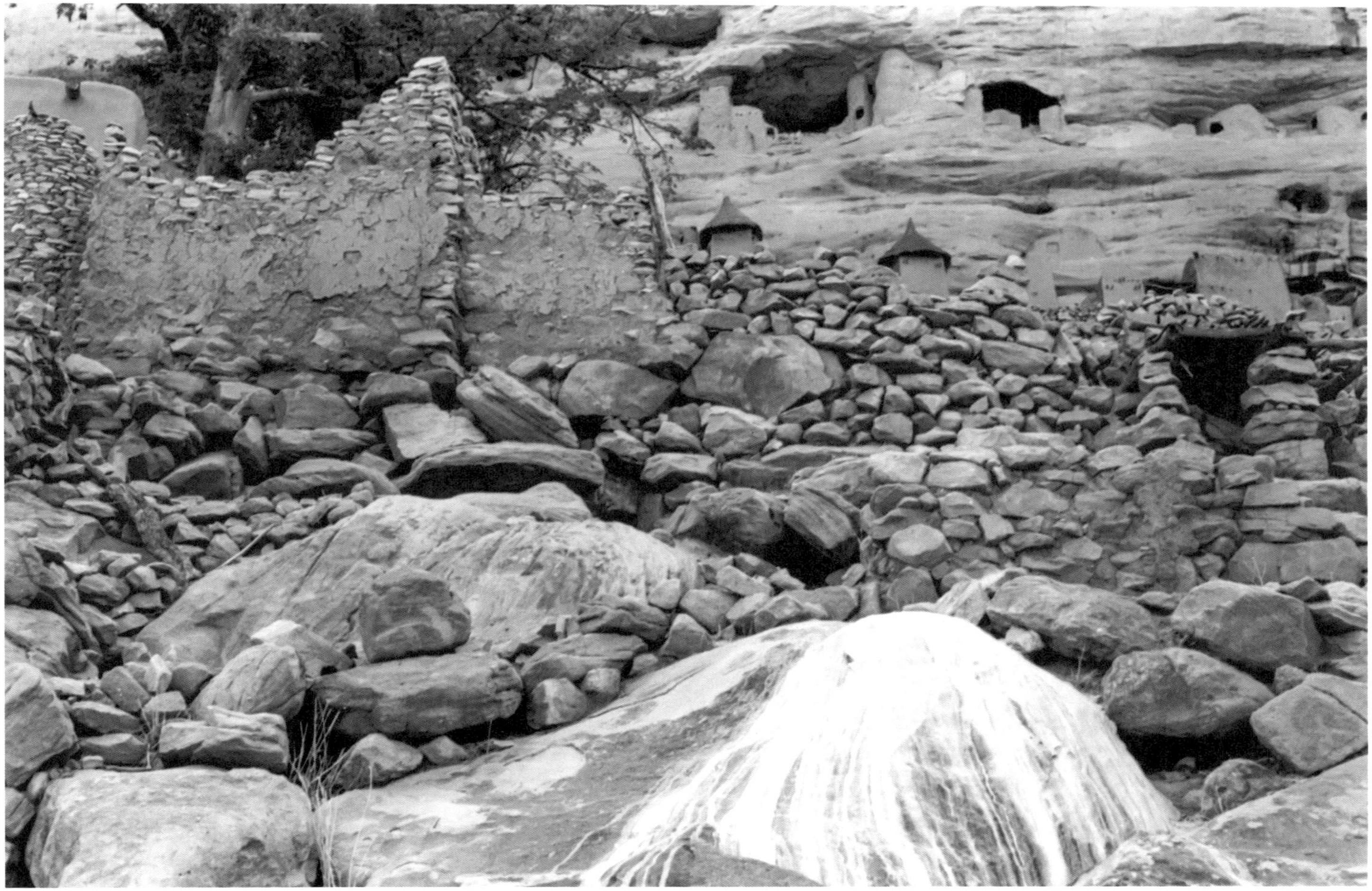

Dogon village Photo by Lucas Kiers

might as well have alighted, with this same thrill of authenticity and sense of estrangement, at a Cro-Magnon fireside or a gilded *salon* of the Enlightenment, as in this Dogon *toguna*. I wonder what we're waiting for.

One of the old men rises, steps out onto the rock outside, and calls over the roofs below. He's calling for a rain dance, the guide says. Directly beneath the lodge is one of the few level places in the village, a small area hemmed in by house walls and rock faces. In the middle is a carefully laid pile of stones like a cairn. In answer to the old man's call, women are arriving down there from every direction, from high and low, most of them in indigo clothing with a few flashes of bright patterned cloth. They are calling out loudly and gathering in a confusion of sound and movement that gradually resolves itself into a dark circle of women who begin to dance around the pile of stones. Eric leans over and points up to the precipitous cliff above us. Three men are climbing slowly to a shrine high up under the overhang. The cliff is riddled with caves up there where the Dogon bury their dead. The climbers are using long flexible poles to fix ropes to the rock above and haul themselves up in stages. They look tiny, black against the blazing rock faces.

The women, meanwhile, are making music for their dance, strong rhythms on calabashes, an iron bell, a rattle. They circle together singing, while three or four others circle counter to them on the inside, exhorting their sisters like cheerleaders, keening and quick-stepping. They go round and round the pile of stones. Overhead, the climbers have reached a cave closed by a wall of stones pierced with a little opening, and are talking into the opening and gesturing animatedly to the ancestors within. They are bending over some kind of ritual and pouring water on the rock, water which spreads down darkly over the cliff face. Below us, the rhythms of the dance have fallen silent. The circling stops. Then an old man steps forward to pour water on the rock pile and on the rock floor all around, where it forms dark pools. The women rush forward, shouting, to run through the water and wet their feet. Another deep silence now as an ancient bent figure hobbles from their midst, approaches the fetish of rocks and throws an egg on it—POP! I look up and around. I can feel it all going on at the same time, now, in this very moment: the green fields are ripening on the plains, the densely staggered village is rising up the cliff, the tiny figures of the climbers are dangling above, talking to the ancestors. At the center, the dark ring of women circles and sings under the sky full of sailing clouds. The dead are supplicated, the rain will fall and the millet ripen. Past, present and future, the human, natural and spiritual worlds have been brought together and made powerfully simultaneous in this moment below the cliffs, above the plain.

The Long Walk takes us winding through other villages along the escarpment, around the gargantuan rubble at its base and out onto the fields of hip-high grain. A wind ripples across them, relieving the heat and bringing snatches of staccato rhythms and high-pitched choruses coming from the immense trees that stand here and there in the fields. On the wide lower branches of these trees, deep within their shade, women and children are keeping birds away from the ripening millet with their rolling, crackling rhythms and volleying song. I shade my eyes and stare across the fields, trying to imagine what it's like to spend all day in a tree with your relatives, siblings and comrades, your whole neighborhood, singing and banging on a calabash.

Finally the path swings back to the escarpment and to a deep cleft that runs right up to the top. Inside the cleft, a stairway of stone lifts us up from the plain past treetops and rockslides and hawks riding on the thermals to a ledge high on the cliff, enclosed by boulders and shaded by the tops of trees that are growing 30 feet below. On the ledge, a fountain of pure water jets out of the rock. From here, we can look back down on the foreshortened villages below, past the hawks wheeling by at eye-level and beyond over the hot plains to the very edge of the Dogon's world. Eric throws off his clothes and stands in the falling water of the fountain. I follow, feeling like a stone in a torrent and taking in great gulps of the water to become pure and cold myself, inside and out.

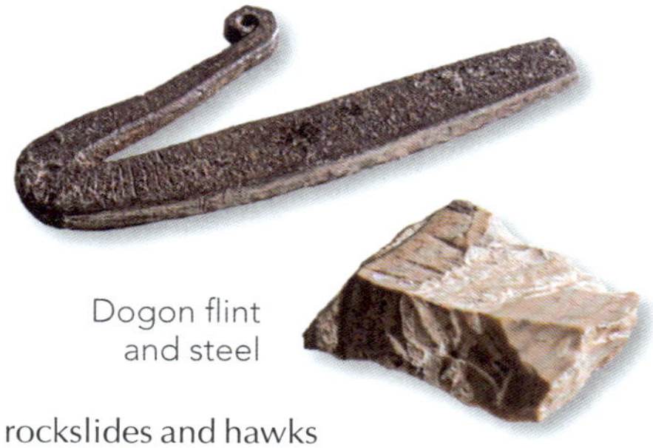

Dogon flint and steel

The next day we are in Bandiagara, in a bus that will take us back to Mopti. I'm puzzling over that feeling I had of being invisible among the Dogon. It's odd that we never experienced the welcome, the mutual curiosity and engagement that we've had everywhere else on our travels. French is not current, to be sure, at least among the villagers we saw. But what about their willful indifference? It wouldn't be surprising if these proud, distinctive, long-independent people resented the Malian tourist officials who oblige them to give strangers a seat in the *toguna* and to allow them to wander through their villages; and resented also the tourists themselves.

A man at the bus window is trying to get my attention and holds up something that he wants me to look at. He hands up a small piece of veined jagged stone, along with a curiously shaped metal object, shiny with use along the bottom: flint and steel, a fire-making tool older than the Dogon. At this moment, the bus gives a lurch and starts forward in a cloud of dust, fast gathering speed. The man's face is aghast, he runs after us. I want to throw the steel back to him before it's lost in the dust, or toss a bill out the window. Another moment and the man is left behind. I'm distressed that he's lost his sale; but I look reverently at the flint and steel, finding in them an omen.

DJENNÉ

During the rains from July to December, many roads across the Inland Delta become impassable and the best way to get around is by boat. So Eric and I are at the Port of Mopti early in the morning of our arrival back from Dogon country, examining the *pirogue* (dugout) that will take us up the Bani River. *Pirogues* are made from a single tree trunk; this one must be more than 30 feet long and only just wide enough for two to sit abreast. Its entire length is shaded under a vault of woven palm fronds. The helmsman sits in the bow and controls the motor astern with cablets that run along the gunwales. Other, similar craft crowd the wharf, many elaborately carved and one with a Dogon-style figurehead, an abstract human figure with raised arms. Our *pirogue* is relatively plain; its name is Air Mali, for better or for worse.

The port is alive with passengers waiting to board, standing in family groups over their bulky baggage of things wrapped in cloth and bound with rope, talking excitedly and calling out to the boatmen. Traders are here, too, men in long robes who imperiously

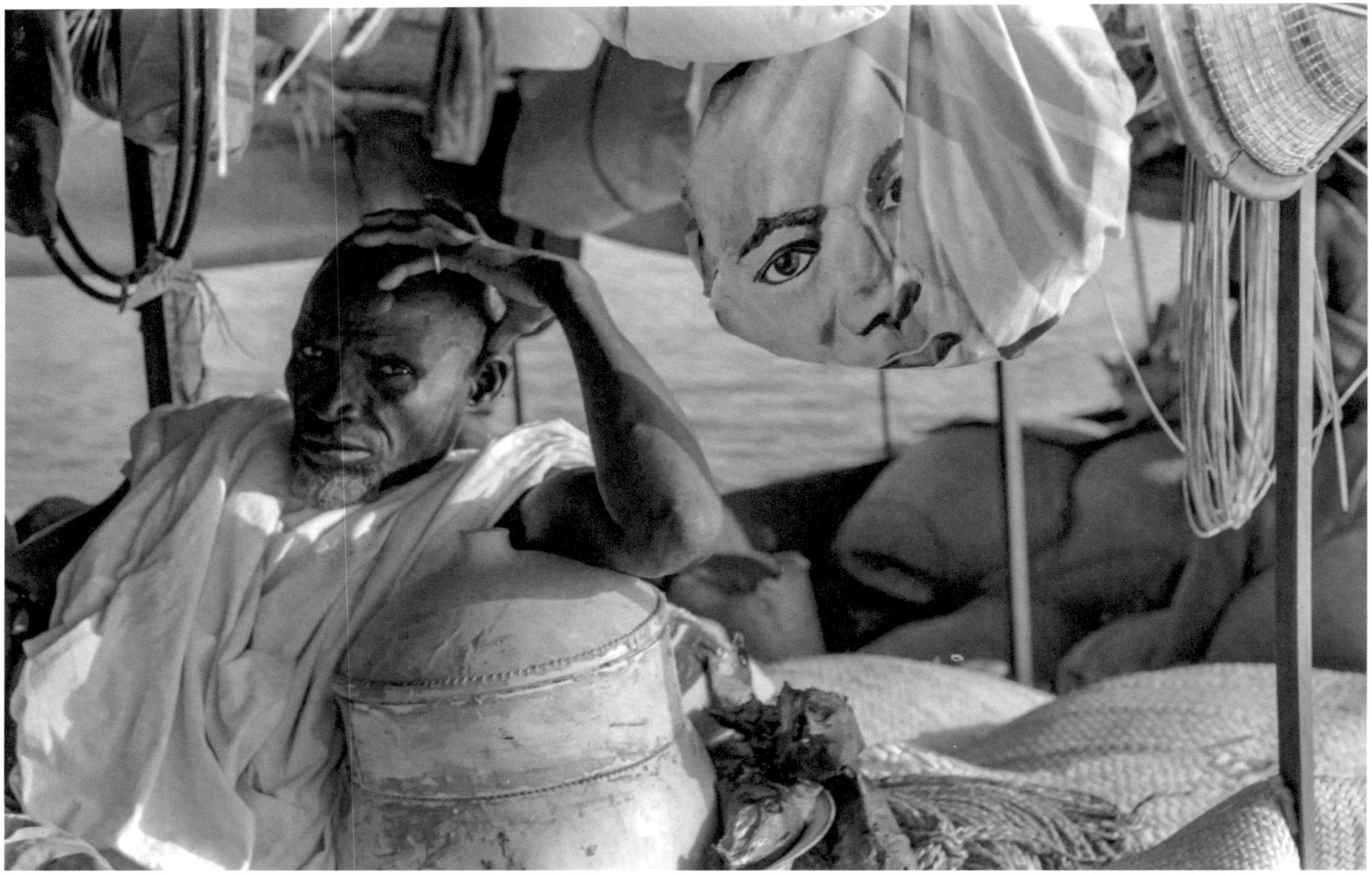

Niger River boat

Photo by Lucas Kiers

order the dock men to fetch or carry their goods. These stevedores appear to live right here on the stone quays in little round huts. River birds call and circle overhead. The "Air Mali" is boarding in a general noise and confusion. Eric and I find seats in the middle of the boat, which is packed with passengers and baggage all along its length. Eventually, the boat edges away from the quay and the hubbub of Mopti falls rapidly astern.

It will be nightfall before we reach Djenné, a city that grew rich on the trans-Saharan trade in salt and gold until the Portuguese in the 17th century opened trading ports on the coast that made the caravan routes redundant. Djenné remains a center of Islamic learning and a city of remarkable adobe architecture.

We're immobilized in the packed boat, and there are no stops along the way. The palm-frond canopy prevents us from standing to stretch our legs, but we're grateful for its shade. It ends well above the gunwales, allowing us to see out to the high riverbanks we sweep by. The river flows somewhat below them and so we don't often have a view over the countryside beyond. Black and white herons are performing their stately predation along the shore, pausing in their unhurried patrols to listen, then plunging a long beak into the water to come up with a frog or fish which they swallow whole, tilting back their head to get it down and giving it a little shake for good measure. Flocks of tiny bright yellow and red birds skim the water, and overhead we see an osprey.

The floodwater is deep and the boat proceeds untroubled by shallows, sandbanks or other craft. The motor is far enough astern not to be intrusive, and there's something hypnotic about our steady, easeful progress between the high unrevealing riverbanks. Sometimes they dip to disclose a village of stacked earthen buildings around a mosque with a crenellated façade. Spiky palm trees or the rounded crowns of acacias show vividly green above the adobe. Occasionally, we pass a settlement of fisher folk in domed huts with a little fleet of beached dugouts and children waving excitedly, or a solitary Fulani shepherd watering his goats. It's as if a camera shutter opens and then closes on these scenes as they disappear rapidly astern.

Soon, however, our reverie is interrupted by an increasing obsession with food. By early afternoon we have finished the bananas and peanuts we bought in Mopti. We've watched hungrily as our fellow-passengers uncover calabashes and enamelware full of stew and rice and fritters whose appetizing odors waft down to us along the length of the boat. It's been impossible to engage with anybody in this extremely confining craft, so we can't count on African generosity. Eric begins to talk about Justin's masterly soufflés, and I recite a list of my favorite dishes. *Crêpes aux volailles,* creamed chicken rolled into a crepe, takes on a maddening clarity: the brown speckling on the crepe, the sweetness of the cream sauce allayed by a touch of cayenne pepper…

By evening, we are approaching Djenné. Fish are jumping and we pass through a weir, a line of fish traps delicately woven of reeds and stretching from bank to bank across the river. Sunset is followed by a long afterglow, but it's fully dark when suddenly, voices are raised, the boat slows and we peer into the darkness on the shore, only to see a darker darkness, a focus of cries and shouts but not a single light. We have to wade ashore. The boat lies-to in the shallows as everyone clambers over the sides, shouting and chattering and carrying their bundles on their heads. Eric has the misfortune to fall into a hole underwater and comes

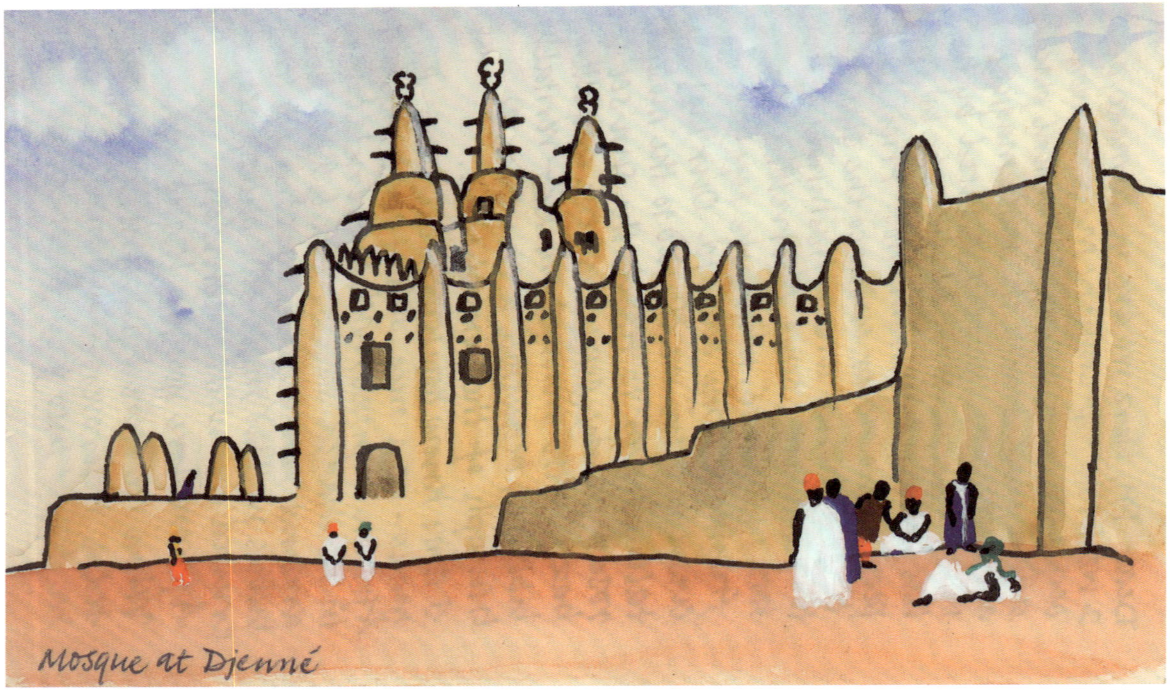

Sketch by the author

ashore soaked from the neck down. Still not a glimmer of light, until a man appears with a kerosene lamp and invites us to follow him to the *campement,* the government bungalow. The unlit streets are silent, deserted and dreamlike, the buildings defined only by their silhouettes against the starry sky. Eric has draped his wet trousers around his neck and walks down the dark streets in his underpants.

The *campement* is welcoming, with several electric lights, at last. Dinner is our first request, and we sit down at a waxed tablecloth under a bare bulb, wondering what we will be served at this late hour in this silent city of night. We fall like wolves on the gratifyingly large omelets that appear—large and surprisingly pungent, for the Djenné *campement,* we are to learn, never serves any other but these huge flavorful duck eggs.

We have duck eggs again at breakfast, fried sunny-side up, showing their chrome yellow yolks. Afterwards, we walk through some of the same streets we arrived by in the dark. Now they teem with passersby, bicycles, pushcarts, donkeys and very occasionally, a car or truck. The sandy streets reflect the brilliant daylight and Djenné is bright and golden with the sun. Imposing old buildings with carved and molded facades grow more numerous as we approach the vast riverside esplanade of the Great Mosque. A bridge on the waterfront crosses the Bani only to end under water on the other side, as the seasonal floods have drowned every road out of the city. Partially submerged plains stretch to the horizon.

The mosque of Djenné is a tremendous structure with walls 16 to 24 feet thick punctuated by square towers bristling with the palm logs we saw in Agadez. Once a year, the whole town turns out to celebrate and replaster their mosque. We crane our necks to look up and imagine those walls swarming with the young men of the city working high above the festive crowd on the plaza. It's almost empty at present. The groups of townspeople gathered here and there are engaged in quiet conversation and seem dwarfed by the soaring walls and wide plaza.

We approach the portals of the mosque hesitantly, aware that this city has seen too many Westerners in local clothing to mistake us for true believers. No one seems to notice as we pass inside. It's cool in here, and sandy underfoot. The vaults, immensely far overhead, are lost in shadow. They are supported by thick columns of adobe so numerous that they seem to occupy half the interior space, and we wind among them as through a forest, looking for a direction to follow. We climb to the roof on a stairway we find in the wall. Djenné fumes and clatters below, a harmonious spectacle of uniformly flat roofs and courtyards, all of the same dun color. Where the city stops, the flooded savannah takes over in a great circle of reed beds, marshes, flooded flats and hummocks of dry land, all the way to the horizon.

We leave the mosque and go down to the bridge over the Bani to watch the men fishing with nets. The river seems especially bountiful to one of them, who hauls in a net full of shimmering fish at every cast and adds them to his already half-filled boat. He holds one end of the net in his mouth as he makes wide, well-set casts, hauling and casting, hauling and casting without stop. His apparently inexhaustible physicality makes him master of the net, but also of the fish and, it seems to us, of the river itself. We're enthralled, he seems like some kind of animating spirit, a fisher of joy in life. He sees us watching him and dives in to come up in his own net like a giant catch, grinning up at us on the bridge. Finally, as the sun gets lower over the marshes, he dives in one last time, rolls over on his back like an otter, spouts water from his mouth and emerges streaming and shining onto the riverbank, where he makes his evening prayer.

Monday is market day in Djenné, and on Sunday evening Eric and I go down to the same bridge to watch the first traders arrive. In the evening glow, the marsh grasses are bright green, frogs begin to bellow, flights of swallows rise, wheel, and dip. Dugouts poled by men standing in the stern and laden with goods for market are coming from every direction through the shallow floodwaters. On the riverbank, the dugouts are drawn up in rows among huge baskets of dried fish and woven cane hampers full of fresh produce. The women are already bargaining. A large woman in regal purple cloth steps out of the bows of an arriving *pirogue* and falls to bargaining before her goods are even unloaded. She is followed by a white-bearded patriarch in a white robe and a younger man with a black beard, who set off towards the mosque. A file of bare-breasted maidens with girdles of cowrie shells, who must be from another part of Mali, comes and goes among the boats with hampers and baskets on their heads. Here and there in the crowd are other figures from far beyond Djenné, men in short tunics or long robes, wide straw hats or embroidered caps picking their way through the hubbub, pausing to appraise, sometimes to buy. The corpulent market women stand arms akimbo over their wares or walk from boat to boat, their bare feet treading the ground heavily, as if they connected to it at each step. A haze is rising, the light retreats across the marshes but reflects orange and red on wisps of clouds. Swiftly even these fade and the mosque becomes a huge dark spiky silhouette as hundreds of people hasten towards it from all over the city, streaming over the esplanade and through the portals to pray. Eric and I walk back to the *campement*.

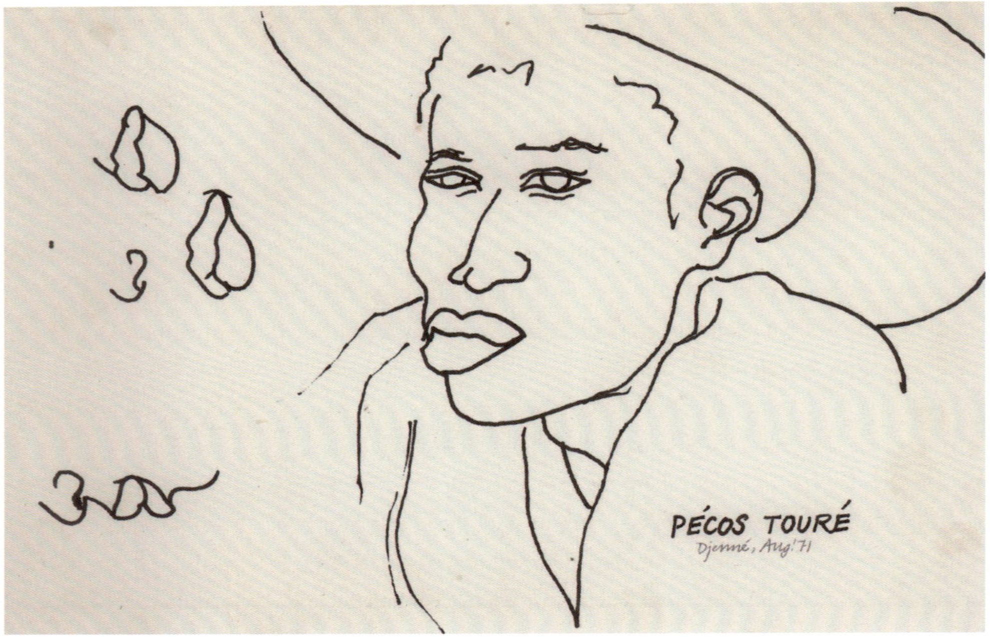

Sketch by the author

We go up to the roof to savor our last evening in the city. Since the buildings are almost all the same height, we can see across to other rooftops where people are sitting in groups on mats or lie propped up on their elbows, talking together, eating dinner. Their quiet voices carry clearly. The evening air is soft and warm, warmth radiates from the adobe we sit on. The whole city seems to be taking its ease together at the end of the day in a scene that looks timeless, unchanged since forever. All around us, thin white plumes of cook fire smoke rise unwavering from the rooftops straight up into the twilight.

The next morning, we are at the waterfront to board a boat back to Mopti. Some friends we've made since our arrival have come to see us off. El Kaya Touré (or Pécos, as he calls himself) loves cowboy movies and can recite whole scenes verbatim, sound effects and all. He is a short man with a compact body like a peanut, and riveting lips. "Gary Cooper," "Eddie Constantine,"

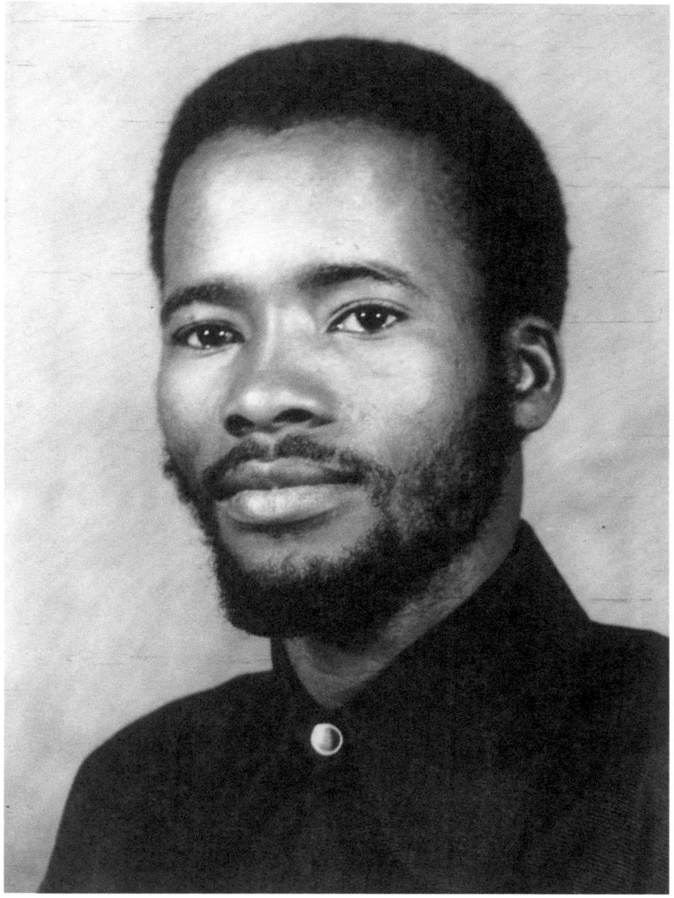

Abdoulhai Sy, goldsmith Bamako, Mali

he says, and I swear I can *see* the words as they come through his lips. Mohammed Nabo is there, too, with the radio he cradles and never seems to be without, swaying and crooning to the rock music he plays, holding the radio like a baby. His French is halting; at parting he can only give us heavy, meaningful looks and stand on the shore, waving.

BAMAKO

We fly from Mopti to Bamako to see friends who live in the capital. Its broad, tree-lined boulevards testify to the colonization of Mali by the French from 1892 to 1960. Passing among the vendors whose outdoor shops crowd under the shade of the trees, disdainful of the noisy scooters, taxis, and trucks whose speed and impunity make ordinary pedestrians dash and dodge, serenely unimpressed, exquisitely wrapped and coiffed, the women of Bamako parade along the boulevards. Gold jewelry gleams at their wrists, necks and ears. Never mind that sometimes these ornaments are made only of raffia, cleverly wound around cores of clay to imitate traditional jewelry and convincingly gilded; the *Bamakoises* are nevertheless among the most elegant women of West Africa.

The real gold is in the city's gold market, where silent men work with small hammers over intense fires. A young man in his uncle's stall shows us how the precious stuff is worked. Abdulhai Sy might one day inherit his uncle's business and join the long tradition of smiths who helped make Djenné and Agadez and Zinder rich and learned cities.

In the center of downtown Bamako, we pass an abandoned

hotel tower that rises fifteen stories above an unkempt lot. Large birds fly in and out of empty windows in the stained concrete of the upper floors. Modern development seems to be making very halting progress here.

We find that there is a train from Bamako to Ouagadougou, the last city on our itinerary. At the railroad station, early in the morning, Eric and I find seats with Takefumi Morioka, a young man traveling solo through some of the same places we have been. Abdulhai Sy has come to see us off and brings us a melon for the long ride over the dry savannah. Suddenly, the Japanese traveler stands, exclaims excitedly and searches frantically around his seat; his camera has been snatched from beside him. The corridor and platform are crowded with people, the train is departing, there's nothing any of us can do. I'm deeply sorry for this distraught young man traveling alone with no way now to share his adventures with family and friends at home. Our mood is dark as the train leaves Bamako behind.

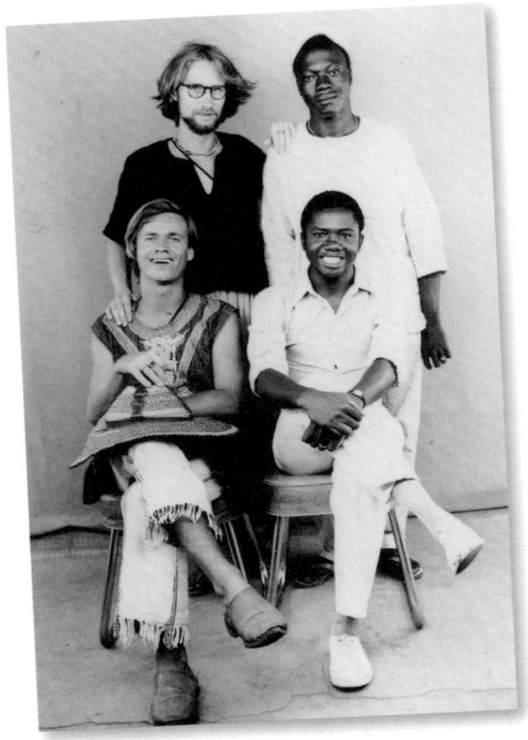

Pascal Kargougou (upper right), Philip, Eric and friend in Ouagadougou

The worn seats and battered interior surfaces of this train don't bother me as much as its apparent fragility. The wooden carriages are lightly built, with large windows opening right on to the noisy track. I'm convinced it was built for a French suburban line forty years ago; but we are hardly passing through quaint *banlieus* or stopping at stations with a *chef de gare* on the platform. All I can see is an endless plain of scrub, inhospitable and apparently uninhabited. The open windows admit blasts of hot air and dust. As night falls, I look searchingly into the dark, hoping for the lights of a settlement. None appear. The train is the only light in this vastness.

OUAGADOUGOU

Eric has made an appointment to see a high government official, a cabinet minister who attended one of the International Dialogues. We go to an imposing building on a wide boulevard and are admitted to a dark office where all the shades are drawn. The minister looks up from behind his big desk. He greets us affably, but his face is set and his eyes downcast. He is preoccupied with shredding documents, tearing them up small and throwing them into the wastebasket. He selects them from boxes on his desk, glances over them and shreds them one after the other as we watch. Political events have gone against him, he explains; he has been driven from office. Eric tries to make small talk about our travels and the conference they attended together, but the atmosphere is melancholy and the conversation lags. After a while, we shake his hand and utter expressions of goodwill and hopes for his speedy return to office. We leave with an appreciation of the precarious nature of political power.

We have really come to Ouaga to see our friend, Mme. Moussa Kargougou. Mme. Kargougou is an adorably cheerful lady full of coy good humor who has visited us in Lomé with her son, Pascal. The family's apartment is in a modern residential tower and is conventionally furnished with chairs and couches, but that doesn't seem to have affected her traditional idea of hospitality. She receives us in the only outdoor space, a narrow balcony spread with straw mats where Mme. Kargougou motions me to sit down beside her. There is something incomparably hospitable about an invitation to sit with someone on their mat. The space it defines is so personal and so clearly delineated that it immediately suggests distinction and a friendly intimacy. Sitting in the sunshine high above the clamorous streets of Ouaga with this amiable lady, laughing and exchanging news, I feel happy with the whole world.[9]

A day or two later, we were back in Lomé.

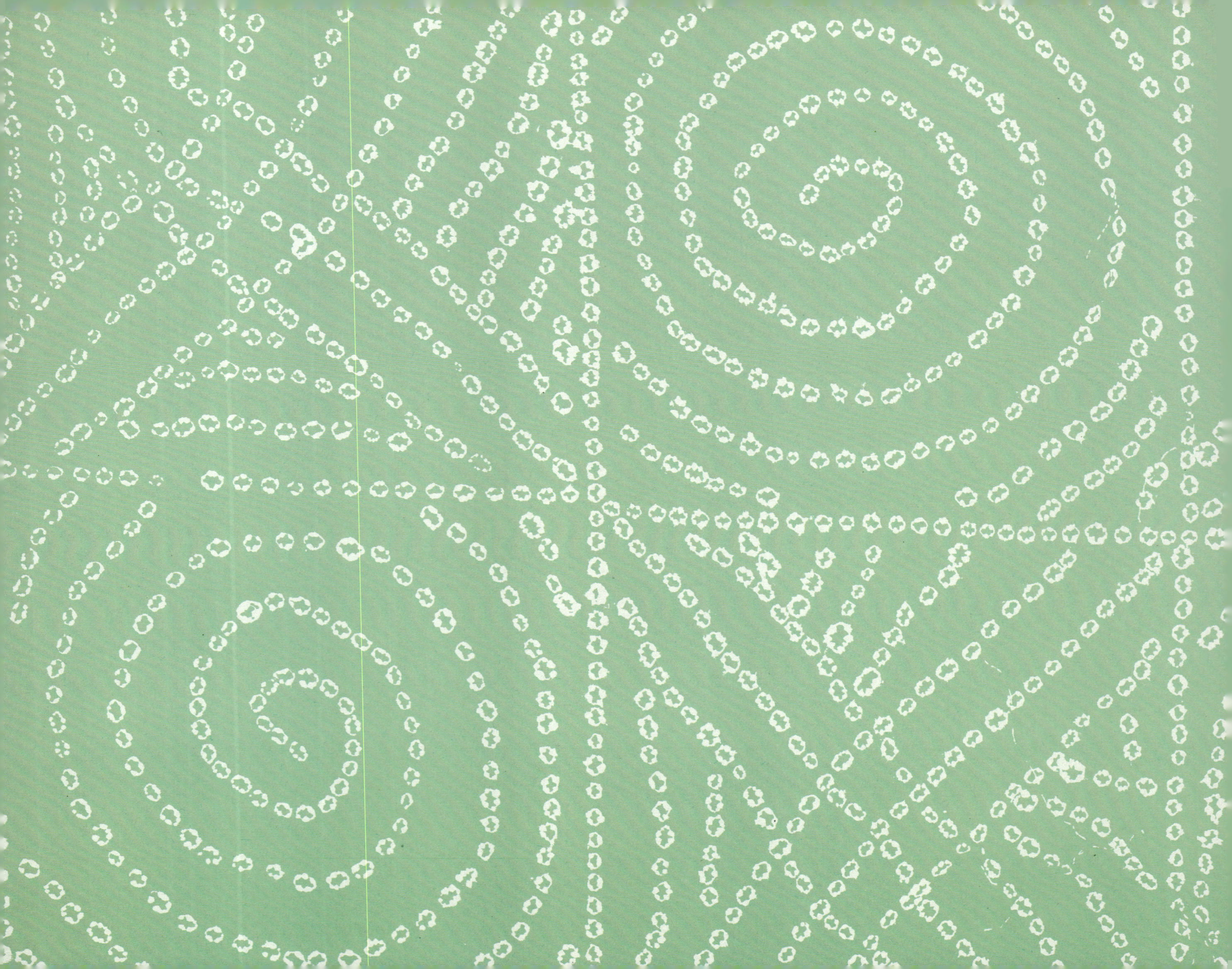

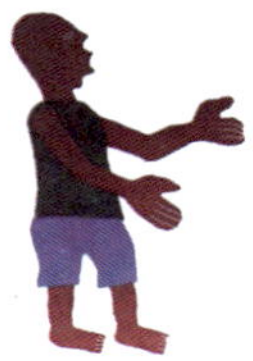

THE SACRED FOREST

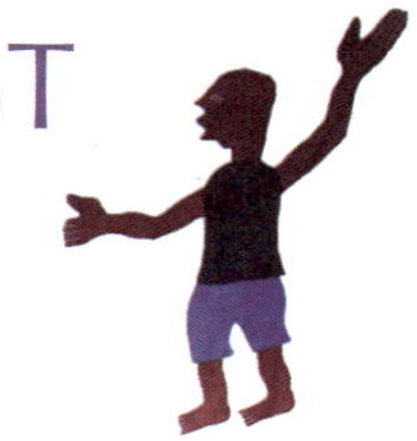

We had barely returned to Lomé from Ouagadougou when an early-morning phone call jarred us awake. Pierre Ametozion was calling to say we must be ready in a few hours. All had been arranged: he was taking us to the Sacred Forest at Togoville.

Pierre was a Togolese intellectual and poet, and the author of articles on his country's traditional culture. He wrote and spoke English and French equally well and worked as an interpreter at the American embassy in Lomé. He was also a member of the clan that dominated Togoville; if anyone could introduce Eric and me to the Sacred Forest, it was Pierre.

These forests, or groves, are centers of traditional spirituality along the coast. Each one shelters a renowned fetish priest and his court, where young women are trained as *fétisheuses* and where local people go to seek advice, a blessing or contact with the spiritual world. They are not necessarily inaccessible—Togoville is barely 20 minute's drive from Lomé, on Lake Togo—but are isolated by an aura of mystery amplified by powerful taboos.

No one Eric knew had ever been to the Togoville forest, and he had begged Pierre to bring him there. Pierre had responded evasively, saying only that he would see what he could do. That had been months ago, and meanwhile we had been far from Lomé and the coast in the arid Sahel. Now we were to be plunged into the humid mysteries of the Sacred Forest, and we had only a few moments to prepare ourselves.

Take a camera, Pierre had said, and some traditional cloth to wrap ourselves in, as European dress was not allowed. The possibility of photography in such a place surprised me; but the injunction against shirts and trousers, hats and shoes seemed to promise a kind of transformation. I blundered around Quaker House looking for film while Eric took a few pieces of his collection of fabric off the wall. We had just time for the hasty breakfast that Justin had prepared. Pierre, we knew, would have to stop in the market for several bottles of gin, obligatory presents for the Togoville dignitaries who would receive us. When he finally arrived with his brother Adolphe, a photographer for a government ministry, the four of us climbed into the Quaker House Peugeot to drive to Lake Togo.

Before we could go into the forest itself, however, we had to be presented to a kind of council of elders who appoint the fetish priest and assure the continuity of the office and the rites. We left the car on the outskirts of Togoville and followed Pierre and Adolphe along the sandy ways between crumbling adobe walls.

As usual, there was no sense of progressing intentionally along streets, but rather of finding our way haphazardly along a wall, across an open space, around a blank façade..... I felt myself abdicating my habitual expectations of purpose, direction and control and followed contentedly over the warm sand, confident that our destination would soon appear. Then Pierre stopped at a door of corrugated tin, opened it and motioned us through.

We were standing in a wide courtyard defined by a number of low, thatched, unremarkable monochrome buildings. A very old woman there greeted us and took our shirts, shoes, cameras and even our wristwatches, while we wound the cloth we'd brought over our shorts. Pierre assured us we'd get everything back, but first we had to meet the elders. He led us towards a building with a columned porch where I could see a number of ceremonial stools all in a row. Then he and Adolphe did an unexpected thing. They stopped short, turned their backs on the porch and dropped to their knees, head down and elbows resting on their thighs. Eric and I had barely time to follow suit when Pierre said, "Clap." So, hunched over, eyes on the sand under our noses, we did as they did and clapped, starting loud and ending soft: CLAP CLAP CLAP CLAP CLAP CLAP—four times.

In the ensuing silence we waited, still hunched over. Nothing happened, which seemed to be okay because Pierre got up and we followed him onto the porch and down its length past the wooden stools, across a small courtyard and, without stopping, through a low doorway.

I got a glimpse of three men sitting in the small dark room; but almost immediately, without a word from anyone, Pierre had unrolled a mat and we were kneeling again with our backs to the three men, clapping again four times in decrescendo. Then we sat up and turned around. Pierre began talking, and I got a better look at the elders.

The one who was talking to Pierre was heavyset and seemed to scowl as he spoke. Perhaps he was presiding, because after the customary responsive greetings, it was he who accepted the gifts we had brought. He clucked happily over the bottle of Gordon's gin and opened with apparent suspicion the piece of paper in which we'd folded a thousand-franc note, before allowing himself to be impressed. The second man was thin and poker-faced. But it was the third who drew my attention most strongly. He sat on a little stool and wore a simple black cloth rolled down to his waist and a string of tiny beads that just circled his neck. His mustache was white and his hair was closely cropped except for a longer tuft on the side of his head that held a white feather. I thought he could be in his fifties, but his torso was slim and knit like a younger man's. He sat unmoving and attentive as the others exclaimed over our gifts. No one addressed him directly, but he seemed increasingly to dominate the little room. Finally he spoke, hardly raising his voice, and everyone immediately fell silent.

He thanked us for the gifts in a grave, level voice, looking intently into our eyes. Certainly his gratitude was ceremonial, but his glance conveyed sincerity and something more, an acknowledgement of each of us that impressed me deeply. Eric, too, I could see, had fallen under his spell. Then his features relaxed, he laughed and proposed a round of *sodabi* from one of several bottles of the native brew that stood by the heavy man. Paul leaned over to say that by custom we should open the bottle of gin, but since someone (I suspected the larger elder) had already

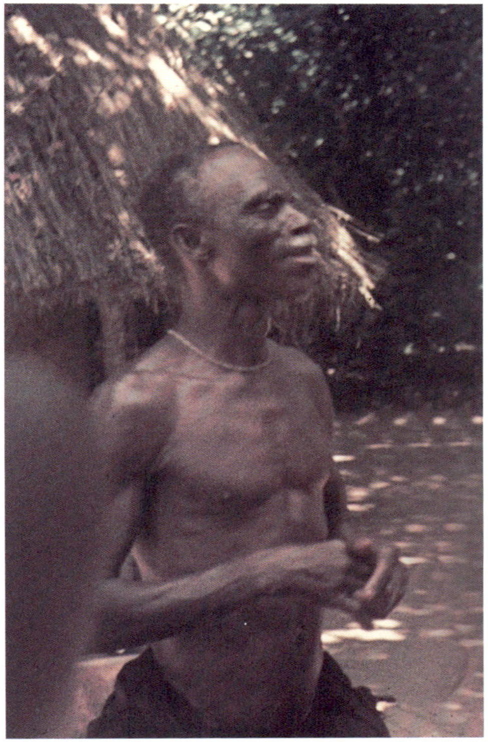

Atoku of the Sacred Forest

been drinking, we would share the *sodabi*. The little glasses went around. The last was poured out on the ground as a libation.

The room grew more animated, and Pierre translated some of the discussion. The quiet man on the stool, he explained, was the true chief here, the administrator of the Sacred Forest, the king-maker of its priests and the human face of its spiritual world. His name was Atoku. The men were debating who would go with us, whether this was the right time of day, how we should go there...... Above the talk, I heard ritual clapping in the courtyard and another elder joined us, a tall thin bug-eyed man with a look about him that demanded respect. Through the doorway, I could see the brilliant sunlight in the courtyard and hear voices over the walls to remind me that everyday life continued outside this otherworldly little room.

An agreement seemed to have been reached. Atoku himself would accompany us and we would leave at once by boat over the lake. Ceremony reasserted itself, we turned our backs on the company, clapped in obeisance and found ourselves in the court-yard again, where the old lady handed us our shirts, wristwatches and other accouterments of material life. Atoku joined us. He had draped his black cloth over his shoulder so that it covered him like a toga and wound a piece of the same material around his head. Two young boys accompanied him. If he were to go out alone, Pierre said, anyone he encountered could claim a gift from him.

We set off with Atoku, the two boys at his side, towards the lakeside landing where a dugout canoe would take us across to the Sacred Forest. Eric and I were very much in awe of our guide, and watched as he stopped to talk to the townspeople who greeted him. Each person received that personal acknowledgement, direct look in the eyes and perfect attentiveness that we'd seen earlier. He was treated with marked respect and responded with a simple dignity that had nothing artificial in it but seemed to come from a natural authority in this deeply grounded man. Pierre said he had been a washerman in Ghana before a delegation from Togoville had brought him back to the town to assume the role he has in the Sacred Forest.

We were poled across the lake by a young boatman intent on his work. There was nothing like a "forest" at the sandy landing, only low impenetrable bush. Again, we shed our shirts and wrist-watches and wound lengths of cloth around our waists. Atoku did the same. To be naked to the waist is a sign of respect, and here even Atoku takes second place to the high priest we had come to see. We set out in single file along a path through the thick, head-high brush, with Atoku and the two boys in the lead. The sun was high, the sand searingly hot under my bare feet. We stopped abruptly; two lengths of bamboo lay in an X across the path. This simple barrier marked the inner precinct of the Sacred Forest—simple enough, but no one without serious business would cross it, Pierre said.

A little further on, we found ourselves standing at the edge of a large clearing bisected by a palm-frond fence behind which rose a grove of well-grown trees. Flanking an opening in the fence were two thatched gatehouses where a dozen or so people were gathered, waiting. As we approached, a bald, imposingly tall man came forward to meet us. *"Le premier ministre,"* Paul whispered—the fetish priest's adjutant. He greeted us formally, accepted our gifts for his master, took his place with Atoku at the head of our procession and led us through the gate in the fence.

The expansive courtyard inside was dazzlingly sunlit, with patches of deep cool shade from the encircling trees. For a moment, before they scrambled to their knees to bow and clap in homage to Atoku, I saw the virgins of the Sacred Forest at their leisure. Dozens of girls, children and adolescents, lay in groups across the courtyard. They sat in the hot sand or lay curled up in the shade, their naked bodies in frank contact with the earth and

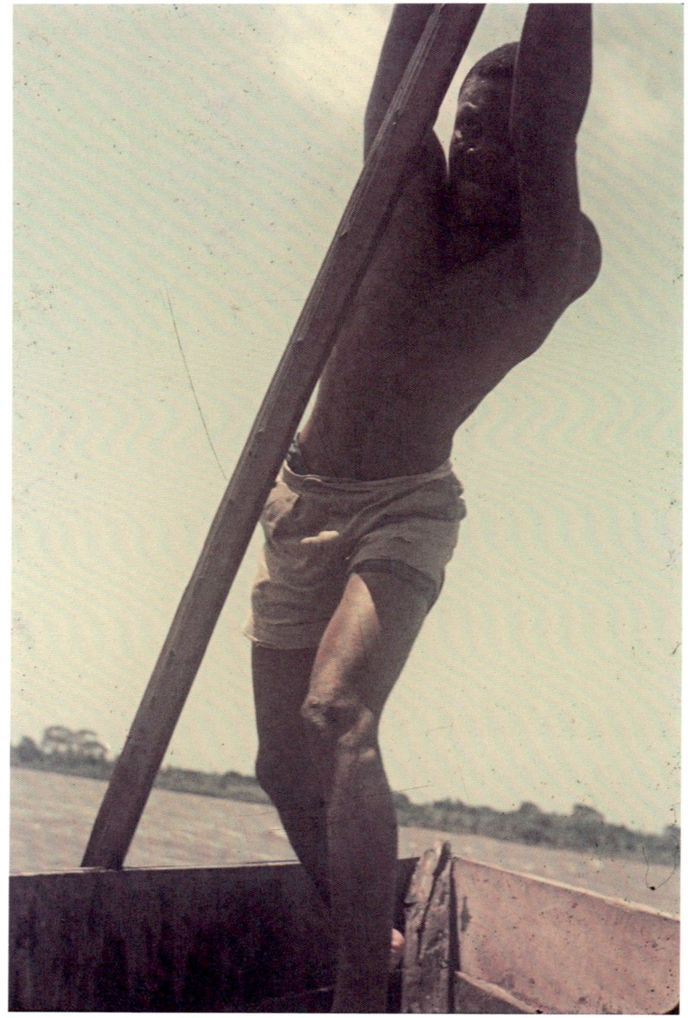

Boatman on Lake Togo

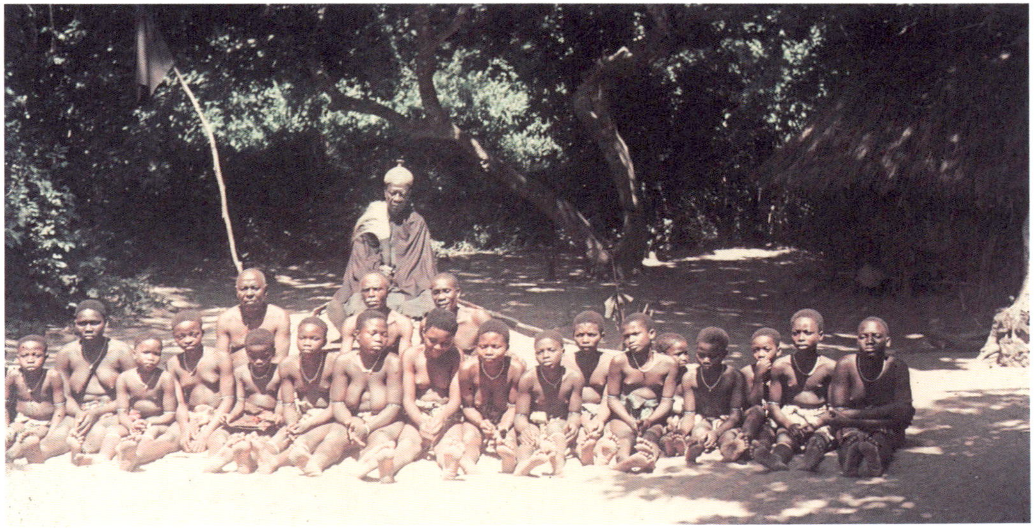

Sacred Forest, Togoville

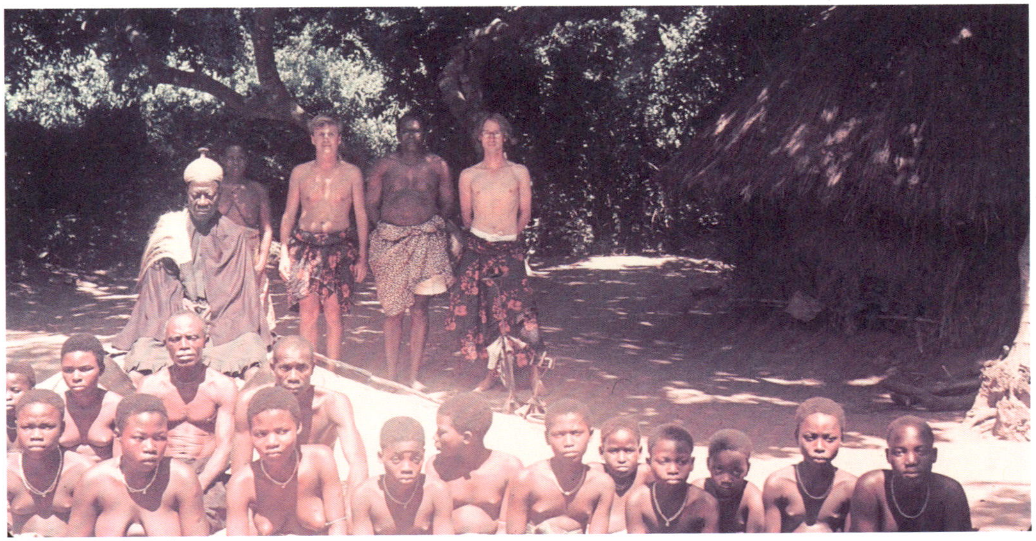

each other. One girl leaned back on another's knees as her hair was groomed. None wore anything more than beads around her waist or at the ear, and all had their hair cut close. They were here to be initiated in the fetish arts and ceremonies and suddenly, after that first unguarded moment, I could see only their glistening backs as they recalled their duty and prostrated themselves to Atoku.

We followed Pierre and Adolphe through the salvos of clapping towards the far end of the clearing where an old man sat alone in front of a round adobe hut. Even from a distance, his eyes were distinct, startlingly yellow in a deeply black face. Mats were unrolled, and we knelt in our turn to the high priest of the Sacred Forest.

He wore a crown of woven raffia shaped like a dome and finial, and a long gray garment covered him from neck to ankles. There was a length of somber native cloth around his shoulders and various objects at his feet: two small wooden figures wrapped in white (suggesting that his wife had had still-born twins), a horse-hair fly whisk and a wooden clapper to call for assistance, as he's forbidden to raise his voice. While his minister intoned an introduction and laid our gifts at his feet, I had a moment to observe him directly. I saw an overweight man with heavy features in a long face. Two deep lines ran from the sides of his nose almost to his jaw. His skin was as dark as any I had seen in Togo and contrasted with prominent eyes that had that yellow tinge in the whites. They looked straight ahead without focus. He seemed unheeding of his minister's address. I wondered whether he might not be ill, and thought of what Pierre had told us when he first described the Sacred Forest: that its high priests never last long. They are already aged when Atoku and the elders select them, and their extremely sedentary way of life, proscribed by ritual, is not a healthy one. Their sole function is to be a conduit between the material and spiritual worlds. They see the ancestors, they speak to spirits and convey their advice, admonishments and blessings to their supplicants, while they themselves increasingly withdraw from outward life to concentrate on voices and powers deep within, until ordinary speech and finally life itself, fail them completely.

At last the old priest seemed to come back to himself. He thanked us for our gifts and looked into my face fleetingly. Something Atoku said drew a smile from him. Then Pierre hauled me to my feet and motioned us to kneel at a heap of sand covered by a leopard skin and ringed by black flags on bamboo poles and iron fetish sticks stuck in the sand, where the priest's minister offered prayers in a monotone. I watched as he poured libations over the strangely configured sticks and was startled to hear our names, *"Eric," "Philippe,"* clearly pronounced amidst his incantations as he recommended us to the spirits. The girls, who had gathered on the other side of the altar, seemed to enjoy this, too, and smiles and giggles broke out in their ranks. In another moment, the prayers were over and we all dispersed, the girls to their chores, Atoku and the old priest into his round hut, and Pierre, Adolphe, Eric and I back through the fence to the gatehouses, where we were to await a further summons.

While we waited, Adolphe, to my private disapprobation, tuned a little transistor radio to the midday news. A car horn honked faintly. Odd to think how this archaic glade could co-exist with modernity. Eric took advantage of this pause to question

Pierre. What becomes of the girls, he wondered, after their term of service? They return to their communities, Pierre told him, ritually scarred and assured of life-long prestige and employment.

Pierre was eager to talk further about the forest. A man condemned for a crime in his own village, for example, might seek sanctuary here. If the priest consented to purify him, he could return to his people in peace; no one could undo the forgiveness he received here.

There were two other Sacred Forests, according to Pierre. They are at Bé, much closer to Lomé, and are visited regularly by the Togoville priest; but the old man has to travel according to strict protocols: only on foot, only on a secret path, only at night, because anyone who crosses his way risks misfortune. A warning bell precedes him and at first cockcrow his party is obliged to halt and spend the day under whatever shelters they can assemble from materials at hand. These are destroyed at sunset and the procession resumes until the next morning. Traveling in this way, it takes three days to reach Bé.

It was pleasant to be waiting in the shade of the palm-frond gatehouse. There were other supplicants beside us, including a young couple from Lomé who looked lovely together; I wondered why they had come. No one seemed impatient or felt that they should try to control the situation. Time spun slowly on itself, as it does in Togo, until the tall major-domo appeared in the gate and welcomed the four of us back into the compound.

We were seated on mats in front of a clear area where all the girls had been marshaled by the old priest's wife. They were wearing far more beads now, gorgets and girdles of bright yellow, blue and red beads. Several girls sat before piles of sand, gently beating rhythms on them. These parures were for a dance; these sand piles were the drums.

It began with a song, as four girls got up and circled before us, stamping and stepping. The rhythms on the sand piles became more emphatic and other groups of girls rose, one after the other, to circle and dance as the songs succeeded each other. The sand drums thumped, the dust rose swirling up along shafts of sunlight,

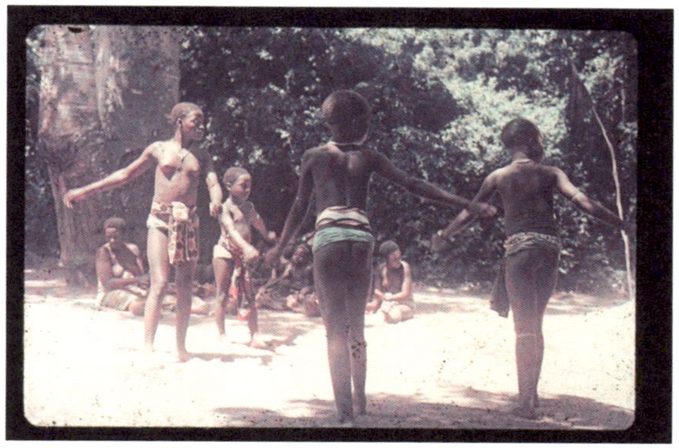

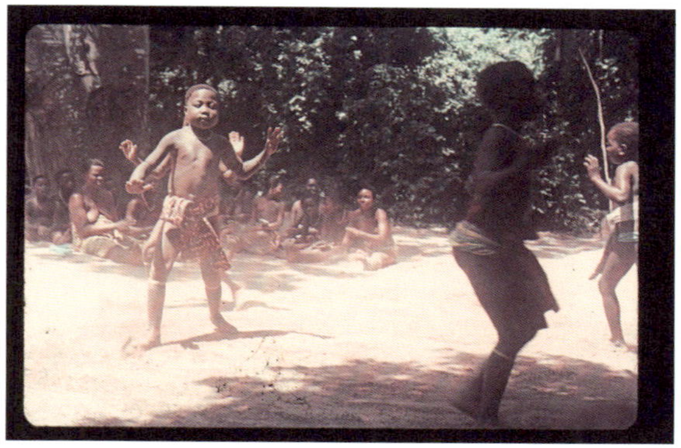

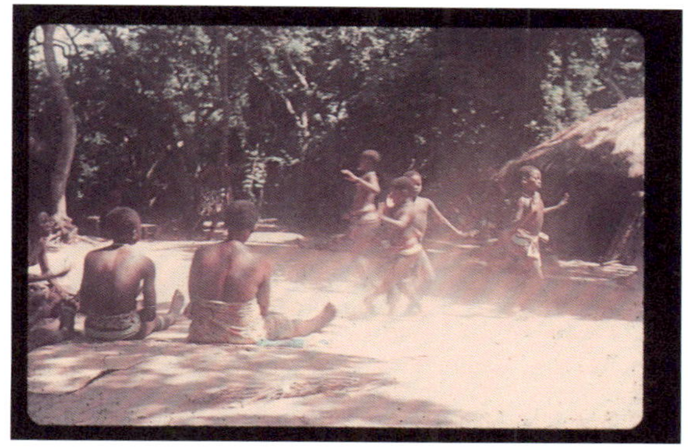

Sacred Forest, the fetish girls dance

the little children stamped bravely while the older girls moved with authoritative grace. Then suddenly they all collapsed at the feet of the old lady and silence fell—too heavy a silence for applause, so Eric and I just smiled and nodded across at the girls as the sunlit dust settled between us.

It is time for the high priest himself to offer prayers on our behalf. We kneel in front of him, elbows on our thighs, heads bowed so low that all I can see is the sand under my nose. But I can sense the old man bending closely over us and hear the low, rapid patter of his invocation, unintelligible except for *"Philippe, Eric,"* which flash out clearly in the flow of words. He is speaking with an animation that belies the withdrawn old man I'd seen earlier. His voice is low, expressive, insistent, intimate and directed downwards only to us—or are there, I wonder, other entities at hand also listening and being addressed, presences I sense but wouldn't see if I raised my head? The forest and its people and my own consciousness seem to be gathered and compressed together into that low compelling voice.

My awareness comes back to the present as a child kneels beside us and places a small bundle of grasses in front of each of us. "Symbols of peace," I hear Pierre whisper in my ear. The old man is speaking blessings over the grass, and I follow the others in making a gesture of cleansing, like throwing water over one shoulder and then the other. The priest, in the same low tones but looking directly at us now, tells us to avoid shaking hands with anyone and to go straight home. Then we are to use the grass to sprinkle water from a bowl—but not a metal bowl—over ourselves, our friends and households, anything that we want blessed. Keep the grass, he said, it will bring you luck. Finally he sat back,

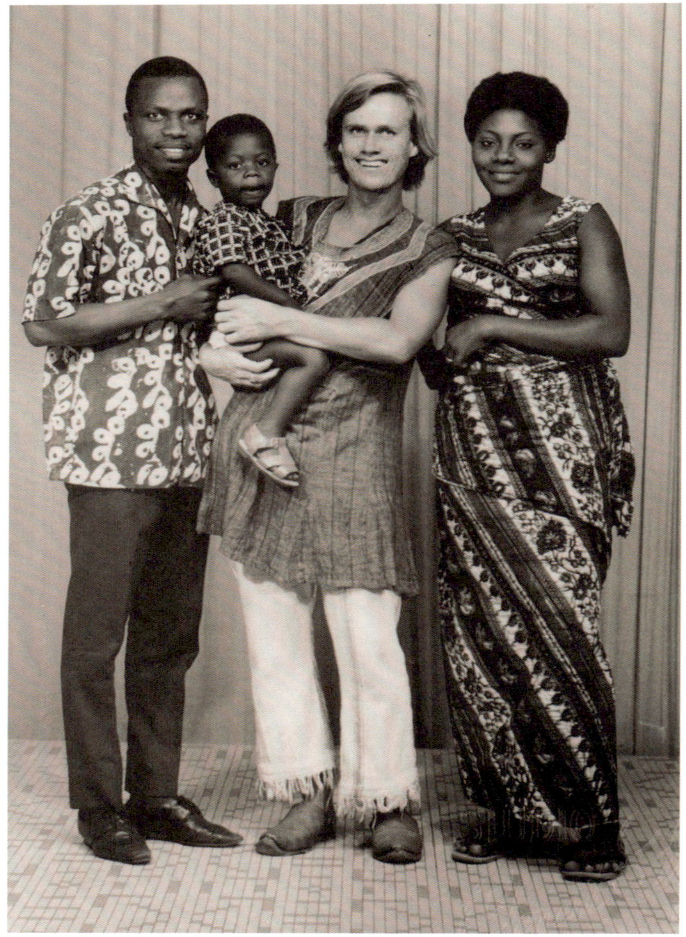

Eric with Bernard and his wife and little Eric, his namesake.

we rise to mumble our thanks, and before we know it we are back at the gate, where Atoku says goodbye and asks Adolphe to send him some photos. When we get our watches back, we see it is 2 o'clock. We have been there three hours. It seemed much longer.

Not long after our visit to the Sacred Forest, Eric moved out of Quaker House. His work with International Dialogues was over and he was returning to New York to work at International House, a social center and dormitory for students from abroad attending Columbia University. It was wrenching for both of us to leave Nyakponapwé, the house and our friends there, especially Justin. Eric missed his garden.

We rented rooms on the other side of Lomé in a neighborhood called *Le Frigo* (there must have been a cold storage facility nearby). Eric had business to wrap up after four or five years in West Africa, and I stayed with him for a couple of weeks before flying back to New York, where he joined me later. Of the compound we lived in, I remember only our wash on the line and the busy street outside the gate. There was a kind of sandbox at the gate, a wooden frame filled with the clean sand that blows so ubiquitously throughout the town, and it was pleasant to lie there under the shade trees that lined the street, and watch the traffic. It was mostly foot traffic, men and women carrying things on their heads or children in khaki uniforms going to or from school, a constant stream of bicycles filling the air with the sound of their bells, occasionally a car or truck passing at reckless speed, blowing its horn and raising a column of dust in the sunlight. It seemed that much of Lomé passed by the sandbox, and it was endlessly diverting to observe leisured townfolk in patterned cloth, country folk in striped homespun, shirtless laborers in stained shorts, Muslims in long robes and caps. The pace was slow and people smiled readily.

Eric's friend Bernard invited us for a farewell lunch. His wife prepared *fufu* and sauce with side dishes while Eric dandled their son, who was named after him. The house was new and sparsely furnished, and after lunch, for want of chairs, we all piled onto the bed. We lay contentedly prone or half upright, closely touching, making small talk and feeling the mattress shake when we laughed. I thought back to Accra and my first experience of this African physical casualness, and felt I'd come a long way.

My Air Afrique flight went through Dakar and Paris. My seatmate was a South Asian man, and he promptly took off his shoes after departure. I noticed how beautifully brown and smooth and natural-looking his feet were, and thought how confining and disfiguring shoes really are; so I took mine off, too. I had been wearing sandals for months, and now I was delighted to see that my feet also looked beautiful, delicately dried, scoured and tanned by exposure to the sun and sands of Lomé and the north. It saddened me to think they would soon have to be shod again.

Passing over France at altitude, I stared down at the strict patchwork of cultivated fields in green and brown that covered the land. At other times, they had looked picturesque to me; but now they seemed harshly rectangular, stifling and oppressive, a slightly terrifying expression of human multitude and exploitation. I sank back in my seat and thought of the exuberant, less defined fields of Palimé and Élavagnon, where the wild and the cultivated flourish side by side, and of the wide empty expanses of the Sahel.

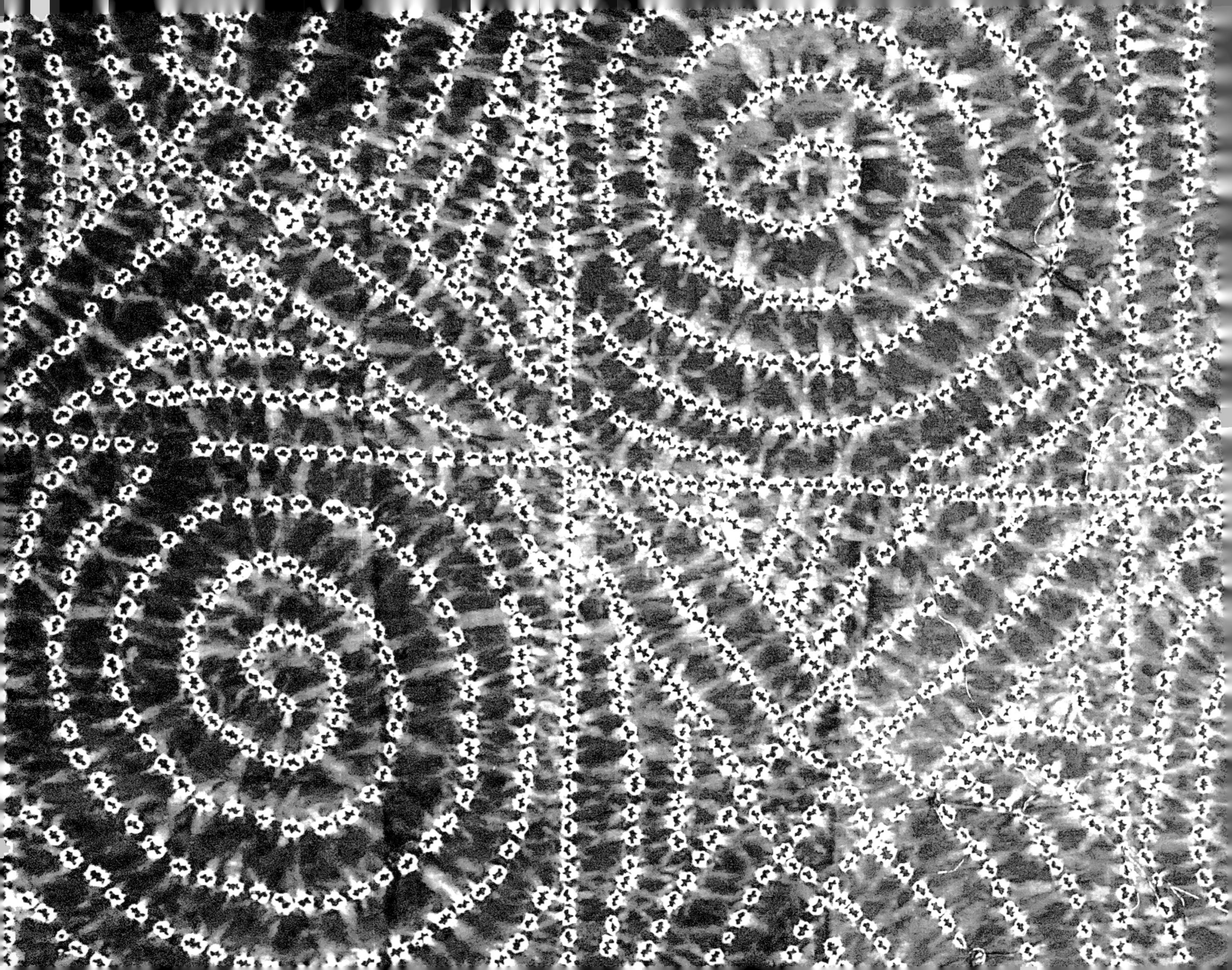

AFTERWORD

BEING HUMAN

"It's not like that anymore." The taxi driver is glancing into his rear-view mirror at me. His eyes, neatly framed in the little mirror, have an amused expression. I've learned that he is from Ivory Coast, a young man with a wife and child in New Jersey, speaking English with me by preference to the French he'd been taught in his homeland—a smart, well-adapted member of the West African diaspora in New York.

I had been telling him about my experiences in Togo, where I'd been excited to find the hippie ideals of my generation—communal living, wholeness of mind and body, harmony with the natural world—being lived every day in the traditional villages there and all over West Africa.

"It's not like that anymore," he insisted. "Everyone watches TV. Everyone wants to be glamorous." And as we drew up to my address, he grinned and said, "Welcome to Togo." I looked into his good-natured face and thought he must mean that now Togo as I'd experienced it almost fifty years ago is wherever I am, and only in my heart and memory.

Of course I know that West Africa is no longer as I remember it. I hear in the news that Togo has become a dumping ground for electronic waste. In Niger, Zinder is a center of human trafficking and Agadez hosts an American drone base. Fulani herders, forced from the Sahel by a drying climate, are at deadly odds over land with the Dogon and the farmers of Northern Nigeria. French troops wage war with jihadists in the Malian desert who in return bomb hotels in Bamako. The Tuaregs want their own country.

My cab driver, however, seemed to be talking about deeper changes. If "everyone wants to be glamorous," it implies that a preening individuality has supplanted traditional communal values. Television programs depict a world free of scarcity where sharing is optional and everyone is connected remotely by the Internet. But scarcity, interdependence and a human scale where villagers interact with each other face-to-face, were pre-conditions of the traditional culture of the West African villages I saw. There, no one was ever alone, time passed without compulsion and handsome, brilliantly clothed men and women smiled easily at each other and at me and moved with unconscious grace.

In a letter my mother wrote me at the time, she warns me, "Don't be sentimental about Africa." My sociologist brother, when I told him I was writing this book, said, "You're romanticizing traditional society." *Romance; sentiment*—it's true, Togo arouses in me feelings of affection, exhilaration and poignant regret, like a long-ago love affair. And like a love affair, it proved fragile. I remember how I regretted to hear West African students at International House in New York glorying in the privacy, personal autonomy and material possessions they found in the city. No more sharing: their brother or cousin or friend had no claim to a new shirt or CD. And they had a door to their own room, a door to be shut against others! They had abandoned so gladly the traditional complex of relationships determined by ancestry, family, village and ethnicity, bolstered by the authority of elders and the machinations of *gris-gris,* which had formed their African identities. To be sure, I understood that these relationships can be stifling, even harmful; but I wonder whether some of these students ever grew to regret what they left behind: to always belong, to be cherished as an individual by their family and village, to be guaranteed status and security.[10]

Traditional ways can be very fragile. On my first visit to Togo in 1969, Eric and I set out into the countryside to find a particular weaver of fine textiles. We had to stop four or five times to ask directions. An old woman tottered out through her doorway to say we were going in the right direction but we should ask the blacksmith under a great tree a kilometer down the road. The blacksmith, stooping down to grin at us through the open car window, told us to turn right at the white flag of the *fétisheuse's* house. The *fétisheuse* herself clapped her hands in encouragement and said we were almost there. Two years later when we sought the same artisan, a sign had been nailed to a tree: "This way to buy woven cloth." I marveled, sadly, how the written word had so completely superseded our friendly interactions with the people who had guided us formerly.

We seem to have a fateful capacity to dehumanize ourselves with our own inventions. The Industrial Revolution and mass production reduced scarcity and the interdependence it necessitated, and now people are widely expected to be, like machines, efficient, productive, and punctual. The Internet connects us all, but only in a zone of virtual reality that distances us from the real world of locality, moment, and sensation. Really *human* connectedness requires the immediacy of face-to-face communication, when all our senses are in play and we discover meaning in each other's eyes, facial expressions and body language. We are present, we feel each other's contexts, we have to acknowledge each other.

In Togo, people were "the measure of all things" in a quite literal way, as scale in the landscape was determined by how far a person could walk, rather than by the range of a vehicle. Cultivated fields were small and nearby. Market villages were at the end of a footpath. The scale and organization of villages were also expressive of people and their relationships. Dwellings built in close proximity spoke of interdependence, while walled compounds expressed the distinction of families. The houses themselves were proportional to a person standing, and their uniformity muted differences in wealth and status.

Time, too, had a human face. Schedules were provisional; events began only when the people had gathered. Regardless of the pace of daily activities, encounters between people created a pause. Greetings had to be exchanged, questions asked and answered, and this obligatory ritual carved out a distinct moment, bringing the flow of time to a stop. When it resumed, it followed the pace of the people's successive activities, and they moved from task to task without the artificial stress of chronology and without haste.

Even the human body seemed more itself in West Africa. Maybe the custom of carrying loads on the head accounts for the relaxed, grounded way that people walk. With no tension in the joints, the limbs are free to move easily and weight sinks downward through hips and legs and passes through the feet, which seem to acknowledge the ground at each step.

Hands also move in a distinctive way. They hang easily on the wrist, rotating without stress. They clap or slap percussively and make real contact with whatever they touch. The African hand seems abler, perhaps because there's less recourse to the myriad time-saving tools we have in the West. Just watching Justin sweep crumbs from a countertop with the edge of his hand, I thought his gesture seemed beautifully sufficient.

Eric liked to say that his Dutch ancestors had spent too many long dark winter nights staring into the fire and deepening the mind-body duality that pervades Western philosophy and religion. Whatever the merit of his idea, it was easy to see an easy-going wholeheartedness in West Africans, a quality of movement and being arising from a continuity of mind and body, a spontaneous wholeness that put them closely in touch with the world around them. All this seemed profoundly human to Eric and me: people whose culture was not modeled on machine or digital technology, who lived in a human-scaled environment, who depended on each other and communicated face-to-face, who moved over the earth earth-like, with their whole selves.

I could never go back to Togo now. Eric and I returned briefly in 1975 on our way home from a long trip through South and Southeast Asia. The political atmosphere was tense following an attempt on the president's life. No one seemed to trust each other, and the Post Office, where every ethnic group in West Africa had formerly gathered, was deserted. The pools of light under the streetlamps where students used to study were empty, too. Even in Élavagnon, our greetings were no longer returned. I felt like a lover spurned and realized it would be foolish to think things would ever be the same.

So now, is the Togo I remember largely only a country in this book? Perhaps, but as the world spins headlong into a global culture based on the Internet and artificial intelligence, we may need to remember Togo and what it is to be human, and how deeply it suits us. I recall with awe the many West Africans Eric and I encountered—the goatherd of Zinder market, the minstrel of Péwa, Atoku of the Sacred Forest—who evinced a remarkable kind of dignity and confidence, arising from an unassuming self-respect and a sure sense of their place among their fellows and in the cosmos. Maybe this confident *belonging* is the best thing that traditional society has to offer to our over-populated, bewildered, warming world.

In a dentist's waiting room recently, I fell into conversation with a fellow-patient and together we deplored the effect of cellphones. We agreed that they often isolate us from the present moment and avoid the messy inconvenience of direct human communication. Face-to-face communication, however, is by nature spontaneous, immediate and problematic. "It's hard work being human", my wise, friendly interlocutor said. Maybe "hard working" traditional societies like Togo's can remind us of the importance of cultivating our humanity, especially as we seem increasingly to be surrendering so much of it.

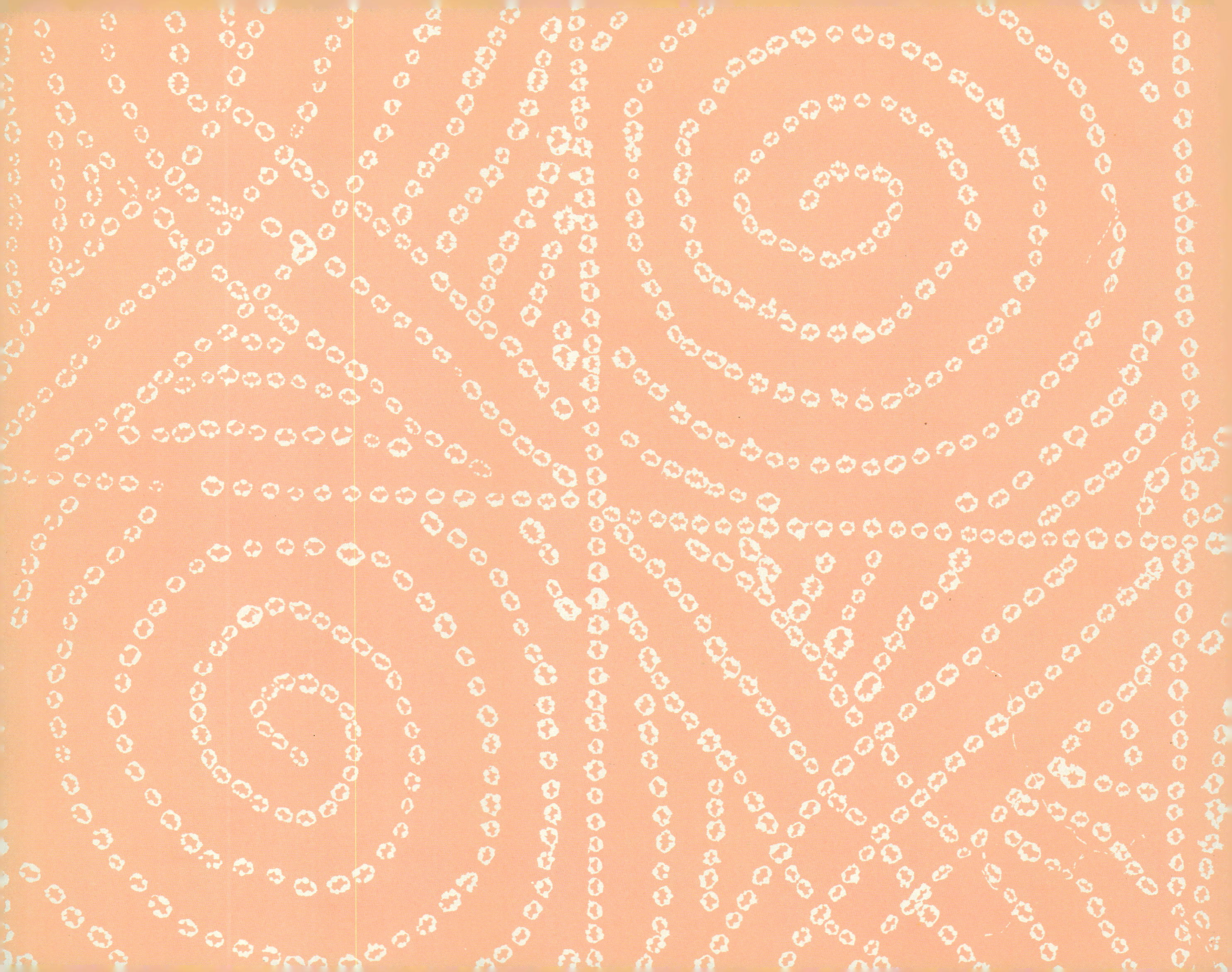

ENDNOTES

1. Years later, I saw these same kind of footpaths from a tenth floor hotel balcony in Brasilia. Oscar Neimeier planned the Brazilian capital with green spaces around dense urban centers connected by highways. From my balcony, I could see that the green areas were laced with red-earth footpaths spreading in all directions, an unplanned transportation network created by the economically poorer residents of the capital who don't have a car and so know the value of a shortcut. None of the paths was straight or level, and they looped and twisted and crossed each other in the same organic way I'd seen in West Africa. They seemed to defy the urban planner's preference for symmetry and right angles, although he had his revenge, perhaps, when a path encountered the highway. There, the pedestrian had to make a perilous dash through the speeding cars, cross a median and dash through traffic again. I could see, however, that the path always picked up on the other side.

2. The market women are a major force in Togo's economy. Eric asserted that, were they all to withdraw at once their deposits from the national bank, it would ruin the bank and might well bring down the government. Together, we go to the national bank building on Friday morning to watch the ladies make their deposits. They arrive in a long line of black Mercedes sedans. As each car stops at the bottom of the steps, the driver jumps out to open the door for his grandly corpulent passenger. The floor of the car seems to sag and then rebound as she steps out. The bank staff, all men in black suits, is waiting behind tables indoors, where each woman unwinds a length of cloth, knotted at intervals, from under her voluminous dress. As the knots are undone, piles of bills and coin spill out and are counted, swept up and deposited. The next Mercedes draws up.

3. Later, traveling in northern Togo, I learned more of *gris-gris'* important social role. I asked my Togolese friends about the abandoned houses I saw along country roads, concrete structures standing derelict in weed-grown lots, vegetation bursting through their vacant window frames and unfinished second stories. My friends called them *"les maisons inachevées"*, or unfinished houses, begun by a prosperous family in place of a more typical single-story concrete or adobe dwelling. Their project would have aroused envy in the countryside and a *fétisheur* had been commissioned to assure that it was never finished. Initiative frustrated, progress sabotaged—I was indignant. The West has long believed in progress, but even its great proselytizer, the Frenchman St. Simon, knew it could be destabilizing, and called for "Order *and* Progress." The Togolese village, like any traditional society, values equilibrium over change. Those who might disturb it, the unfortunate who drag it down or the

fortunate who challenge it, have to be re-integrated into the community. The village cares for its poor and works *gris-gris* on its rich.

Trevor Noah writes of the same equilibrium in his account of growing up in South Africa, *Born a Crime*."The biggest thing in the hood is that you have to share. You can't get rich on your own….. Everyone must know that your success benefits the community in one way or another, or you become a target." Trevor Noah, *Born a Crime, Stories from a South African Childhood,* Spiegel & Grau, New York 2016, pp. 218,219.

4. In Greece, I had visited the excavations of King Nestor's Minoan palace at Pylos. Homer writes that Odysseus's son, Telemachus, stopped there and was bathed by the women of the palace. Our guide even showed us where the bathtub might have been. I couldn't help thinking that my bath in Élavagnon was a distant, folk-culture echo of this ritual bath of welcome, especially as it was never repeated. Ritual is not, after all, something offered lightly; and what a lot of work, I thought, to carry water up from the stream and gather firewood to heat it, to say nothing of the extravagance of so much soap, so much talcum powder!

5. Here is Stephen's song:

There are many many changes in the world,*
There are many many changes in the world,
There are many many changes in the world,
So, you no go see anybody like me.
You go walk-walk so-so you go tired,
You no see me anywhere you go,
There are many many changes in the world,
So, you no go see anybody like me.

*differences

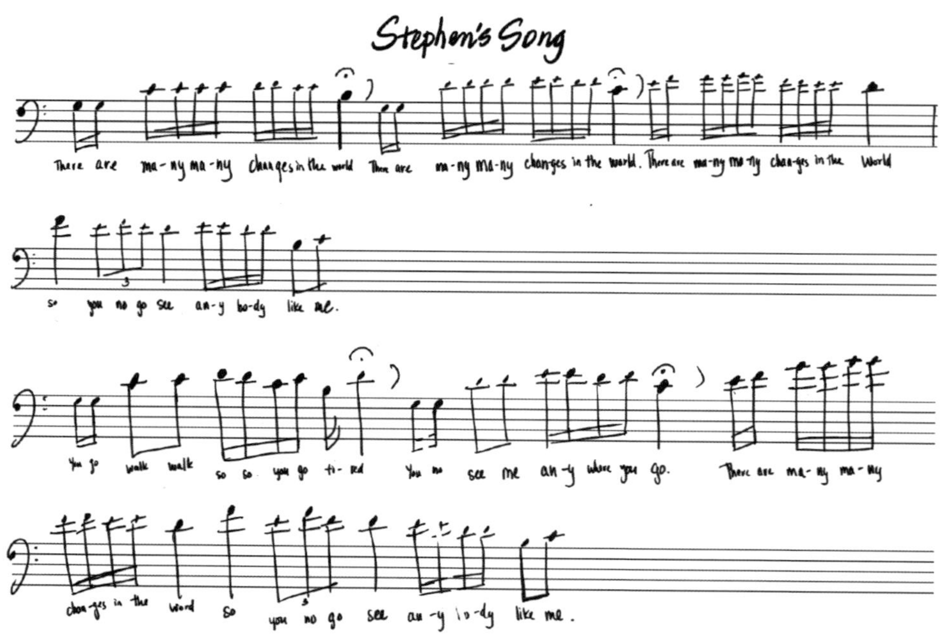

6. I dislike being taken for a missionary, remembering the destruction they have wrought on other cultures and their role as fifth columnists of colonization. Those who have mistaken me for a missionary, however, never seemed to mean it as a reproach. On a mountain road I hiked once in Haiti, where the farmers were singing as they worked in their fields and a clean breeze swept down from green heights, I thought to enhance my contentment with some marijuana I'd rolled into a joint in Port-au-Prince; but I had no matches. Coming down the road opposite me was an elderly farmer smoking a pipe. I asked him, would he light my joint? For a moment, we were head-to-head there, inhaling in unison as the marijuana took fire from his tobacco.

"*Merci, mon ami,*" I said.

"Ce n'est rien, mon Père" ("Don't mention it, Father"), was his reply.

How could he think I was a priest?

7. On my return to New York I joined the choir of the First Tabernacle of Deliverance Spiritual Church on 125th Street in Harlem. The preacher railed at us that "God is an on-time god" and exhorted us to be in our places for Sunday service at 11 o'clock sharp. I noticed, however, that we rarely started until most of the congregation had arrived, sometimes well after 11:00. "11 o'clock CPT" (Colored People's Time), my fellow choir members called it. Humanity rules!

8. The grand adobe architecture I saw in Kano was a world beyond the comparatively plain buildings I knew from New Mexico. My aunt Dorothy Brett's small house in Taos, built for her by craftsmen from Taos Pueblo, had the characteristic thick walls of adobe bricks — earth mixed with straw and dried in a mold— plastered over with a layer of wet mud. The roof was flat, supported on wooden beams exposed on the interior ceilings. The interior felt like spaces scooped out by a big hand rather than something plumbed and squared, and the walls of the rooms swelled irregularly and flowed seamlessly into each other and into the floor and ceilings. Where my aunt had pierced a wall to add a room, the opening gaped like the entrance to a cave. The Pueblo itself was built the same way, but vertically, in several stories of this heavy adobe material. Once I climbed to the top story on exterior ladders to visit my aunt's friend, Pete Concha. In a small, high room, cool despite the heat, we sipped orange sodas in the dim light of a single tiny window.

9. Pascal Kargougou was a teenager at this time, a shy serious young man who lived for pop music. We developed a correspondence that continued from 1970 to 1976. I learned of his evolving aspirations to be a teacher, a translator, a scientist, a businessman, a computer programmer, as he went from high school to university in Niger and back to Ouaga. Vacations in Kaya, his father's hometown, were full of dance parties and attempts to start a discotheque with his band of friends, who called themselves the "Black Needles." Pascal's letters often included lists of his favorite hits, some of which I was able to send him. In exchange, I received a Fulani shirt, fringed and covered with buttons, an elaborately worked leather wallet to be worn around the neck, a horse-hair fly whisk and beautiful open-backed shoes.

Through these letters, I was also able to follow the career of Pascal's father, Moussa Kargougou, as he went from Minister for Rural Education to member of the National Assembly, and eventually, Minister of Foreign Affairs. In one letter, Pascal alludes to his father's 23 children! The last letter I received included a photo of Pascal at his wedding with his wife and witnesses, everyone splendid in traditional dress.

10. Alexandria, the Johannesburg suburb where Trevor Noah spent some of his adolescence, afforded him some of the same advantages. "The hood is a low-stress, comfortable life.....you don't have to ask yourself any of the big questions. Who am I? Who am I supposed to be? Am I doing enough?.....You never feel like a failure in the hood, because someone's always worse off than you, and you don't feel you have to do more, because the

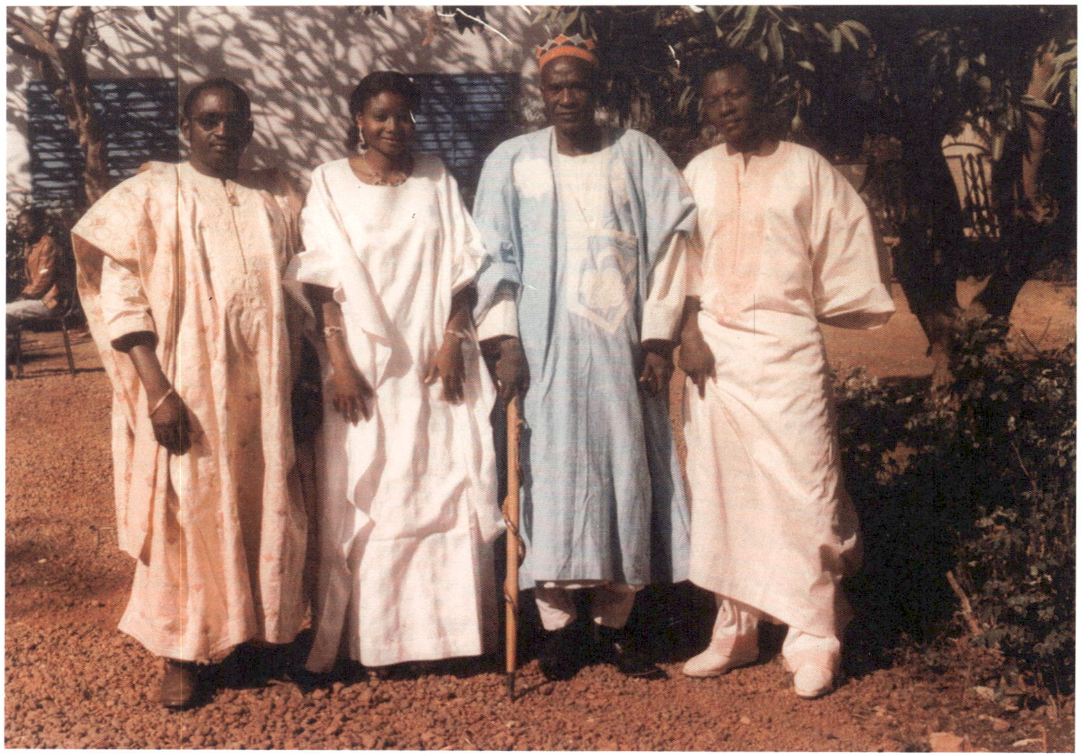

Pascal Kargougou (far right) at his wedding

biggest success isn't that much higher than you, either. The hood has a wonderful sense of community to it, as well. Everyone knows everyone, from the crackhead all the way to the policeman. People take care of one another." Trevor Noah, *Born a Crime, Stories of a South African Childhood,* Spiegel and Grau, New York 2016, p. 218

Designed by Claire MacMaster
Barefoot Art Graphic Design, Gloucester, Massachusetts.
Set in Zapf Optima Regular and printed on 156 GSM
Art Matte paper in Shanghai, China in the fall of 2021.

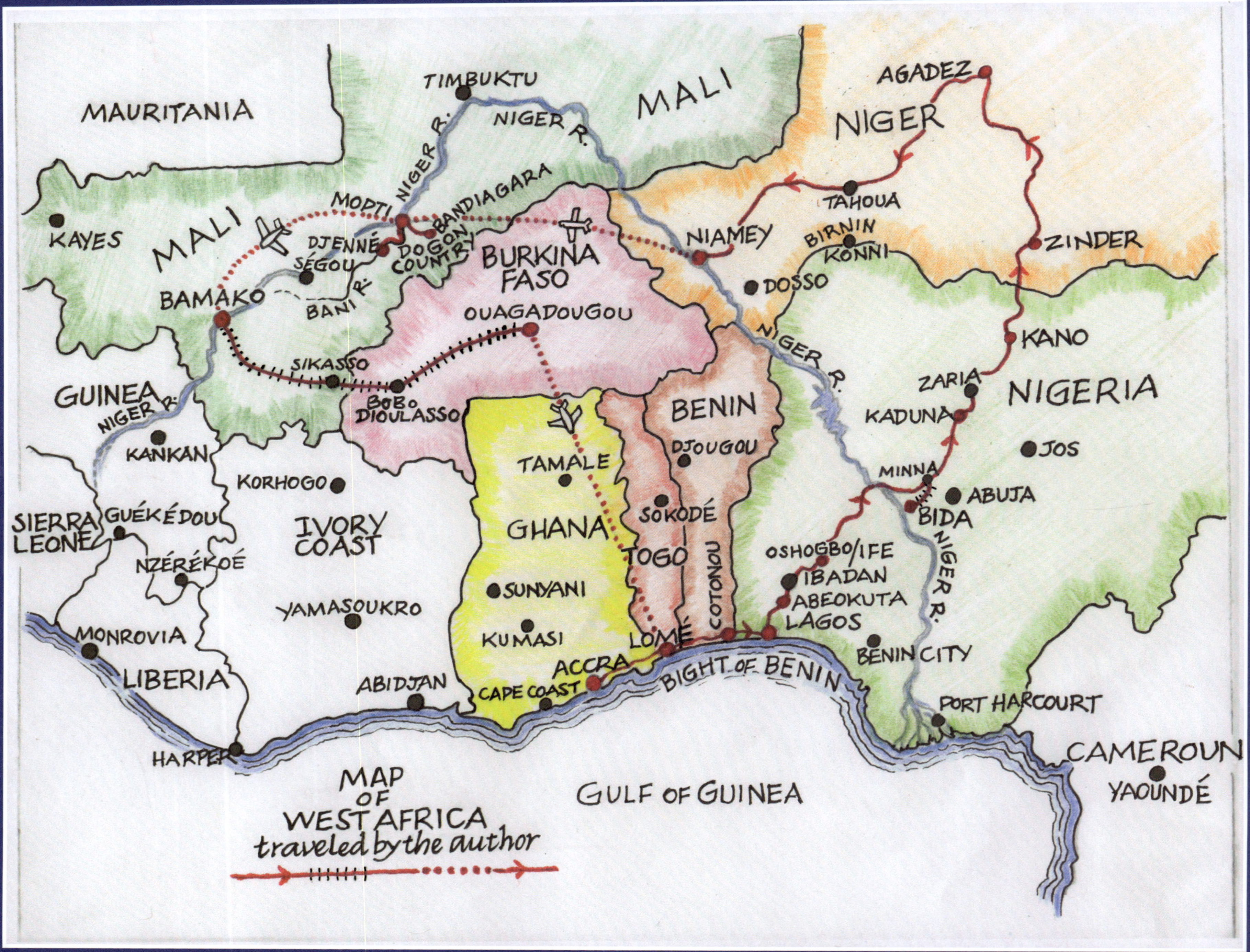
MAP
OF
WEST AFRICA
traveled by the author
MAURITANIA
TIMBUKTU
MALI
NIGER R.
AGADEZ
NIGER
MALI
KAYES
MOPTI
BANDIAGARA
DJENNÉ
DOGON COUNTRY
SÉGOU
BANI R.
BAMAKO
BURKINA FASO
NIAMEY
TAHOUA
BIRNIN KONNI
ZINDER
DOSSO
OUAGADOUGOU
SIKASSO
BOBO DIOULASSO
GUINEA
KANKAN
BENIN
KANO
ZARIA
KADUNA
NIGERIA
JOS
MINNA
ABUJA
BIDA
DJOUGOU
TAMALE
KORHOGO
SIERRA LEONE
GUÉKÉDOU
IVORY COAST
NZÉRÉKOÉ
GHANA
SOKODÉ
TOGO
COTONOU
OSHOGBO/IFE
IBADAN
ABEOKUTA
LAGOS
SUNYANI
YAMASOUKRO
KUMASI
LOMÉ
MONROVIA
LIBERIA
ACCRA
CAPE COAST
ABIDJAN
BIGHT OF BENIN
BENIN CITY
PORT HARCOURT
HARPER
CAMEROUN
YAOUNDÉ
GULF OF GUINEA